DiMag & Mick

Books by Tony Castro

Chicano Power:
The Emergence of Mexican America

Mickey Mantle:
America's Prodigal Son

The Prince of South Waco:
American Dreams and Great Expectations

DiMag & Mick

Sibling Rivals, Yankee Blood Brothers

Tony Castro

LYONS
PRESS

Guilford, Connecticut

An imprint of The Rowman & Littlefield Publishing Group, Inc.
4501 Forbes Blvd., Ste. 200
Lanham, MD 20706
www.rowman.com

Distributed by NATIONAL BOOK NETWORK

British Library Cataloguing in Publication Information Available

Library of Congress Cataloging-in-Publication Data

Names: Castro, Tony.
Title: Dimag & Mick : sibling rivals, Yankee blood brothers / by Tony Castro.
Description: Guilford, Connecticut : Lyons Press, 2016. | Includes bibliographical references and index.
Identifiers: LCCN 2015042698 | ISBN 9781630761240 (hardback) | ISBN 9781493039517 (paperback)
Subjects: LCSH: DiMaggio, Joe, 1914-1999. | Mantle, Mickey, 1931-1995. | Baseball players—United States—Biography. | New York Yankees (Baseball team)—History—20th century. | BISAC: SPORTS & RECREATION / Baseball /History.
Classification: LCC GV865.D5 C37 2016 | DDC 796.3570922—dc23 LC record available at http://lccn.loc.gov/2015042698

ISBN 978-1-4930-3951-7 (paperback)
ISBN 978-1-63076-125-7 (e-book)

∞™ The paper used in this publication meets the minimum requirements of American National Standard for Information Sciences—Permanence of Paper for Printed Library Materials, ANSI/NISO Z39.48-1992.

Printed in the United States of America

For Renee

It is possible to be a master in false philosophy, easier, in fact, than to be a master in the truth, because a false philosophy can be made as simple and consistent as one pleases.

—GEORGE SANTAYANA

CONTENTS

PROLOGUE

New York, 2014

"Above Grand Central Station, there used to be this incredibly fabulously opulent apartment that looked like a palace that the original architect built as part of the original design, and in 1951 I knew someone—I knew a lot of people even then—who arranged for me, for us, to stay there one night that summer. And so Mickey and I spent one of the greatest nights of our lives there. It was a romantic, magical evening. We made love all night. We were both young and in love, and he wanted to marry me and spend the rest of our lives together."

Her eyes welled up, and Holly Brooke cleared her throat. She was recovering from a bad cold that came on over the holidays and hadn't retreated much, and her face slackened, making her voice parched and masking the gentle lilt of earlier conversations about days now more than six decades ago. Although she was small and fine-boned, any hint of frailty was deceptive. She was a hard-edged New Yorker at heart, and, from her 10th floor apartment just off Central Park near Trump Tower, had the view of Manhattan to match. As she sipped her afternoon tea, it was evident that her mind remained wit sharp, unbothered by her age. Holly would be 91 that coming June—June 7, she emphasized because the number had always been special. So special, she said, that in that late summer of 1951, when she was in Kansas City living with the love of her life, she had begged that when he returned to New York from his minor-league demotion, he ask the Yankees to change his uniform, to take back the jersey with the number 6 on the back and to give him the jersey with the numeral 7.

"It will bring you luck," she told me she said to Mickey. "I promise."

Mickey Mantle would do just that when the Yankees called him back to the majors that August, tearing up Triple-A pitching with a vengeance in only 40 games with the Kansas City Blues. Some skeptics feared that Mantle, who would not turn 20 until the end of October, was washed up for good when he went into a slump after a magnificent start to his rookie season. However, his manager Casey Stengel had dismissed that kind of talk, telling reporters who asked if Mickey was finished playing, "You wish you were through like that kid's through."

On August 22, 1951, the Yankees' new prodigal son returned to New York, arriving with Holly on a Super Chief train at Grand Central Station and passing through what was then known as the "Kissing Room," where travelers once embraced their sweethearts, friends, and family, and offering cozy access to the Biltmore Hotel above. That was where Zelda and F. Scott Fitzgerald had honeymooned, she whispered to Mickey as they snuggled arm and arm with the crowd.

"I don't know if Mickey knew who F. Scott Fitzgerald was," said Holly, smiling as she dreamily remembered that day. "I shouldn't say that. He was a very smart man. He just didn't like to show it, but his mind was like a steel trap. Once he heard or saw something, he knew it by heart. I suspect that's what helped make him such a great hitter and ballplayer. But I think he enjoyed being seen as that good ol' country boy.

"We had a drink at the Kissing Room. We had come in a day early, and Mickey didn't have to report back to the team until the next day. He didn't want to go to the Concourse Plaza where they had a room for him. That was all the way out in the Bronx, and we were in Manhattan and at Grand Central Station, and we had the day to ourselves, and I had come to think that we would have the rest of our lives together as well.

"'Holly, I want you to marry me,' Mickey said to me that night. He had said it earlier, but I think, returning to New York, he knew he now had it together. The Yankees wanted him back in the majors, and this time he knew he was going to stick with the team for good, and that he would live up to all they were expecting of him. We had talked about marriage. *He* had talked about marriage. He had talked about wanting to marry me and about adopting my son. But this time was different. He was so insistent. And when he asked me to marry him this time, it wasn't like the other times. He knew the only person who could stand in our way was his father. But Mutt had seen us together in Kansas City, just as he had seen us together here in New York before Mickey was sent down. And in Kansas City, I think he saw in Mickey's face his determination to be with me.

There in front of me, Mickey said to his father, 'Dad, so what if she's older than me? She's seven years older than me. Mom was ten years older than you when you married her, and she had been married before as well. If it can work out for you and Mom, why couldn't it work out for Holly and me?' I thought Mutt was going to cry. He left our room, and I wouldn't be surprised if he did shed a tear later. You could tell that Mickey had hit a soft spot. So that night back in New York, Mickey says to me, 'Dad won't like it. You saw what he's like. He wants me to marry Merlyn, but I can't. I'm not in love with her. I'm in love with you. So I'll bring him around.' And, of course, I said, 'Yes, Mickey, I'll marry you. I love you.' And he told me he loved me, too. 'You're the love of my life, Holly.' And that's how we left it. Mickey was going to talk to his father—'Come hell or high water,' I think is how he said it—and we were going to get married as soon as the season ended. Mickey said the only thing that would be more perfect was if the Yankees won the World Series as well."

I knew of Holly Brooke almost forty years before I met her, though I don't think I expected to ever meet her, much less interview her. In 1970, I was a young newspaperman in Dallas, doing what all cub reporters at big city papers do, hustling for stories while working long hours, often on the lonely night shift in the newsroom where there is little to do but hope and wait. There was a giant Rolodex on the city desk, and one night I found myself flipping through it and stopping at the name and phone number of my childhood hero. Over the coming days I must have called a dozen times trying to talk to him in hopes of setting up an interview, though neither the sports nor city editors showed much interest in a story on my hero in retirement. Gay Talese's *Esquire* profile of Joe DiMaggio in 1966 remained the standard for that kind of story, and I had hoped to model mine in a similar fashion, the silent season of DiMaggio's successor.

When my father returned to the United States from overseas at the end of World War II, he had fulfilled one of his lifelong dreams of watching the New York Yankees play at Yankee Stadium. He attended two games that September of what had been a miserable season for the Yankees. It was the third straight year that the Yankees had been without the services of Joe DiMaggio, my father's favorite player, who had enlisted in the Army Air Forces. That alone made DiMaggio even more special in my father's eyes—he was a decorated army veteran—and he had returned home to Texas with a life-size portrait of "The Yankee Clipper," as he was affectionately known by fans, that later hung in my bedroom alongside a similar large picture of Mickey Mantle. My mom, a devout Roman Catholic, often complained that my bedroom was more of a place of worship to my hero, than to God. Maybe she was right. I did have a crucifix on a wall; however, it was dwarfed by those giant pictures of Mantle and DiMaggio, each with their own piece of wood in their hands. Fittingly, each night my nightly prayers that began with "Now I lay me down to sleep . . ." ended with a special request that God watch over Mickey, who had bad legs and was often injured.

Mantle had retired to Dallas in 1969, and Dallas in this period was like a baseball purgatory for him. It was a big city in America without a Major League Baseball team. As the country finally exited the troubled 60s and entered the 70s, Dallas was also a city still in mourning for the most defining event of the recently completed decade, or of the century for that matter. The Kennedy assassination had left Dallas not only with a civic black eye but also at a loss for a national identity beyond the Dallas Cowboys, the city's National Football League franchise. That alone said volumes. Dallas was a big enough city to have its own professional football franchise, two of them, in fact, when the Dallas Texans of the old American Football League had been around before their move to Kansas City where they became the Chiefs. However, it wasn't a big enough city to have its own Major League Baseball franchise. When big-league baseball did come to the area in 1972 with the move of the Washington Senators, Dallas would share the franchise with Fort Worth, and the games would be played in Arlington, midway between the two big cities. Mantle, though, was hardly a newcomer to Dallas. He had lived there since the 1950s and in that time had irked local sportswriters more than any other sports figure in town. His drinking and carousing in the heart of the American Bible Belt, a sports star's bad boy exploits which were then rarely reported in newspapers or on television, had already become legendary in Dallas, where he had also earned a reputation for his boorish behavior, especially toward members of the news media.

When we finally met, it was at one of those quaint restaurants of that time littered with peanut shells on the floor in the trendy Turtle Creek area of the city. It took all my willpower to stop staring at him. I was nervous and didn't know if I could actually talk to him until Mantle gave me a handshake worthy of a lumberjack. I was surprised, though, to find that he was only a couple of inches taller than I, maybe 5'10". But he was massive, as if chiseled from flesh and muscle. He had the shoulders of a linebacker and the arms of a bodybuilder.

He was also sloshed and slurring his words. What broke the ice was golf. He played almost every day, and I had been a golfer growing up in Waco, Texas. I also now lived with my wife in a town house community in North Dallas with a golf course off it that Mickey said he knew.

Mickey Mantle was drunk. Just how drunk I didn't realize. He was trying to balance peanuts, still in their shells, on his nose. He would perfectly balance a peanut on his nose, snap his head upward so as to pop the peanut in the air, and then catch it between his teeth. Mickey had wanted to bet $10 that he could catch 10 peanuts in a row that way but so far he hadn't been able to make it past six. It was amazing he could even get that far given his condition. I had heard stories of Mickey having slugged prodigious home runs while hung over, so perhaps catching half a dozen peanuts in a row between his teeth shouldn't have been so amazing, but it was. We also had attracted the attention of the patrons sitting at the tables around us, and they were all now engrossed in watching a grown man behaving like a drunken adolescent. Worse, a couple of the men looking on appeared to recognize him.

"Is that Mickey Mantle?" one of the men whispered to me as Mickey began making another run of peanuts.

I ignored him but could hear him and his lunch partner whispering as to whether it was.

"That's Mickey Mantle?" the other man said, disbelieving.

"Yeah, it's gotta be him. Look at his arms."

"Nah, I don't think it is. What would he be doin' here?"

It was a late spring lunch at which I was supposed to be meeting my childhood hero. Instead it felt like what I imagined having lunch with my father would be like when he was on one of his drunken binges, which had been often when I was growing up. The restaurant served its beer in 16-ounce Mason jars, and Mickey had insisted each of his beers be served in a fresh jar and that the jars be left at our table, as if some marker of what we had drunk.

"What the fuck!" Mickey finally gave up trying to make it to 10 peanuts in a row. "I feel like I'm in some god-awful dream where the peanut man at Yankee Stadium's been using me as a fuckin' dartboard." I had to be drunk myself, I thought, to be sitting here watching Mickey Mantle play a silly peanut catching game and listening to him talk about some baseball peanut vendor in a nightmare. "What the fuck!"

The afternoon had been full of *What the Fucks*. "What the fuck" came out of Mickey's mouth the way other people use you-know, as in "What the fuck, this has been the shittiest year. What the fuck, how long's it fuckin' gonna take to get these fuckin' burgers?"

Mickey said the words flowingly, though, not like an angry piece of off-color language but as if it were the name of a country tune on some imaginary jukebox that the restaurant didn't have. He said it a decibel or two just above a whisper. *What the fuck.* Half wonderment and half frustration. I could imagine not even paying attention to him saying it after a while. This was Mickey *fuckin'* Mantle, after all, easily recognizable, even out of uniform, in a football town at that, and no one seemed to mind it—least of all the waitresses who likely assumed that a star this big and with people sending notes to our table, was tipping big.

Actually, I left the tip that afternoon after Mickey had insisted on paying and snagged the check from my hand. "Let's see how you tip," he said. Mickey noticed a photograph of a woman behind a plastic covering in my wallet and motioned to look at it.

"What the fuck, who's that knockout?" he demanded.

"That's my wife, Mickey." I pulled the photograph out of the wallet so that he could get a better look.

"What the fuck, she looks like a movie star, Waco," he said. I had told him I was from Waco, Texas, south of Dallas, and that had been a mistake because he started calling me "Waco," after that. "Talk about marrying the hell up! Tell me about it."

"We got married two years ago," I said. "Secretly."

"You eloped?"

"Yeah, and no."

"What the fuck, you did or you didn't."

"We did," I said. "We'd been dating secretly for a year. Then got married and kept it a secret for almost another year."

Mickey let out an unexpected laugh and lost the gulp of his last beer. I began telling him my crazy story of being 20, in college, falling in love with a high school cheerleader who was only 16, and whose parents objected to her dating me.

"I would, too, Waco. You're lucky her old man didn't shoot your fuckin' ass off."

"That's why we decided to get married," I said. "So if they found out we were dating, we could say, 'Hey, we're married. Fuck off. You can't do shit about it.'"

"What the fuck, Waco, you fucker, you're fuckin' lucky her old man still didn't shoot you!"

Then, for what seemed like an eternity, Mickey Mantle continued to give the photograph a cross-eyed stare. He turned it around and studied the picture as if it were a puzzle he had to decipher. A smile darted across his eyes, as endearing as the crooked grin that had been locked on his face for much of the afternoon.

"She's awfully purty," he said, his words growing more slurred every time he spoke. "She reminds me of my first."

"Merlyn?" I asked, thinking he was talking about his wife.

"Naw, Merlyn wasn't my first," he said. "I'm talking about a girl I met in New York my rookie year. Her name was Holly. Holly Brooke. She was a redhead like your wife."

If there was any doubt that Mickey was drunk, this was a dead give-away. My wife was a blonde, and the color picture I had shown Mickey had actually made her hair look even lighter than it was. So there was no reason for mistaking her for a redhead unless you considered that Mickey was seeing what he wanted to see.

"Mick," and, as I said the name, I mentally pinched myself. I was sitting here talking to my childhood hero, calling him "Mick" as if I had known him for years, and talking about women in a way I had never spoken to anyone. I'm not sure how the interview, whatever there was of an interview, had taken a turn in which Mickey had begun quizzing me about being new to Dallas, about having recently graduated from college, and about my wife. He had noticed my wedding ring, and he had wondered why I had married so young. He should talk. I reminded him he had gotten married after his rookie season, when he had barely turned 20.

"I know, but that was a long time ago," he said. "We were kids. We were foolish. I don't know if we woulda done that today."

Then he went back to looking at the photograph of my better half. I wouldn't understand until years later when I finally saw a picture of Mickey with Holly Brooke in that year when he was young, in love, and happy.

CHAPTER ONE

Endings and Beginnings

Heroes are people who are all good with no bad in them. That's the way I always saw Joe DiMaggio.

—MICKEY MANTLE

"WELL, MICKEY, THIS IS ANOTHER SEASON FOR ME," JOE DIMAGGIO SAID to the Yankees' celebrated rookie who wasn't even sure if he was starting his first season in the major leagues or back in the minors. "Of course, this is the first season for you here in the major leagues. How do you feel about this first trip for the first game you're going to play?"

"Well, Joe, I'm pretty nervous about it all," said a shy and, yes, nervous Mickey Mantle. "It's all really new to me."

"Well, I'll tell you, Mickey, I felt pretty nervous the first game I played," said DiMaggio, obviously trying to make Mantle feel at ease. "As a matter of fact, I can recall I missed 17 games at the opening of the season and finally I got back in there. When I did play my first game, I swung at the first pitch and was very fortunate to get a base hit and that took all the tension out. Now are you going to do the same thing for us?"

There was a moment of nervous laughs the two shared.

"Well, I don't know," said Mickey. "I'll probably swing at the first pitch no matter, but I don't know if I'll get a hit."

"Well, I hope it's a hit, Mickey," said DiMaggio, offering encouragement, "because from there on in, you'll go from there."

It was the morning of April 16, 1951, and Joe DiMaggio and Mickey Mantle were with their New York Yankees teammates about to board a train to Washington for the season's Opening Day against the Senators. They were being detained for a few minutes for recorded interviews for CBS Radio's famous news program *Hear It Now* when a remote microphone picked up DiMaggio and Mantle's unrehearsed conversation, a conversation that unfortunately would be soon forgotten and overlooked.

The veteran DiMaggio, who only weeks earlier had announced he would retire at the end of the 1951 season, appears enthusiastic and supportive, engaging Mantle in a genuine manner that is both refreshing and surprising. All spring training much of what the press had been reporting was young Mantle's superman-like heroics at the plate, especially since the Yankees appeared to be grooming him as DiMaggio's replacement.

DiMaggio's surprisingly gracious remarks to Mantle were all the more unselfishly magnanimous because in the following years much of what was written about the relationship between the two men would suggest just the opposite. They were, after all, the legends of the greatest team in the greatest era of the game at the greatest time in America—Joe DiMaggio and Mickey Mantle—and seemingly forever they have been depicted as bitter enemies who could make each other physically ill over just which of them could be, or was, the greatest New York Yankee. DiMaggio almost always had been cast as an aloof, bitter aging star who resented the presence of any heir apparent but especially someone as different from him as Mantle appeared to be.

Unfortunately, deeply held notions can be long lasting, especially if they have been repeated without question and then reinforced by reports and books based on little more than misperceptions, no matter how mistaken. There were also the misguided recollections of teammates who might have been put off by DiMaggio's aloofness and his unwillingness to party and carouse with them, while they may have been more receptive and sympathetic to Mantle, who quickly in his career became a party animal and a favorite among his fellow players.

If you believed those stories that have been retold many times in the biographies of both players, DiMaggio never said anything to Mickey all season long in 1951, not until the second game of that year's World

Series. That was when Mantle tore up a knee when he caught his cleat in an outfield drain while avoiding DiMaggio as they both chased Willie Mays's fly ball. After making the catch, DiMaggio ran over to check on Mantle, offering reassurance and trying to allay his immediate fears. "Mantle said it was their first conversation of the year," one major biography of Mickey maintained. However, that was far from the truth, as the April 16 recorded conversation shows. It is also at the heart of an overwhelming amount of material documenting that the true relationship of DiMaggio and Mantle, contrary to the long-held myth of the two men being unfriendly antagonists, was actually that of symbiotic teammates and heroes cast into the national spotlight in 1951—DiMaggio's final season and Mantle's rookie year—and lasting until Mantle's death in 1995.

Merlyn Mantle, for one, didn't believe those stories about Mickey and Joe DiMaggio disliking one another.

"That's not true, not true at all," Merlyn said to me in one of our conversations recounting stories she said Mantle had told her of quietly spending time with the famously private DiMaggio out of sight of writers and fans. "Mickey said he wouldn't have made it through that first season if it hadn't been for the words of encouragement from Joe. I don't think Joe made a big public fuss of it in front of even teammates. I don't think that was Joe. I think it was more like a wink and a word here and there. I don't think Joe was a big rah-rah kind of guy, was he? And I think that kind of thing rubbed off on Mickey, too. That you were a good teammate, that a word here and there meant more than showy speeches."

Woe, however, to anyone else casting doubts on the myth that the brooding, unsentimental DiMaggio was some kind of evil von Rothbart, the antagonist to Mantle as Prince Siegfried and seeking to enchant and steal his princess talent in baseball's ballet of the game's immortals. Yet that was the classic tale, as fictional as *Swan Lake*, which sportswriters of newspapers and books chose to write—of a rift between the two Yankee heroes—and one of the reasons both DiMaggio and Mantle went to their graves cursing those who wrote about them.

"If there's a place for sportswriters in heaven," Mantle told me in a 1970 interview, "I'll just gladly sign those dozens of balls for St. Peter at the Pearly Gates and then go to the other place. Ya know, I sometimes found it easier to tell writers what they wanted to hear, even if it wasn't the truth because they wouldn't know the truth if the lord gave it to them . . . I don't believe half of what I read in the papers. Why should I? I know that at least half of what I told writers wasn't true. It's what they wanted to hear and wanted to write, and if they want to be that goddamn stupid, then fine. It's not too hard to help them since they're usually already there!"

The DiMaggio-Mantle relationship, including conversations, had begun that spring training in Arizona. Anyone who has ever been to a spring training camp and spent any time there with the players on the field can attest to the fact that it is unlike anything you will see in the major leagues insofar as the camaraderie and *esprit de corps* that quickly develops. It more closely resembles a frat house environment than a camp that soon determines who the club will keep, who will move over to the minor-league camp, and who is being carefully considered for a roster spot on the major-league team. The Yankee spring training of 1951 was no different, and Mickey quickly moved into that group of younger play-ers who had a good chance to be a major-league Yankee. The surprise with Mantle was that he had just completed a season in Class C minor-league baseball, and no minor-league player had ever made the jump from Class C baseball to the Yankees in one year. So the veterans as much as anyone else were keeping an eye on Mickey, and DiMaggio was no different.

Strange dynamics also happen when grown men get drunk together and talk honestly about their lives, their women, their work, their lies, and, most importantly, their goddamn lies. Almost 20 years after that 1951 season, the subject of DiMaggio and his alleged resentment of Mickey were brought to Mantle's attention over drinks at the Preston Trail Golf Club in Dallas. Mantle and I had played golf several times a week that summer of 1970, the result of my call to him months earlier and Mickey learning that I played golf and could get away early and play anywhere in Dallas, often with the green fees "comped" just because it was Mickey Mantle playing on the course.

Mickey's drinking problem was well established by then, and perhaps I was on my way to a similar demise, especially given that I came from a family of hard drinkers who denied their alcoholism. What that meant was that from my early childhood I had learned to negotiate my way around drunks. Long before I had graduated from college, I had a life's lesson degree on how to handle a drunk whom you loved, that being my father. From there, sensing how to handle a drunken Mickey Mantle, my childhood hero, was almost second nature.

When drinking, Mickey delighted in telling stories, especially about life as a New York Yankee. Everyone in the clubhouse from Pete Sheehy, the clubhouse attendant, to the lowliest player had their own imitation of DiMaggio, Mickey told me, and they would often do these impersonations while Joe was sitting in front of his locker, his back to his teammates, seemingly self-absorbed in his brooding.

"Joe was just too easy to make fun of, and I guess I saw all the other players do it that it seemed easier to be that way than to be as serious as Joe always was," said Mickey. "He wasn't much for having friends on the team, and I think it was that way his entire career. I know that by '51, which was the only year I played with Joe, he was someone you just left alone. If he wanted to say something to you, he would. He did offer advice, I'll say that for him, and I think he might have wanted to be a good teammate—and don't get me wrong, on the field, in a game, there was no better teammate, and he was hurtin' that last year. Later in my career, when I practically needed a wheelchair most of the time just to make it on to the field, I thought of Joe in '51, and it occurred to me that that son-of-a-bitch was hurtin' just like that. And to be honest, it became a kinda backhanded inspiration because I figured if old man Joe could suck it up and go out that last year the way he felt, goddamn if I wasn't gonna try to do the same."

One of the first times Mickey recalled DiMaggio coming over and saying something to him was on May 1 of that 1951 season, shortly after Mantle hit his first home run off of right-hander Randy Gumpert in Chicago, a 450-foot drive into the White Sox bullpen beyond right field.

"Joe came over to me on the dugout bench and said, 'Mickey, Gumpert oughta thank you. You just put him in the history books,'" Mantle said. "I wasn't sure what the hell he meant until later. He meant people would remember he was the first pitcher I homered against. So I guess Joe knew I was going to amount to something."

CHAPTER TWO

America's Hero

I want to thank the Good Lord for making me a Yankee.

—JOE DIMAGGIO

IT'S BEEN SAID THAT JOE DIMAGGIO, IN TRUTH, WAS A MAN WHO COULD not be written about with any degree of accuracy under the old rules of journalism and biography. It was difficult to strip away the facade that he, like most celebrities, used to protect himself from an adoring public. DiMaggio, especially though, was not merely a sports legend, but as David Halberstam once described him, "a kind of icon of icons, the most celebrated athlete of his age, the best big game player of his era and a man who because of his deeds, looks and marriage to the actress Marilyn Monroe, had transcended the barriers of sports in terms of the breadth of his fame."

But he remained an icon in America about whom a great deal had been written, especially at the height of his glory in the 1940s but yet about whom little was known beyond what protective sportswriters shared about him in his day. Nevertheless, when he died in 1999, DiMaggio had gone from the heights of hero-worship to virtual ridicule for the exact way in which he had carried himself above everyone, writers, fans, and teammates alike but especially Mickey Mantle.

In what was widely lauded as one of the best baseball books ever written, the late Richard Ben Cramer in *Joe DiMaggio: The Hero's Life* opened the book with a scorching prologue portraying the Yankee Clipper as a sad, miserly old man who might have sold nine of his ten World Series rings and then returned to Yankee Stadium on September 27,

1998, for Joe DiMaggio Day where he was presented replicas of those rings. He was pictured riding around the perimeter of the stadium in a 1956 Thunderbird convertible waving to fans like the pope as if his hands were blowing blessings to the crowd. However, according to Cramer, Joe had wanted this celebration not for the rings but for special commemorative Joe DiMaggio Day baseballs authenticated by Major League Baseball—15,000 that would be given to him—that would fetch DiMaggio at least $400 per ball. Joe was still seething, the book contends, from not only having to attend the special Mickey Mantle ceremonies at the stadium in 1995 honoring Mickey who had just died, but also learning that the Yankees were using in the game a special Mantle commemorative baseball that collectors and memorabilia dealers were already selling for $300 a ball—twice what DiMaggio's signed baseballs were commanding.

"For sixty years, writers had to make up what Joe cared about," wrote Cramer. "So they wrote about remembered autumns of glory, about the love affair of the Yankee hero and the Yankee fans."

DiMaggio himself had once said: "They used to write stories about me like they were interviewing me, and never even talked to me."

So with DiMaggio reluctant to say much, writers jumped to conclusions and went for the best angle they could conjure up on a story. In 1951, that angle was Mantle, who was there to replace DiMaggio. He was getting all the attention in the press, and manager Casey Stengel loved him like a son. So naturally, the writers figured, there had to be some resentment from the somber DiMaggio, some bad will from the prince of the city guarding his throne from the young upstart who now did all the things DiMaggio used to do with more power and more speed and was always seen with a smile on his golden face, as if he didn't have a care in the world.

"The whole Joe DiMaggio Day," Cramer had concluded, "wasn't about rings but about history and Joe's need to win; about Mickey Mantle and the way Joe resented him; and money, mostly money, as it mostly was with Joe."

How did it get this way for DiMaggio, so that his latest biographer, a highly respected journalist and Pulitzer Prize recipient for international reporting who had authored a solid biography of Ted Williams and a marvelous book about the presidential campaign Bill Clinton won in 1992, had portrayed him as little more than baseball's Ebenezer Scrooge—and without a final act of redemption?

Had the world that once worshipped and adored Joe DiMaggio now at the new millennium turned on the very same national hero who made the war-turmoiled middle decade of the American 20th century not just bearable but joyously celebrated and triumphant? The Golden Age, America had come to call, that period of the national pastime but of the country as well. For DiMaggio, correctly or not, had come to symbolize the greatness of America and its conquest of Adolf Hitler and the Nazi threat to freedom. Americans sang songs about Joltin' Joe, as he was known, and his nickname the Yankee Clipper conjured up the image of the elegant New England schooners developed in the Chesapeake Bay before the American Revolution. And in 1951, America seemed united in sad regret that the great DiMaggio, after many glorious years in baseball was about to hang up his spikes and that his pending retirement threatened to extinguish the glitter that his heroics had bestowed on the nation.

Of course, it may not have been coincidental that DiMaggio was leaving the baseball stage, making a farewell tour, though it never was that, in the same year that Mickey Mantle was making his debut. It was in essence a changing of the guard not unlike the significant changes that were underway in the world. President Harry S Truman was nearing the end of his tenure in the White House as the country had used his caretaker years to acclimate to life without Franklin D. Roosevelt. In a sense, then, America was looking for new heroes to lead the nation into the second half of the century and to cheer on in its national sports obsession.

The postwar America of the mid-20th century was like all societies with the need for heroes, not because they coincidentally made them up on their own but because heroes like DiMaggio and Mantle express a deep psychological aspect of human existence. They can be seen as a metaphor for the human search for self-knowledge. In their time, DiMaggio and Mantle showed us the path to our own consciousness through the power and spectacle of their baseball heroics, often backlit by the cathedral solemnity of Yankee Stadium. In the atomic age of the 1950s, the tape-measure blasts in our national pastime became peacetime symbols of America's newly established military dominance.

For America, just six years removed from World War II, was already involved in another foreign conflict, the Korean War, and a new conflict at home, the war against communism and the "Red Menace." In 1951 Ethel and Julius Rosenberg were sentenced to death, eventually becoming the only two American civilians to be executed for espionage-related activity during the Cold War. The United States had opened the Nevada Atomic Test site in January and tested its first hydrogen bomb in May. It was a new age, even in sports which witnessed the first coast-to-coast telecast of a live sporting event on television which that year also premiered two of its landmark shows, *I Love Lucy* and *Dragnet*.

As Mantle was to say about himself in the 1950s, as well as of DiMaggio in the previous two decades:

"I guess you could say I'm what this country's all about."

Perhaps it wasn't so much that age and time weren't good to Joe DiMaggio as that his biographers and writers sometimes had the last word, something for which he may have been partly to blame. Joe didn't give of himself, especially to those he knew wanted to write about him. He wanted to keep himself, his life, his loves, his fears, all to himself. In protecting his privacy, however, he had failed to put forth his own story, his own autobiography, to put on the record, as he wanted, his life. God knows he had grand opportunities, perhaps the best having been someone who might have been the most sympathetic, the author and writer Gay Talese. They were both Italians with an American heritage and legacy of greatness in their two chosen careers. If ever there was a writer whom DiMaggio should have allowed inside, to have befriended really, it would have been Talese.

In 1966, *Esquire* magazine, at what many have said was the height of its cultural relevance, published Talese's fabulous profile of DiMaggio under the headline "The Silent Season of a Hero," that portrayed him as a brooding, chain-smoking loner hiding figuratively behind his fame and more literally behind the protective walls of his restaurant on the San Francisco pier.

It would have been an unprecedented opportunity for DiMaggio to allow himself to be known personally by an entirely new generation that knew of him only through the ancient reminiscences of old men who had once seen the great DiMaggio play. And, lord, did America want to fall in love with DiMaggio again, or someone like him. It would be another two years before the film *The Graduate*, starring Dustin Hoffman and Anne Bancroft, popularized the Simon & Garfunkel song "Mrs. Robinson," though most would remember it for the famous line bemoaning the loss of DiMaggio from the national consciousness. The song had put DiMaggio's name on the lips of an entirely new generation, and it may possibly have generated the most favorable reaction Joe was to ever have from a national audience that otherwise would not know him, except perhaps when he became a commercial spokesman for Mr. Coffee machines in the 1970s.

But DiMaggio was an unwilling profile subject, effectively alienating someone who could have gone a long way in shaping his image for the rest of his life.

Talese was surprised, having thought he had an agreement with the baseball icon who had been his boyhood idol. In 1944, when the Yankees moved their spring training to Atlantic City because of wartime gas rationing and travel restrictions, 12-year-old Gay Talese had taken a trolley car 11 miles up the coast from Ocean City, New Jersey, to watch DiMaggio. In 1965, when he left the *New York Times* to write full-time for editor Harold Hayes at *Esquire*, Talese met DiMaggio at the 1965 Yankees Old-Timers' Game, introduced by their mutual friend, *Times* photographer Ernie Sisto. After chatting a few minutes, Talese told DiMaggio, "I'd love to come out and see you sometime in your hometown, and maybe write a piece about you."

"Sure, sure, anytime," said DiMaggio, who told him he could reach him at his restaurant.

DiMaggio, however, hadn't been forthright and wanted no part of it. When Talese showed up unannounced at DiMaggio's restaurant, he was at one point confronted by an angry DiMaggio, shouting to him over the phone that he had better get a lawyer.

"*You are invading my rights. I did not ask you to come. I assume you have a lawyer. You must have a lawyer, get your lawyer!*"

All the while Joe was just in another part of the restaurant.

"Look," DiMaggio told Talese when he finally spoke to him, "I do not interfere with other people's lives. And I do not expect them to interfere with mine. There are things about my life, personal things, that I refuse to talk about. And even if you asked my brothers, they would be unable to tell you about them because they do not know. There are things about me, so many things, that they simply do not know."

"I don't want to cause trouble," Talese said, trying to assure him. "I think you're a great man, and . . ."

"I'm not great," DiMaggio quickly said. "I'm not great. I'm just a man trying to get along."

Talese persisted. He didn't write about this in the piece, but he personally appealed to DiMaggio's close friend Lefty O'Doul.

"I'm not going to write about Marilyn Monroe," he told O'Doul. "I'm not here as an enemy. I don't do hatchet jobs—look at my work."

O'Doul interceded and got Talese an invitation to accompany DiMaggio and his pals on a golf outing during which, in a three-piece suit and street shoes, he foraged in the brush and woods, finding three of Joe's errant shots.

"That was when I started having access," Talese said.

DiMaggio began inviting him on outings, even over to his house and on a flight to the Yankees' spring training camp in Fort Lauderdale. Talese included some of this in his story, though, unfortunately not about their flight together where they spoke about Truman Capote's just-published nonfiction novel, *In Cold Blood*. DiMaggio told him he was enjoying the book and even started "talking about the opening scene, of the wheat fields in Kansas, and the Cutter family."

"And he started telling me," Talese would later tell an interviewer, "what a wonderful way it was to begin a book, and then I think he even read me a few lines. And I thought, '*This is the side that the sportswriters don't know of Joe DiMaggio.*'"

For whatever reason—Talese said he didn't want the *Esquire* story to be a first-person piece—this, perhaps most touching of all personal anecdotes, wasn't included in the article, this side that not only sports-writers didn't know about DiMaggio but neither would Talese's readers.

DiMaggio was furious when he read the story in the magazine. *Esquire* had been unable to locate him to shoot the cover photograph and had to do something imaginative, showing someone in a business suit swinging at home plate and looking like DiMaggio in front of an empty Yankee Stadium. But it wasn't DiMaggio, who later told the magazine's advertising editor, "Well, I wouldn't have posed for it. But I've gotta tell you—when I saw it . . . it brought tears to my eyes."

DiMaggio, though, apparently never forgave Talese, who ran into Joe in 1998 at a black-tie dinner at Radio City Music Hall when *Time* maga-zine celebrated its 75th anniversary and had invited every living person who had ever appeared on its cover. Talese and his wife Nan attended the dinner, as the guests of then–executive editor Norman Pearlstine and his wife, Nancy Friday. While at the dinner, Talese spotted DiMaggio, who was heading up to say hello to the political consultant Ed Rollins, at a nearby table.

"I saw him walking up right by me," Talese recalled. "And I said, 'Hello, Mr. DiMaggio.' He looked at me, and he recognized me, and he said, 'Are you still working for that rag?'"

The DiMaggio profile would become one of the cornerstones of Talese's career. Pulitzer Prize–winning journalist and author David Halberstam called the piece the best magazine story he had ever read. Ultimately, Talese became one of the most revered, celebrated writers and authors of his time, linked with Capote and Tom Wolfe as one of the pioneers of the so-called New Journalism spawned in the 1960s and 1970s, nonfiction writing that often employed the techniques of fiction.

"This is part of the New Journalism," Talese said of his work. "It takes certain liberties, if you will, from formal journalism—formulaic journalism."

However, there is no denying that Talese would have been the ideal writer in whom to confide, the perfect observer to allow into Joe's small circle of friends. Talese himself made no secret of having a unique con-nection to some of the personalities he profiled.

"I understood it because I'm an Italian," he said in an interview with the Nieman Foundation of Harvard. "My position, with regard to Sinatra and DiMaggio and Joe Bonanno and Joe Girardi—all those people—comes out of . . . (a) personal and prescient place in an ethnic culture. I have that in the Italian-American."

For Talese, and especially for DiMaggio, the missed opportunity would be an immeasurable loss.

CHAPTER THREE

The Yankee Legacy

Baseball didn't really get into my blood until I knocked off that hitting streak. Getting a daily hit became more important to me than eating, drinking or sleeping. Overnight I became a personality.

—JOE DiMAGGIO

SO HOW DID IT COME TO BE THAT THE LEGENDS OF THE GREATEST TEAM in the greatest era of the game at the greatest time in America—Joe DiMaggio and Mickey Mantle—would seemingly forever be depicted as bitter enemies who could make each either physically ill, as was the story with Mantle, or jealously angry, as DiMaggio was characterized as reacting to Mick, presumably feuding over just which of them could be, or was, the greatest New York Yankee?

Virtually every biography ever written about DiMaggio or Mantle portrays them as rivals, an idea stamped indelibly on the minds of most by Billy Crystal's sentimentally brilliant 2001 HBO film *61*. And who is a bigger Mantle and Yankee fan than Billy Crystal? However, all of us of his generation have depended heavily on those biographies as well as the sports literature of that era, and the sources often have been the teammates of both players. It is no secret that Mantle was far more popular among his teammates than the brooding, standoffish DiMaggio. However, not even the teammates of his own time were close to DiMaggio, and many resented him for keeping his distance especially during his greatest seasons when he appeared to bask in his glory alone, as if baseball were a game of individuals like tennis or golf.

"Before a camera or a group of people, I didn't have a performance to give," DiMaggio said in a 1983 interview. "I was very, very shy. I wanted to be away from people. I thought I didn't have that much to offer, that much to say, so I used to go into my shell."

Few baseball writers were close to DiMaggio. But then, sportswriting was different in that era. There was almost no intrusion by writers into the personal lives of sports figures, and athletes' personal lives were rarely written about in the newspapers. College football game programs of the day often carried newspaper advertisements promoting their sports sections with the line, "sports writing isn't a profession—it's an art." As a result, sportswriters often thought too much of themselves, believing they were the chroniclers of games that had taken otherwise shiftless men off the streets. "Without sport, what would Mickey Mantle do? He would drive a fork lift," Texas author Gary Cartwright wrote in his hilarious 1968 *Harper's* magazine memoir "Confessions of a Washed-Up Sportswriter." "Joe Namath raised carrier pigeons and sold hubcaps. Roger Maris operated a liquor store on the Illinois-Missouri border. Bud Wilkinson was Norman Rockwell's chauffeur, and Vince Lombardi operated an academy for the sons of South American dictators."

Baseball, the game itself, also could be a tedious cure for insomnia for some, and a church for most who followed and wrote about it, and their prose the gospels of this unique American religion. The stars and heroes of the game were viewed as gods to be measured by their records and their statistics, making them in the eyes of sportswriters even more competitive among themselves than they already were. Had Babe Ruth been the greatest Yankee, or had that been Lou Gehrig? They had been teammates for years and bitterly feuded late in Ruth's career, a feud that lasted for years up until July 4, 1939, the day the dying Gehrig delivered his "I consider myself the luckiest man on the face of the earth" speech. A teary-eyed crowd at Yankee Stadium bid its farewell, and Ruth had rushed to the stadium, the first time he had seen his friend in years, for a bear hug embrace that would become one of the most famous photographs of the two. Or was DiMaggio the greatest Yankee, or could it be in 1951 that the usurper was actually the Mantle kid? The sportswriters chronicling the incredible rookie spring training

Mickey Mantle enjoyed as a 19-year-old had held him up as the next Ruth, Gehrig, and DiMaggio all wrapped into one and set in motion a narrative that wouldn't be true—but who would dispute the authors of the gospel?

"Mickey said that was all so much rubbish," Greer Johnson, Mantle's companion the last 10 years of his life, told me in a 2001 interview. "Mickey would have laughed at the way he was portrayed in *61*—disliking Joe [DiMaggio] so much that he became physically ill every time Joe came to Yankee Stadium. I wasn't with Mickey in those years, but he spoke often enough about Joe for me to know they weren't feuding rivals. Heck, how could they have been? Mickey was a rookie in 1951, and that was the only year they played on the Yankees roster together. Joe DiMaggio retired after that season. Maybe there was some sense of a rivalry from Joe's side about their legacies. I don't know. But weren't they different kinds of hitters? I think the only regret Mickey really might have had about Joe DiMaggio may have been that they didn't play longer together, when each was at the top of their game."

DiMaggio's longtime friend Reno Barsocchini, who was his best man when he married Marilyn Monroe in 1954, told me almost the same thing, insisting in several interviews in 1978 and 1979 that biographers and the sportswriters of his time had wronged Joe. Barsocchini, who met Joe when they both played for the San Francisco Seals of the 1930s, was saddened that the DiMaggio–Gay Talese relationship in 1966—which he tried so hard to repair—had soured and been a lost opportunity for both men.

"That could have been such a great friendship and who knows where it might have led," Barsocchini said in one of several visits I made to his bar in San Francisco. "It might have been a great book that would have allowed the world to know Joe. Some of us close to Joe didn't think the [*Esquire*] article was a bad article, and to this day I don't know who it might have been who got to Joe first and said, 'Clipper, it was a crappy hatchet job,' but that's all it took: For one person Joe trusted to dump on the article, and the die was cast. Joe isn't the kind of person who asks anyone else's opinion of something once he's gotten it in his head that it was an unkind article. Gay Talese just had the poor misfortune of meeting Joe at the tail end of his experience with writers he felt he couldn't trust. He paid for the crimes of all those writers who had crossed him all those years."

The best authority on how there had been no feud between the two heroes, however, may have been the one person who played an extraordinary role in Mantle's life in New York during much of the 1950s, almost anonymously because she slipped through all the Mickey Mantle watchers of that time without raising an eyebrow.

Her name was Holly Brooke, a young divorced mother from New Jersey who would, in Mickey's words, become "my first" and hold on to his affection for years. The New Yorkers who knew her, or, more accurately, knew of Holly dismissed her as the showgirl who in the spring of 1951 had been involved in some reportedly sketchy scam to take advantage of the dazzling Yankee rookie.

"I became the showgirl who tried to scam Mickey Mantle," Holly reminisced half a century later. "Oh, if they had only known. I loved Mickey. Mickey loved me. Mickey had great years in his career. I was with him in New York those years, too. Many of his fans would tell you that 1956, when he won the Triple Crown, was his favorite year. And it was his best season. But if you had asked him, he would have said that 1951 was his favorite year. It was his favorite year because it was our year."

CHAPTER FOUR

Now Batting, Jack Daniels

When I got to New York, Casey [Stengel] told everyone I was gonna be the next Babe Ruth, the next Lou Gehrig, the next Joe DiMaggio. I didn't believe that. I don't think Casey really believed that. But New York was a circus, and Casey was like the circus barker trying to get people into the big tent.

—MICKEY MANTLE

IF ONLY THE YANKEES HAD KNOWN IN HIS ROOKIE YEAR WHAT THEY realized in the coming seasons—that despite the country boy appearance, their switch-hitting kid from Oklahoma with a guileless grin was a party animal with a penchant for alcohol and a recklessness no one could have foreseen—the story of Mickey Mantle might have been different. There were clues, but the Yankees and almost everyone else mistook them for the innocent signs of adolescence, especially since on the field Mantle appeared to be the prodigy the team expected after his spectacular spring training. However, those incredible talents carried with them monstrous appetites for the kind of life Mickey couldn't have found in the backwoods of Oklahoma but which was readily available all around him in New York. And Mickey didn't waste time connecting. When veteran Yankee outfielder Hank Bauer took him under his wing early in the season, he found Mickey moving into an apartment they shared above the Stage Delicatessen at 54th Street and Seventh Avenue carrying a bottle of Jack Daniels.

"I had drunk some in Oklahoma with some of my pals back in high school when someone would sneak us a bottle," Mantle told me in 1970. "But it wasn't something I was about to do much with my dad always looking out for what I was doing. But in New York, once we got there that [1951] season, it didn't take long for me to find what I liked, and it didn't seem to matter that I was under-age. There was always someone willing to buy it, even though I don't think I would have had any problem buying it myself. But there was usually someone there, and it had nothing to do with Billy Martin. I know everyone likes to blame Billy for my drinking, and the Yankees even ran his ass off thinking that would be the fix. But, hell, I was drinking long before Billy and I started hanging around. He just made it more fun!"

Was it Holly Brooke who got Mickey drinking? Years later, she would wonder and feel partly responsible, though there were many others to share the blame, if blame were to be assigned. Just how Mickey began drinking his rookie season was never clear, or maybe he just didn't want to say. He remembered that one night, while having a meal with some teammates, drinks were brought to their table. "I think it might have been a fan or someone who knew us who sent over drinks," Mickey recalled. "We had a good time, and the next morning I wake up hung-over and with an awful headache, and we had a game that afternoon."

This would become typical for Mickey in the years to come. In that rookie season, the drinking was like a baptism under fire into big-city life, for which he seemed totally unprepared, but then what 19-year-old would be? He was a kid in a man's body believing he could do things other men did, and perhaps be just as foolish.

Mickey was also too trusting of strangers and became easy prey for con men and scam artists. From one hustler, Mantle bought what he thought was $200 worth of sweaters for $30 only to learn that they were made of a cheap, highly flammable material. Then there was the Broadway opportunist named Alan Savitt, who in the early weeks of the season convinced Mantle that he needed him as his commercial agent. Savitt promised Mantle he could get him $50,000 a year in endorsements and personal appearances, which they would split 50-50. Mickey had no experience with agents. His father, after all, had naïvely undersold his own son's talents to scout Tom Greenwade and the Yankees without so much as waiting to see what other clubs offered. Mickey was also too shy to broach the topic with his teammates. The best friend Mantle had in those early weeks was Hank Bauer, who in Mickey's first days in New York had taken him out shopping and bought him two suits with his own money.

Bauer and several other Yankee players were represented by Frank Scott, who had been the team's traveling secretary through the late 1940s. Bauer soon learned about Mickey's deal and enlisted both Scott and the Yankees' help in trying to extricate Mickey from the deal with Savitt. Bauer and Scott even developed a clever plan for Scott to seek out Mickey as a client. For a country rookie, however, Mickey could be unusually stubborn.

"I've got bad news for you," Mantle told Scott when he approached Mickey about representing him. "This fellow wants to be my agent, and he's giving me a contract that guarantees me $50,000 a year."

Although skeptical, Scott said he couldn't offer any guarantees but would only take 10 percent, which was a more typical agent's fee. Scott also advised Mickey to have the Yankees' lawyers read over the contract. Mickey, however, was naïve enough to believe he had somehow latched onto a better deal than anyone else. When Scott again ran into Mantle a few days later, Mickey informed him he had signed the contract.

"Did you take it to the Yankee lawyers?" Scott asked.

"Nope," said Mickey, confidently. "I didn't have to. This fellow had a lawyer for me."

Mickey had been conned and this wasn't the end of it.

Savitt himself didn't have any money, so to pay Mantle an advance he promised him, he tried selling shares in the deal. However, he had no legitimate investors either. Instead Savitt tried hustling shares to struggling actors and Broadway show people and anyone else he could find. An investment of $1,500 could get you a part of Mickey Mantle, he promised. He got little interest except from an actress in her mid-20s named Holly Brooke, and she refused to turn over the money to Savitt until she could be introduced to Mickey and see for herself that Mantle was actually involved.

"There was an ice cream parlor and drug store in the 50s—it was the most inexpensive place around, and Alan Savitt came in and asked if anyone knew Mickey Mantle," Holly told me years later. "The fellas in the crowd did. I didn't. He asked if we'd invest $1,500. No one had $1,500. I asked my brothers and fathers. They knew of [Mantle], and they got the money together for me. Alan Savitt asked me if I wanted to meet him. I said, 'Yes, if I'm investing money, I want to meet him.' I was staying at a hotel for women. Danny's Hideaway was across the street from me. So I said that's the best place to go because the models and actresses would go in there and eat lunch because Danny's would always give us everything at half price and then sometimes we'd get things free. So we'd all go in there to eat. So I asked him if we could come in there. Mickey and I and Savitt, and he asked, 'Do you mind if we take pictures?' and I said, 'I don't mind. Ask him.' He didn't mind. So he took photographs of Mickey and me, that's the one you have in [*Mickey Mantle: America's Prodigal Son*]. And Mickey and I, I don't know. For some reason we clicked. I don't know what it was. And he asked if he could see me again, and I said yes. And then I saw him after that every single day that he was in town . . . He was incredibly handsome and muscular, and he was very young. I told Savitt I was in and I thought, 'Okay, Holly, I've just bought a quarter interest in a ballplayer.' I started to leave, and that's when Mickey asked if he could see me again."

It didn't matter to Mickey that he was engaged to his high school sweetheart, Merlyn, who was still in Oklahoma. Holly Brooke was stunning, as beautiful as any of the starry-eyed young actresses who hung around the Stage Deli or Danny's Hideaway in those days. "I thought she looked a little like Rita Hayworth," Mickey said years later. "I had never seen anyone that beautiful in the movies. You know how people wondered later why Joe [DiMaggio] would fall so hard for Marilyn Monroe? Well, when you've grown up the way Joe did in San Francisco and I did in Oklahoma, poor and the smell of fish and coal in your nostrils that you want to choke, and then someone like that—someone you would only see in your dreams or on the movie screen—taking any kind of interest in you, well, there's no goddamn way you're going to walk away from that."

Mickey began seeing Holly every day that the Yankees were in New York. Holly, who was seven years older than Mickey, showed him the New York nightlife that he wouldn't see with any of his Yankee teammates that year. "I guess I developed my first taste for the high life then," Mantle later said, "meeting Holly's friends, getting stuck with the check at too many fancy restaurants, discovering scotch at too many dull cock-tail parties."

However, that wasn't exactly true. Mickey didn't get stuck with many checks. The Stage Deli especially was often Mickey's security retreat from the intimidation of the big city. Max and Hymie Asnas, who owned the delicatessen, befriended Mickey and often made him special meals that were not on their menu. "Like all shy people," said Mantle, "I had a hard time going into new restaurants, not knowing whether to grab a table or wait to be shown, afraid to order something different for fear of making a jerk of myself, unable sometimes to tell the waiter from the busboy. But in the Stage Delicatessen I might have been in my home town." Much the same was true at Danny's Hideaway and many of the places where he went, where there was always someone picking up the tab. If someone wasn't paying for Mickey and whomever he was with, the places he went to were always too happy to comp him his meals and his drinks. It was a big deal to have a New York Yankee who was a regular hanging out in your place, and early in the season Mickey was the toast of the town.

"Mickey was the prince of the city," Holly said. "And he was having the time of his life. He loved every minute of it."

It didn't even seem to matter to Mantle that Savitt had failed to deliver on the $50,000 guarantee he had promised him to sign a contract for representation. Soon the Yankees got involved, as general manager George Weiss called on Arthur Friedlund, Yankee owner Dan Topping's personal lawyer, to finally extricate Mickey from the contract with Savitt.

Mickey, though, likely could have called on any of his new acquaintances he was meeting on what was known as "Steak Row" on East 45th Street to help him get rid of the sleazy Savitt. His favorite hangout quickly became Danny's Hideaway at 151 East 45th Street, which Clay Cole, a popular New York disc jockey from that time, described as "a restaurant for stand-up guys: Boxing champs, saloon . . . actors, teamster bosses, well-heeled merchants and well-mannered mobsters." It was the place to be seen, and Mickey was. Holly Brooke was invariably always with him, expanding her own networking, hoping it could further her own career.

"Mickey may have been that hillbilly hick everyone loves to say he was when he first came to New York," Holly said in an interview. "But it didn't take him long to fit in. Alan Savitt taught him a big lesson about fast-talkers in New York; and before you knew it, it was the other way around. He may have been a rookie and only 19, but in those first weeks in New York he quickly became a star. And people treated him that way. He rarely had to pay for anything. Not just drinks. People would pick up the check for dinner as well, especially at Danny's. They wanted to be in that circle of people who could say they bought the new Yankee star dinner and drinks. Men who owned clothing stores who would be in Danny's—and there were a lot of them—would come up, give Mickey their cards, and tell him to stop by and they'd take care of him. Mickey was one of the lowest paid players on the Yankees that year, but you'd never know it from looking at him because he was soon dressing like he was making the kind of money Joe was being paid."

It wouldn't take long before Mickey and Holly were being ushered out of sight, to the VIP Room at Danny's. By 1951, Danny's was no longer the one-room bistro seating six that it had been at its beginning. It had expanded to a four-story building, with 11 dining rooms, with two separate kitchens and two completely stocked bars on each floor. Mickey got to know the layout as well as the Yankee Stadium outfield, Holly said, and on any given night when the Yankees were home, Mantle would be there for hours before he would emerge, slightly inebriated. He would sign a few autographs and leave.

Mickey didn't even realize that DiMaggio was also an occasional regular at Danny's until the night when Mantle and Holly were arriving and found a horde of men and a few women packing the front of the restaurant, not moving nor allowing anyone to enter or leave but instead straining curiously to move closer to the center of the commotion. Holly thought someone dining there that night might have had a heart attack or fainted. She had seen that happen in the past. However, that night there were no signs of anyone panicking or needing help. As men slowly moved away, Mickey and Holly saw what everyone had wanted a glimpse of.

It was Joe DiMaggio. He was surrounded by well-wishers enthralled at just being near the great Yankee Clipper who had become even more popular, if that were possible, in New York in the weeks since his announcement that 1951 would be his final season. Everyone seemed to be lobbying for him to play at least another year: "Joe, you're still the man"... "Joe, please don't retire"... "Joe, you're still the best." DiMaggio had a reputation of rarely going out for dinner, ordering room service instead, but that had changed since the breakup of his first marriage. He had been seen the past year often at Toots Shor's restaurant and at Danny's where he loved the manicotti. Usually he was quickly escorted past the adoring fans, many with their jaws dropped at the surprise of personally seeing DiMaggio just feet away. He was always impeccably dressed, trim and looking taller than most imagined him to be, and nodding at anyone he personally recognized. Of course, there was always one diner who, not wishing to miss the opportunity, would stop Joe by extending a handshake that he would quickly firmly acknowledge and slide past.

"Joe, are the Yanks gonna take it again this year?" asked a man who stood up and patted his arm.

"We're going to try," DiMaggio said.

"Joe, you look like you could play another five years," said another well-wisher.

"I'm just looking to play this year," said DiMaggio, who was already ailing in the young season.

"Joe, are you thinking of managing?" asked a third man.

"No, the Yankees have a manager."

Mickey was frozen taking in the scene, Holly recalled. He watched as DiMaggio weaved through the people milling around him, totally in command. Mantle felt awkward even in small crowds, never knowing what to say and now seeing that all he had to do was to converse in the simplest manner, the way DiMaggio was doing, and to remain cordial.

DiMaggio seemed surprised to see Mickey arriving, and he was especially pleased to see the pretty redhead at his side. Mantle introduced Holly to his teammate, and Joe made an innocent mistake.

"Good to meet you," he said. "You're from Oklahoma, too, I understand."

Joe saw Holly and Mickey exchange nervous looks, and quickly realized he had said something wrong.

"No, Joe, I'm from Jersey," Holly said, smiling and putting DiMaggio at ease.

"I'm terribly sorry," said Joe. "Please accept my apologies. Mickey, I'm sorry . . ."

"Don't be silly, Joe," said Mickey. "I met Holly here. She's an actress."

"Anything I might have seen?" Joe asked.

"A couple of things," said Holly.

Then, as Holly mentioned a couple of recent off-Broadway shows in which she had parts, DiMaggio asked if he could buy them dinner. Mickey was shocked. He had heard clubhouse stories of how DiMaggio could be distant and how few players could say they ever dined with the legendary Yankee. That night DiMaggio not only dined with his rookie teammate and his date but also recounted a story about his mishap in his own rookie season in 1936 that got him off to a late start.

In spring training his rookie year, DiMaggio told them, he burned his foot in a diathermy machine, a device commonly used in sports medicine. Joe said he was so shy that he didn't dare ask anyone why it was that his foot was getting so hot in the treatment machine. When the treatment ended, the trainers discovered that Joe's foot was red and blistered so badly that he had to sit out the Yankees' season opener against the Washington Senators at Griffith Stadium where President Franklin D. Roosevelt threw out the ceremonial first ball. DiMaggio not only sat on the bench but he was also unable to play for several weeks, not making his Yankee debut until May 3 when he singled twice and tripled in six at-bats in a come-from-behind 14–5 win over the St. Louis Browns. DiMaggio went on to have a brilliant season—batting .323 with 44 doubles, 15 triples, and 29 home runs—and would have undoubtedly won Rookie of the Year honors if the award had been given out. The Rookie of the Year Award wasn't instituted until 1947, when Jackie Robinson won it.

"I've heard stories over the years about how Joe DiMaggio was standoffish, unfriendly, and not a very nice person," Holly said years later. "And I don't know who they could be talking about because it wasn't the Joe DiMaggio that I knew. I wasn't a close personal friend, and the only time I was around him was when Mickey and I ran into him or the times we had dinner with him—and once later when he was with Marilyn in New

York. But the Joe DiMaggio I got to know was a sweetheart. That first night at Danny's, I think that went a long way in making Mickey feel comfortable around him. I remember Mickey later saying that Joe seemed to be all business when he was in the clubhouse and at the stadium. 'He acts like the president of a bank, all serious all the time,' Mickey told me. And I said to him, 'Well, Mickey, the Yankees are like a bank aren't they? All those salaries, all that responsibility, and if Joe is who everyone says he is—Mr. Yankee—then he is like the president of the bank, isn't he? Hasn't Joe been that for as long as he's been a Yankee? Hasn't Joe been the reason that the Yankees have remained the greatest team in America after Babe Ruth was gone and after Lou Gehrig was gone? Mickey, who could ever know the pressure that Joe DiMaggio's been under to keep the Yankees from being anything less than the New York Yankees?'"

Mantle came to that realization thanks to Holly, and perhaps that is what Mickey meant when he told me that she had been the best business-woman he had ever known.

"If she hadn't been there," he said, "I don't think I would have made it that first year. She made me understand that I was no longer just a base-ball player. I was a *professional* baseball player. I tried to live up to that. Sometimes I didn't do too good a job of it, but I kept tryin'."

Until Holly, Mickey had never fallen head over heels for any woman, but Holly was unlike anyone he had ever known, he would tell her often, especially in their first days together, though he might have said that about any beauty he might have gotten to know then. Holly lived in an all-women housing complex near the theater district, but it wasn't unusual for men to be snuck in, as she often did with Mantle. Soon, though, she found her own apartment where Mickey began spending as much time as he did at the Concourse Hotel in the Bronx or the place he later shared with teammates above the Stage Deli. Bauer and fellow Yankee Johnny Hopp each had their own bedroom in that place, and Mantle would sleep on a cot in the living room. "I don't think they knew when I wasn't there," Mickey said of his roommates. "I was always there when it came time to leave for the stadium or to get to the train station, and I think that's what they figured was important."

CHAPTER FIVE

The American Dream

"I would like to take the great DiMaggio fishing," the old man said. "They say his father was a fisherman. Maybe he was as poor as we are and would understand."
— ERNEST HEMINGWAY, *THE OLD MAN AND THE SEA*

IF HIS FATHER GIUSEPPE HADN'T DREAMED OF A BETTER LIFE IN AMERica, Joe DiMaggio might have been born to be a fisherman in Isola delle Femmine off the coast of Sicily, or worse a victim of the life that befell Sicilian men of that age. It says enough that the island's name, translated to English as "The Island of Women," apparently came from a women's prison there in the 16th century. The town's government in a community of now fewer than 8,000 residents was eventually shut down because of "Mafia infiltrations," *La Cosa Nostra* having become the island's most famous export. Giuseppe married hometown girlfriend Rosalia Mercurio, whose father had gone to America and immediately thrived as a fisherman in Martinez, California.

Rosalia was pregnant with their first child when her father wrote to her with the advice that Giuseppe could earn a better living in California. So on February 25, 1889, at the age of 25, Giuseppe along with his older siblings, brother Francesco and sister Michelle, left Naples on the SS *Kaiser Wilhelm II* for California, arriving at Ellis Island March 9. Giuseppe was already gone off to the new country when Rosalia gave birth to their daughter. He had planned to be apart from his young family for no more than a year, but it took him longer than he had imagined to acclimate to his new homeland and to the competitive fishing environment he found in Martinez. Rosalia finally joined her husband in 1893, and they wasted little time in quickly expanding their family. On November 25, 1914, Joe was born, delivered by a midwife identified on his birth certificate as Mrs. J. Pico. Joe's name on that birth certificate was Giuseppe Paolo DiMaggio in honor of his father and Giuseppe's favorite saint, and he was the DiMaggio's fourth son and eighth child.

When Joseph Paul DiMaggio Jr., the Americanized name he would take on and one day have listed on his death certificate, was barely a year old, his family moved to the Italian neighborhood of North Beach in San Francisco where Giuseppe hoped to make a better life in a still more favorable fishing environment. Giuseppe also figured he would have a lifetime of help from his four sons. For in the old country, any fisherman with that many healthy boys would have been considered having been blessed by God, for these would be trustworthy helping hands who could build a solid family fishing business. The DiMaggios, after all, had been fishermen for generations. Soon there also was a fifth son, but Giuseppe's dream of a DiMaggio fishing family would never be realized.

"My father," DiMaggio said in a rare interview in 1978, "would curse the day his sons learned about baseball. I think we can all agree, can't we?"

DiMaggio asked the question of the handful of friends surrounding him at his friend Reno Barsocchini's bar in San Francisco, and as if a chorus to a maestro, they all toasted not Giuseppe DiMaggio but Joe.

"To the Clipper!" said Barsocchini.

"To the Clipper!" roared the chorus.

Giuseppe DiMaggio would never know this part of his great son's life. He would eventually come to accept it, grudgingly at first though he would have little choice. Although two of his older sons would follow Giuseppe into the family's fishing trade, arguably the three most gifted physically did not. The smell of the sea can be an enticing, romantic calling to men who have it in their blood, but it wasn't in the hearts of three of the DiMaggio boys. Joe, in particular, found the smell of fish and the sea nauseating.

Even before Giuseppe lost Joe to the national pastime of the family's new country, the older DiMaggio son had drifted away to a game that their father didn't understand. What were the odds that an immigrant

fisherman and his wife would produce three major-league ballplayers—
and all who would play center field—especially without their father ever
once picking up a baseball to play catch with them? But this would be the
family patriarch's legacy.

For the litany of the DiMaggio sons' legacy in baseball would be
the stuff of Americana. Vincent Paul "Vince" DiMaggio, who was two
years older than Joe, would go on to play in the majors for the Cincinnati
Reds, the Pittsburgh Pirates, the Philadelphia Phillies, and the New York
Giants. He would pave the way for Joe in semi-pro and minor-league
ball on the West Coast, softening their father's hard-line opposition to
baseball when he began to make money by playing on a semi-pro team
in Northern California. Joe would attend his older brother's games, and
by then he had become a good enough ballplayer in 1931 to attract the
attention of another semi-pro team in San Francisco. However, Joe was
still a minor and needed his father's approval. Joe, a Roman Catholic, said
he never made the sign of the cross outside of church except once that he
could recall.

"I crossed myself and handed my father the contract," he said. "I was
only 16. He could have said no."

Giuseppe, however, acquiesced.

Vince would open the door for Joe a second time the next year when
he was playing for the San Francisco Seals of the Pacific Coast League.
With his team needing a shortstop for the last three games of the season,
Vince suggested his brother, who was so impressive that he was invited
to join the Seals for their 1933 spring training. Joe, by then 18, did more
than earn his roster spot. He set incredible records, among them hitting
in 61 consecutive games, smashing the league record of 49 games that had
existed since the year he was born.

Joe DiMaggio was so spectacular so quickly that it was impossible
for his talent not to catch the attention of major-league teams. In 1934
the Yankees bought DiMaggio from the Seals, paying $25,000 and five
players, but agreeing that Joe could stay with the Seals through 1935 to
heal a nagging injury. In that final season, Joe missed hitting .400 by two
percentage points but was named the Pacific Coast League's Most Valuable Player while leading the Seals to the league championship.

The third of Giuseppe's sons to choose baseball over the life of a fisherman was Dominic Paul "Dom" DiMaggio, two years younger than Joe, who played his entire 11-year baseball career in the 1940s and early 1950s for the Boston Red Sox. Smaller than Vince or Joe, Dom's small 5'9" frame and eyeglasses quickly earned him the nickname "The Little Professor." Joe was unquestionably the best ballplayer among the DiMaggio brothers, but his siblings acquitted themselves well. Vince became a good journeyman player, and Dom was a legitimate All-Star. He was the Red Sox's leadoff hitter, batting .300 four times and leading the American League in runs twice and in triples and stolen bases once each. Defensively, Dom even had his supporters who argued he was on par with Joe. He led the league in assists three times and in putouts and double plays twice each. Offensively, Dom had one record even his illustrious teammate Ted Williams couldn't match: His 34-game hitting streak in 1949, which would remain a Red Sox record. There was even a ditty Red Sox fans used to sing: "Who hits the ball and makes it go? Dominic DiMaggio. / Who runs the bases fast, not slow? Dominic DiMaggio. / Who's better than his brother Joe? Dominic DiMaggio. / But when it comes to gettin' dough, they give it all to brother Joe."

"If anyone wants to know why three kids in one family made it to the big leagues, they just had to know how we helped each other and how much we practiced back then," Joe DiMaggio said looking back. "We did it every minute we could."

But, of course, it was Joe who became a legend. Even after another injury kept him out of Opening Day of his rookie year, DiMaggio batted .323 with 29 homers and helped the Yankees win an American League pennant and a World Series title his first major-league season. Joe also was voted to the 1936 All-Star Game, as he would be every year of his career. Then DiMaggio only got better. In 1937, his 46 home runs and 151 runs scored led the league. In 1939, he won the batting crown with a .381 average and was voted the league MVP. Meanwhile, the Yankees were winning four consecutive American League pennants and four World Series championships, becoming the first Major League Baseball team in history to do so. In 1940, Joe led the league in batting average again with a .352 mark, but the Yankees slipped to third place.

Then came the defining moment of DiMaggio's career. World War II was looming in Europe when Joe DiMaggio captured the imagination of America with an incredible achievement spanning two months in the summer of 1941. On May 15, DiMaggio singled in a game against the Chicago White Sox. At that moment it might have seemed like an inconsequential hit in a career that had already in the previous five seasons produced many memorable achievements. For the next 63 days, the nation virtually stopped what it was doing when the Yankees played, waiting on word from radio reports as to whether DiMaggio had gotten a hit in that day's game. Joe hit safely—getting a single, double, triple, or home run—in 56 consecutive games, an unheard of feat that would became baseball's most cherished record along with Babe Ruth's 60 home runs 14 years earlier in 1927. It would even outlive Ruth's mark, which fell in 1961 to Yankee Roger Maris and was then surpassed numerous times during the Steroid Era. However, DiMaggio's consecutive-game hitting streak lived on, perhaps never to be broken.

"It was as if I were in a dream—a ballplayer's fairy tale," DiMaggio would say of it, looking back almost in disbelief though clearly proud of his feat.

In 1941, America celebrated each time Joe shattered a previous consecutive-game mark. The Yankees' longest hitting streak had previously been 29 games. Joe broke that in mid-June. One by one, they all fell. The more modern major-league record of 41 consecutive games with a hit had belonged to the St. Louis Browns' George Sisler, who had achieved that mark in 1922. The all-time record of 44 games, set in the so-called Dead Ball Era, had been set by Wee Willie Keeler of the Baltimore Orioles in 1896. The country was spellbound, and Les Brown and his orchestra even recorded a song titled "Joltin' Joe DiMaggio" that became a popular tune on the radio.

America needed DiMaggio's 56-game hitting streak and Ted Williams's .406 batting average—the last time a big leaguer hit .400 or better—that season in 1941 as an escape from the real world. Just as it needed Orson Welles's *Citizen Kane* as well as *The Maltese Falcon*, both released that same year. Just as it needed Frank Sinatra on the radio, on records, in nightclubs. Outside the baseball stadiums and the movie theaters, and the airwaves, the real world in 1941 was full of calamity, uncertainty, and trag-edy. In Europe, Nazi Germany was in the midst of its aggression against the world. That summer, on June 22, 1941, Adolf Hitler launched a mas-sive attack against the Soviet Union. In August, President Franklin D. Roosevelt effectively committed the United States to the fray, meeting with British prime minister Winston Churchill at sea where they drafted the Atlantic Charter that aligned America with Britain and worsened relations with Japan. Ultimately, Japan's surprise attack of Pearl Harbor on December 7, 1941, plunged the United States into the war. Four days later, in a speech to the German Reichstag, Hitler declared that Germany was at war with the United States.

In 1941, Mickey was 10 years old and still being shaped in the mold of Mickey Cochrane, his father's favorite player. He was an undersized catcher and presented a fascinating sight. "Soaking wet," his mother remembered, "he didn't weigh more than eighty or ninety pounds. When he squatted down behind the batter wearing that [chest] protector that was too big for him, you couldn't see his feet. About all you could see of him—except for his arms—were those two little eyes sticking out of the protector like a scared turtle looking out of its shell." And, like other young boys his age, each day Mickey hung on word from his father or friends or anyone else who had listened to the radio to learn whether DiMaggio had succeeded again in hitting safely.

The Streak, as it came to be called, produced drama both on and off the field. In late June, as DiMaggio closed in on Sisler's record, Joe appeared at a hospital in Philadelphia to cheer a dying boy identified in the papers as 10-year-old Tony Morella, urging him at his bedside to lis-ten to the radio the next day and promising to get a hit for him.

"You be listening to your radio tomorrow, Tony," DiMaggio told the youngster, "and hear me break that hitting record for you. That's a prom-ise, kid."

That next day, June 29, the Yankees played the Washington Senators in a sold-out doubleheader in the nation's capital. DiMaggio tied Sisler's record in the first game, and sportswriters began preparing their Joe Cures Dying Boy stories. Behind the scenes, however, there was panic in the Yankees dugout. As the second game was about to begin, DiMaggio couldn't find his favorite bat, which he had named "Betsy Ann," the bat he had used throughout the streak. Between games the bat apparently had been stolen from the bat rack near the dugout. DiMaggio, ever superstitious about his bats, was furious, and in the second game failed to hit in his first three at-bats, heightening the tension. Finally, Joe turned to teammate Tommy Henrich, to whom he had lent one of his bats earlier in the season to help him snap a hitting slump. Henrich returned the bat, and in his last at-bat DiMaggio drove a ball into left field, establishing a new record.

In the next day's newspapers, accompanying the story of Joe breaking the record was the sidebar of DiMaggio's hero-cure of little Tony Morella. Unfortunately, few of those overanxious sportswriters reported the fact that poor little Tony had actually died before the start of the first game of the doubleheader, and fewer still noted that they had had the child's name wrong to begin with. His last name was actually Norella. But then, why ruin a good story.

DiMaggio continued the streak for another 15 days, hitting safely in 56 straight games until July 17, 1941.

By then, DiMaggio was even the pride of his parents' home where there had been a dramatic change of heart. On the day that Joe was trying to break Sisler's record, Giuseppe had spent the afternoon pacing "like a panther at the zoo," in the words of his oldest son, Tom, in front of the family house at 2150 Beach Street in San Francisco. Giuseppe had once made life almost unbearable for his three baseball-playing sons, who had endured a tumultuous rite of passage in abandoning their father's expectations to assist him in the fishing business to chase their own dreams on the ball field. The DiMaggio family patriarch had chastised his sons as being "lazy" and "good for nothing," criticism that Vince and Dom laughed off but which Joe took to heart. It would tear away at him for the rest of his life.

"When it came to his father, Joe couldn't reason right," said his longtime friend Reno Barsocchini in a 1978 interview. "Even after he became Joe DiMaggio, you know the 'greatest living ballplayer of his lifetime,' he had a difficult time coming to grips with having disappointed his father. Most men, we live our lives living our dreams out through our sons and that's what our fathers did through us. But it was different for Joe. His father's dreams for him bore no resemblance to the life Joe wound up living. You know, I sometimes wonder if that's not why Joe has to hear himself called, over and over, 'the greatest living ballplayer.' It's an ego thing but not why most people think. I don't think it has anything to do with 'lording' over another ballplayer. Joe needs that. It's almost as if he's hoping that wherever he is, his father is hearing that. It has to do with Joe. A lot of that just comes from being Italian and Catholic. Well, Joe was riddled with guilt. One time I asked him, 'Say, Joe, whacha got to be so guilty about anyway?' He steps away and looks at me and says, 'Reno, the same things that craw away at you and make you crazy, fuckin' dago!'"

DiMaggio's guilt was also that of any immigrant who finds that his upward movement in America has brought success but at a cost of building a barrier often separating them from their parents with their old-world ways, customs, and traditions. Joe would be no different. His greatest triumph, the 56-game hitting streak in 1941, would be immediately followed by what became his worst family crisis. In the aftermath of the bombing of Pearl Harbor and after America's entry into World War II, Giuseppe and Rosalia DiMaggio were among the thousands of German, Japanese, and Italian immigrants classified by the United States as "enemy aliens." With Italy allied with Germany and Japan, the DiMaggios were forced to carry photo ID booklets at all times and were not allowed to travel outside a five-mile radius from their home without a permit. Giuseppe found himself barred from the San Francisco Bay where he kept his boat, which was seized, and where he had fished for almost half a century. The DiMaggios, in part because of their limited English, had not become citizens. It would not be until 1944 that Joe's mother became a citizen, and his father followed in 1945.

Giuseppe and Rosalia's troubles also became a public relations embarrassment to the military. Their case eventually came to the attention of General John L. DeWitt, who was in charge of the internment of Japanese-Americans during World War II and also directed the classification of so-called "enemy aliens." His aide, Colonel Karl R. Bendetsen, wrote to DeWitt:

. . . there has been a great deal said in the papers about people like Joe DiMaggio's father, that is Italians who have never become citizens but concerning whom, it seems at least in the press, I don't know what their backgrounds are, there is no doubt as to loyalty. [James Rowe asked me] whether any of them need to be excluded.

DeWitt answered unsympathetically:

No you can't make an exception. If you start that you're in an awful mess. I had one man speak to me about it the other day. He happened to be the editor, Mr. Patterson, I think of the New York Sun. *He was in here and he asked me about Joe DiMaggio's father, and I said yes, he's got to go. You can't make a single exception because if you do that you're lost.*

Although DeWitt wanted to round up Italians much like the Japanese and remove them from their homes, his superiors were more sensitive to the ramifications of placing Italians and Germans in detention camps and stopped such action. The day after President Franklin D. Roosevelt signed Executive Order 9069 ordering the "evacuation" of Japanese residents, Secretary of War Harry Stimson wrote DeWitt:

In carrying out your duties under this delegation, I desire, so far as military requirements permit, that you do not disturb, for the time being at least, Italian aliens and persons of Italian lineage, except where they are, in your judgment, undesirables or constitute a definite danger to the performance of your mission.

Giuseppe and Rosalia DiMaggio were free to remain at their home, but there were severe restrictions. There was a curfew every evening, from eight at night until six in the morning. They couldn't travel more than five miles from home, and they weren't even supposed to have a radio. Before the war, Giuseppe had managed to open a little restaurant on the wharf where he enjoyed being known as Joe DiMaggio's father, and now he could no longer even go there.

"Just when Joe should have been basking in the sun for the greatest accomplishment in baseball," Reno Barsocchini told me years later, "there was incredible sadness at what his mother and father were forced to endure. It was a disgrace. It was a tragedy. I think it had an impact on Joe. I think it changed him. He came to realize that anything he gained could be taken away, and I think that's why he vowed this would never happen again."

CHAPTER SIX

The Oklahoma Kid

Mick was from Oklahoma. That's a hard part of the country to be from. It's a testament to Mick—and to his character.
—JOE DIMAGGIO, RENO'S, SAN FRANCISCO, 1978

THAT MICKEY MANTLE WAS BORN AT ALL IS A MINOR MIRACLE, OR PER-haps just the good fortune of fate giving biology a helping hand. Who hasn't wondered at some time how different life might have been, being born to a different mother or another father. Years later, after the Hall of Fame career and the New York fast life and long after he had become accustomed to the role of being Mickey Mantle, Mickey Mantle occasionally would chuckle with a hint of curiosity at the thought that he might easily have been his aunt's child. For before his father, Elvin Clark Mantle, had his eye on the woman who would give birth to Mickey, he had had designs on the woman's younger sister, a neighbor in the mining town of Spavinaw in Mayes County, Oklahoma. Elvin, the first of four children who from his crib days had been known as Mutt, was in his mid-teens. Lovell Richardson, the woman who would one day be Mickey Mantle's mother, was a grown woman 10 years older than Mutt and, at the time, married to her first husband, William Theodore Davis, a farmboy from nearby Craig County with whom she ran off at the age of 17. She bore two children by William Davis, Theodore and Anna Bea, before divorcing. Later, she explained her marital breakup to Mickey by simply stating, "We had a bad misunderstanding." Lovell Richardson, a tall, slender woman with gray eyes and reddish-blond hair, returned to her parents' home where she met Mutt one day when he came to court her sister. Months later, at the age of 17, Mutt Mantle married Lovell in a civil ceremony.

Mickey Mantle was born October 20, 1931, in an unpainted two-room house on a dirt road outside Spavinaw, Oklahoma, a town of a few hundred people about 35 miles southwest of Commerce in the flatland northeast corner of the state which was also the hub of the Oklahoma mining district. Spavinaw was in the heart of Cherokee Indian country and was part of the legendary Dust Bowl, the Oklahoma plains where red dirt blanketed everything when the wind blew. The Missouri state line is just 10 miles east, and Kansas is five miles to the north. On the day they finished the last section of Route 66 at the Kansas-Oklahoma state line, Cherokees came down from their reservation to watch, squatting along the highway, wrapped in blankets, to glumly witness the passing of an era.

The world in which Mickey Mantle was born and experienced his childhood is so closely linked in our minds with America's worst economic depression that it has become almost impossible to view it historically as anything other than cheerless. A period of drab and desperate existence, spiritually void and mired in hopelessness, the 1930s for most people evokes the stolid and stunned faces of tenant farmers immortalized by James Ageé and Walker Evans in *Let Us Now Praise Famous Men*. In the country as a whole, this era of economic debacle was also filled with more major political, social, and intellectual developments than the nation had ever known. In Oklahoma, however, the 30s reflected the uprooted, impoverished existence of a Steinbeck novel. Baseball, already ingrained as the national pastime, was both a diversion and a summertime remedy. To raise funds to help the unemployed in the Depression, in September 1931, the Yankees, Giants, and Dodgers played a series of benefit games that raised more than $100,000. In a pregame fungo-hitting contest, Babe Ruth, normally a left-handed hitter, batted right and drove a ball 421 feet into the center field stands.

The 1930s were hard times in the Oklahoma plains. In Spavinaw, many of the Mantles' neighbors who were unable to make a living moved out to California, far away from what would become an ecological and human disaster in the southwestern Great Plains region. It was caused by misuse of land and years of sustained drought. During the years when there was adequate rainfall, the land produced bountiful crops. But as the droughts of the early 1930s deepened, the farmers kept plowing and planting and nothing would grow. The ground cover that held the soil in place was gone. The Plains winds whipped across the fields raising billowing clouds of dust to the skies. The skies could darken for days, and even the most well-sealed homes could have a thick layer of dust on the furniture. In some places the dust would drift like snow, covering farmsteads. At the same time, the country was experiencing the Great Depression, the worst economic slump in United States history, and one that spread to the entire industrialized world. The Depression began in late 1929 and lasted for about a decade.

It was into this America, scandalously troubled economically but holding on to a moral purpose of unwavering optimism, that Mickey Mantle was born. As in the life of every man, the intricacies of his nature can be traced back to where he came from and to those who shaped him. For Mickey Mantle, it all started and ended with his father, a teenager when Mickey was born but ultimately the most influential person in his life. Mutt Mantle held the same dreams for his first son that other fathers have had for their children since the beginning of time. With Mutt, however, it is fair to say his dreams for Mickey were obsessive. "The feeling between Mutt Mantle and his son," Merlyn Mantle once said, "was more than love. Mick was his work of art, just as much as if his father had created him out of clay. He spent every minute he could with him, coaching, teaching, shaping him, and pointing him toward the destiny he knew was out there. Baseball consumed Mickey. He talked, when he talked, of little else. It was the number one priority in his life and, in a way, always would be."

Mutt Mantle found the 1931 season a fortuitous one. Months before Mickey was born, Mutt had decided that his son would be named after one of the princes of his beloved game. "If my child is a boy," Mutt told his friends, "he's going to be a baseball player. I'm naming him Mickey—after Mickey Cochrane." The catcher and spark of the Philadelphia Athletics' championship teams of 1929–31, Mickey Cochrane had a .346 batting average for those three years. He later would lead the Detroit Tigers to two pennants and a World Series championship in 1935. In 1947, he and

A's battery mate Lefty Grove would be elected to baseball's Hall of Fame. But in 1931, as he helped the Athletics win the American League title, Cochrane also caught Grove's historic 31-win season. On October 10, 10 days before Mickey was born, Mutt Mantle got the best of both worlds. His favorite player, who had hit .349 that season, made it to the World Series, but his favorite team, the St. Louis Cardinals, won the championship, defeating the A's, in the seventh game of the series. On the day Mickey was born, Cochrane was still playing baseball, part of an all-star squad on a barnstorming trip to Hawaii and Japan. On that day, too, Frankie Frisch, the Cardinals' fiery leader and another of Mutt's heroes, after hitting .313 and a league-leading 28 stolen bases, was named Most Valuable Player of the National League.

"Mama says dad showed me a baseball before I was twelve hours old and it almost broke his heart when I paid more attention to the bottle," Mickey would say years later. "Baseball, that's all he lived for. He used to say that it seemed to him like he just died in the winter, until the time when baseball came around again. Dad insisted on my being taught the positions on the baseball field before the ABCs. He was that crazy about baseball . . . I was probably the only baby in history whose first lullaby was the radio broadcast of a ball game. One night, mama says, I woke up during the seventh-inning stretch. She pleaded with dad to please cut off that contraption and let me sleep. 'You got Mickey wrong, hon,' dad said. 'I don't blame him for screaming. He knew the situation called for a bunt instead of hitting away.'"

Mutt named his son Mickey Charles Mantle, after both Cochrane and his own father. He apparently was unaware that Cochrane's given name was actually Gordon Stanley and that "Mickey" was an informal name that had been derived from the nickname "Black Mike" that Cochrane had been given at Boston University for his competitiveness on the football team. Mutt, though, was not one who was too concerned about the exactness of names. Mickey spelled his father's name "Elvin"— which was also the way Mickey's middle name was spelled. But Mutt Mantle's Oklahoma driver's license spelled his first name "Elvan," and it was spelled "Elven" on his headstone at the Grand Army of the Republic Cemetery between Miami and Commerce, where he was buried after his death in 1952. It was also spelled "Elven" on the birth certificate of Mickey's youngest brother, Larry. "I'm not sure how he spelled his name," daughter Barbara later said. "The only way I ever saw him sign anything was 'E.C. Mantle.'"

From his father, Mickey inherited something far more important than a name: an incredible, almost mythic physical strength that one day would produce his prodigious home-run power. Mutt Mantle was a lead and zinc miner who had played semi-professional baseball, and his father Charles Mantle had played baseball on a mining company team. Mickey was to later look back on his father's baseball talents with a son's wishful memory, saying he believed Mutt could have been a fine major-league baseball player if he had been given the chance. But, it turned out to be the mines that were in Mutt Mantle's blood. Mutt worked in the lead and zinc mines of the area but had also worked as a tenant farmer both before Mickey was born and later when Mickey was in his teens. For his entire life, Mickey was to lament the life that fate had placed on his father. "I always wished my dad could be somebody other than a miner," a regretful Mickey would reminisce. "I knew it was killing him. He was underground eight hours a day. Every time he took a breath, the dust and dampness went into his lungs. Coughed up gobs of phlegm and never saw a doctor. What for? He'd only be told it was 'miner's disease.' He realized that if he didn't get cancer, he'd die of tuberculosis. Many did before the age of forty. 'So what the hell? Live while you can,' he'd say and light another cigarette. A confirmed chain-smoker, I hardly remember him without one stuck in the corner of his mouth."

Mickey Mantle's parents, Mutt and Lovell, were raised in a town of dissimilar personalities and cultures, so it is no surprise that they, too, were a study in contrasts. Those two different personalities were to equally polarize young Mickey's own self-image and emotional development.

"My father was a quiet man, but he could freeze you with a look," Mickey said once. "He never told me he loved me. But he showed that he did by all the hours he spent with me, all the hopes he invested in me. He saw his role as pushing me, always keeping my mind on getting better. I worked hard at doing that because I wanted to please him. He would drape an arm around me and give me a hug . . . I adored my dad and was just like him in many ways—I was shy and found it hard to show my emotions. I couldn't open up to people, and they mistook my shyness for rudeness." Sadly, the way he was molded by two unemotional parents would influence the way Mickey himself would model his relationships with his own sons. "He had been brought up a certain way," son Mickey Jr. said of his father, "and if he couldn't deal with his feelings, he buried them. He paid a high cost for packing away the affection that was so close to his surface. For most of our lives, when we greeted each other after a separation of weeks or months, we would shake hands. It wasn't just him. Everybody in his family, my uncles, his cousins, kept the same distance."

For Mutt Mantle, that emotional detachment had been a method of self-survival. As a young man, Mutt had been forced to grow up quickly and dropped out of school to take a job grading county roads. Not long after marrying Lovell and having Mickey, however, Mutt lost the grading job and thought seriously about taking his young family to California. Instead he became a tenant farmer, working 80 acres of land but seeing little in return. Lovell, meanwhile, was busy raising her own two children as well as Mickey and she was pregnant with the second of the five children she would have by Mutt. Lovell was a devoted wife to her second husband. What they shared in common bonding them together was that both came from a long line of Oklahoma people, five generations of Americans with family bloodlines of English, Dutch, and German stock. At one point, there was unfounded speculation, in part spurred by Mickey's pride in the American Indian heritage of his beloved Oklahoma, that his mother was part Native American.

What is undeniable is that Mutt fell in love with a woman not only significantly older, but also more distant personally than even he himself was, and with a greater difficulty in showing her emotions than he had. For young Mickey, the impact may have even been greater. Lovell, the daughter of a carpenter, was reticent even with her loved ones, and Mickey would later say that his mother "didn't lavish affection on us either . . . when mom wanted to show her love, she fixed a big meal." However, one of the few times that Lovell did show some emotion, she overdid it. Once, when Mickey's twin brothers Ray and Roy were playing high school football and a fight broke out, Lovell ended up on the field slapping the opposing players on their helmets with her purse. Still, it was not until later, at her 80th birthday party in Oklahoma City, that she was to tell Mickey and the family why she had married Mutt: He was tall, handsome, and a real gentleman under the rough exterior.

Merlyn Mantle's recollection of her mother-in-law seemed to capture the essence of Mickey's mom best: "Lovell was not a warm or openly affectionate woman, but she was a tireless and protective mother. She had seven children, two by a first marriage, and I never saw anyone do as much laundry. She did it by hand, on a washboard in the back yard, and hung it on row after row of clotheslines to dry. They lived in the country and didn't yet have electricity."

As poor as they were at the time, however, Mickey always looked back with pride at how his parents persevered without reaching out for charity or even credit. "We were about the only family in Commerce that didn't buy groceries on credit," he remembered. "We only bought what we needed, and my dad paid cash. The grocer appreciated it so much that he let us kids pick out a free bag of candy."

The Mantles did not have much of a traditional spiritual life, surprising considering they lived in a community of God-fearing neighbors in the heart of the Bible Belt. Commerce had four churches. Mickey later said he had been in all of them at one time or another, "yet nobody in my family took religion seriously. I suppose it was my dad's influence. He used to say, 'Religion doesn't necessarily make you good. As long as your heart is in the right place and you don't hurt anyone, I think you'll go to heaven—if there is one.' Mom felt the same way. She backed him no matter what he believed."

If Lovell Mantle was not a God-fearing woman in a traditionally God-fearing community, she did have her own fears for her children— the biggest of which was a local area known as the "Alkali." This was a flat stretch of plain in Commerce where the lead-mine shafts had been sunk and then left abandoned, and where tall piles of exhausted ore stood like miniature pyramids. The plain of the "Alkali" was used for sandlot baseball games where a ball that got past the outfielders often rolled undisturbed for several hundred feet. Mickey would later joke that playing there as a boy with the endless outfield was what had convinced him to be an infielder. Mickey, however, wasn't even supposed to be playing ball on the makeshift "Alkali" baseball field. His mother had strict rules forbidding him to play there. According to Mickey, his mother "would haul me home and really warm my britches" on the few occasions when she caught him disobeying her. The reason for Lovell's concern was the caved-in old mine shafts, which were closed off only by sagging fences that were regularly climbed over or cut through by curious youngsters. She had grown up with stories about children who had fallen into the cave-ins and died in the black holes and worried, like other mothers, of such a disaster taking one of her own.

Lovell Mantle, though, also had a dark side to her, something that wasn't talked about until years later. While there is no documentation to suggest that she was an abusive mother, Mickey later would reluctantly talk about whippings he had been given by his mother. Years later, too, Mickey would see some of his mother's dark side in her treatment of little David Mantle, who would describe his grandmother as "always mean to me." David also remembered his grandmother with sadness. "She used to chase me around and hit me with a broomstick," he said. "Maybe it was because I was so hyper. One day I was sitting on a stool in her kitchen, and I did something a kid would do. Dad told me she just backhanded me and knocked me off the stool. After that, he never let her watch me any more because it really hurt him that she would give me that kind of swat. He said she used to whip him, too, something he didn't like to admit. She was still dad's mother, and I respected her, but I didn't have the love for her that I did for mom's folks."

That coldness that could sometimes border on cruelty was just one of many ways in which Lovell and Mutt were so dissimilar. Whereas he was occasionally carefree, rugged, athletic but overly demanding of Mickey, she tended to be a loner, if not lonely, emotional on occasion and subservient to her younger husband in his wishes on how Mickey would be raised. Yet Mutt, despite his unquestioned love for his oldest son, was far from possessing the emotional maturity ordinarily necessary for being the dominant parent in a family. Mutt was not even 10 when his mother had died of pneumonia, just a week after giving birth to her fourth child, Emmett. Charles Mantle would struggle to raise his three oldest children, while an aunt and uncle raised the baby. As the oldest child, Mutt became in charge of brother Eugene and sister Thelma while Charles put in long hours as a butcher in Spavinaw. Mutt's own childhood effectively was sacrificed to help his father raise the family. Raising your own family, however, can present an altogether different challenge, and it can be strongly argued that Mutt fell into the same trap that has ensnared fathers throughout history. In raising Mickey the way he did, obsessed from the cradle with his son becoming a professional baseball player, Mutt imposed upon him the pressure of not only fulfilling his own dashed dreams but also a level of expectation of almost immortal achievement.

Year later, fans and friends were often touched to hear Mickey lament that he had not been the same kind of father to his own oldest son. "If my father had been his father," Mickey said on more than one occasion, "Mickey Jr. would have been a big leaguer." To which, Mickey Jr. voiced some serious reservations. "I'm not so sure," he said. "More likely, if Dad had cooped me up in the back yard for three or four hours every day, playing catch and pitching to me, I would have run away from home."

Mickey's wife Merlyn would be convinced that Mutt's overbearing fathering unchecked by Lovell's own detached manner left Mickey emotionally and psychologically traumatized and unable to turn even to his loved ones for help:

"The early pressure on Mickey to play ball and his self-imposed drive to play it better than anyone, caused real emotional problems for him. A lot of the conflicts in him later had their roots in those years. Mick wet his bed until he was sixteen years old. I would hope that this would not be taken as demeaning him. But it is important, I think in understanding what he went through, and how much he wanted to please his dad. This is what the pressure of wanting that approval did to him. He told me that he knew from the time he was five years old that he wanted to be a ballplayer, and how he could never face his father if he didn't make it to the major leagues. Interestingly, the bed-wetting stopped when the Yankees sent him to Independence, Kansas, for his first season in Class D. He had to solve the problems before any of his teammates found out. He could not abide anyone making fun of him. He stopped by asserting his own pure willpower, because the pressure didn't end then, or with the Yankees. It never ended. I know exactly how much he ached for his dad's approval . . . His father had this wonderful but obsessive dream for Mickey, and only for Mickey. He was anointed from the cradle. When his dad would pitch to him for hours, out of a hundred pitches, Mick would be in terror of missing one and looking bad, and having his father frown or criticize."

Mantle would later talk about the bed-wetting on a 1970 *Dick Cavett Show* on which songwriter Paul Simon was also a guest. It was Simon, in a nostalgic expression of longing for the innocence and simplicity of an earlier and happier time, who had written in the lyrics for the popular song "Mrs. Robinson" of the 1960s the iconic line wondering where Joe DiMaggio had gone. In that talk show, Simon was dumbstruck by the revelation of another of his heroes and expressed the shock of millions: "Mickey Mantle wet his bed?!" Sportswriter Phil Berger would observe of Mantle's relationship with his father: "Anything short of success would be an affront to Mutt, and the thought of disappointing his father weighed heavily on him. The wetting of his sheets was an early and vivid indication of the burden under which young Mickey toiled, and the pressure it exerted on him."

However, there was one childhood trauma that Mickey never spoke about publicly. Around the age of four or five years old, his half-sister Anna Bea and some of her teenage friends sexually molested him. He was humiliated in such a demeaning manner that he could never bring himself to tell anyone. Only much later, in the year before his death, would Mickey be able to confide to wife Merlyn the sexual molestation he had suffered. Anna Bea would toy with him sexually, pulling down his pants and fondling his penis, often as her girlfriends watched and giggled, howling their laughter and derision at the times when he would get a tiny erection. The molestation and the teasing continued for several years until Anna Bea moved out of the house, but the traumatic scarring would last a lifetime. Merlyn would suspect that it was the source of his unhealthy relationships with women—that it was a reason he never respected women, his affairs, his one-night stands, the crude and vulgar language he used around women when he drank.

Mutt would never know of the molestation. Like other abused children, Mickey felt shame and guilt over what had happened. Beginning in childhood, he would go to great lengths not to disappoint his father. Mickey himself would later say of his childhood relationship with his father: "No boy, I think, ever loved his father more than I did . . . I would do nearly anything to keep my father happy . . . He never had to raise his hand to me to make me obey, for I needed only a sharp look and a word from him and the knowledge that I had displeased him to make me go and do better . . . I knew from the time I was small that every small victory I won, and every solid hit I made or prize I was awarded, brought real joy to my father's heart."

CHAPTER SEVEN

The Making of a Legend

My dad taught me to switch-hit. He and my grandfather, who was left-handed, pitched to me every day after school in the backyard. I batted lefty against my dad and righty against my granddad."
—MICKEY MANTLE

STORIES OF THE YOUNG MICKEY MANTLE LEARNING TO SWITCH-HIT and being pitched to for hours on end every afternoon by his father and grandfather became as much a part of the Mantle lore as the young Arthur pulling out Excalibur from the stone is central to the legend of Camelot. In 1934, when Mickey was three years old, Mutt took a job as a shoveler at the Eagle-Picher Zinc and Lead Co. and moved his family from Spavinaw to Commerce, near Interstate 44, which connects Tulsa and Joplin, Missouri. Commerce was a small town of fewer than 3,000 people, where the main street was only seven blocks long. This was a town so small it was once called simply North Miami because it was only four miles north of Miami, Oklahoma, in Ottawa County. But in 1914, lead and zinc mines were booming, so businesspeople thought Commerce would be a better fit. The same year the Mantles moved to Commerce, on April 6, 1934, the notorious outlaws Bonnie and Clyde got stuck in the mud on the road between Commerce and Miami. At gunpoint, they forced a trucker to pull them out. A passing motorist happened to notice a bullet hole in Bonnie and Clyde's car's windshield and called the police. In the ensuing shootout, the Commerce police chief was taken hostage and the constable was killed.

Life was a lot calmer at 319 South Quincy Street, a four-room clapboard house that became home to the Mantles for the next 10 years.

Mutt, by this time, had become a ground boss in the Eagle-Picher lead and zinc mines, earning $75 a week, extremely good pay in the 1940s in Oklahoma or anywhere else in the country. Mutt, however, was supporting not only his growing five children and a wife but his father Charles as well. The house on Quincy Street would become the one that Mickey would most associate with his youth. It was situated some hundred yards off the highway on a gravel road leading down to the house from the family mailbox. Often Mickey would wait at the mailbox for his father to come home from the mines, and they would walk together down the road to their house talking about baseball. From the time Mickey had been in his crib, Mutt had made sure his son had a baseball cap nearby. Lovell Mantle had used material from some of her husband's old baseball pants and shirts to fashion miniature uniforms for her son. Here, on Quincy Street on the edge of town, sometimes in uniform and sometimes without, young Mickey began honing his swing with a tin shed for a backstop.

"You take this bat," Mickey remembered his father telling him, "and you try to hit the balls we throw to you. We won't throw them hard, so don't worry about getting hit. Anyway, these tennis balls won't hurt you."

Mickey took the bat and swung it enthusiastically right-handed. Mickey was a natural right-hander.

"Now there's one other thing I want to tell you," Mutt explained to his son. "When I throw the ball, you go ahead and swing the way you're doing it now. But when Grandpa Charley throws the ball, I want you to turn around and swing the other way. Understand?" Mutt pitched left-handed. Charles Mantle pitched right-handed. In conventional baseball wisdom, right-handed hitters generally have greater success against left-handers and left-handed hitters greater success against right-handed pitchers. A right-handed pitcher's curveball will break away from a right-handed hitter, usually making him harder to hit against, and vice versa. Mutt calculated that switch hitters—hitters who could hit both right-handed and left-handed—were a valuable commodity in professional baseball. In 1938, about the time Mickey's switch-hitting lessons began, there were only 11 switch hitters on the rosters of major-league teams. In 1951, there would be only 10 major-league switch hitters, counting Cleveland Indians pitcher Early Wynn. But by 1971, in the generation of players influenced by Mantle, major-league rosters would have 41 switch hitters. So in the front yard of 319 South Quincy Street, at the age when other children were playing cowboys and Indians, Mickey Mantle began learning the art that would one day make him the greatest switch hitter in the history of the game.

"Mickey didn't like it at all in the beginning," Lovell Mantle recalled, "but I know now that he is glad he listened to his father."

At first, Mickey found it extremely difficult to switch-hit, especially to hit left-handed. But the practice continued, day after day, starting around four o'clock in the afternoon as soon as Mutt returned home from his day at the mines and continuing until nightfall. It was not unusual during the summer when there was no school for Mickey to put in as many as five hours a day taking batting practice with his father and grandfather pitching. "Once I learned to hit a ball with a bat," said Mickey, looking back, "I needed none of my father's urging to play the game. Knowing that it pleased my father to see me do well at the game only made it twice as much fun to me."

Soon Mutt and Charles began throwing harder and tossing the incredible curves that can be thrown with a tennis ball. However, when Mickey turned six, real baseballs replaced the tennis balls. To sharpen Mickey's interest in the game, Mutt and Charles devised a set of Quincy Street ground rules. A line drive was a single. A ball hit off the side of the house became a double. A ball off the roof was ruled a triple. A ball hit over the house or into the adjoining lot was a home run. Mickey, who often listened to radio broadcasts of St. Louis Cardinals' games with his father, imagined himself to be a slugger with the Cardinals' legendary Gashouse Gang.

This was Mickey's childhood in which his two closest friends and playmates were his father and grandfather. Mickey's first real friend his own age was LeRoy Bennett, who lived up the street on Quincy. His other close childhood pal was Nick Ferguson, who lived on Vine Street, about eight blocks away. But each afternoon, as the time neared that Mutt returned home, Mickey's mother could often be heard yelling out "Mickey Charles!" Neighbors even used to joke: "When Mutt comes home from the mines, Mickey has to stop playing and start practicing."

Mickey himself would look back on the long ritual of hitting drills with fond memories: "The practice paid off. By the time I was in the second grade, I was hitting them pretty good from the right side. But dad also wanted me to bat lefty, which I hated. When it got dark and supper was ready, dad would turn me around, from righty to lefty. 'Your belly can wait,' he'd say. Then he'd start pitching again. He believed that any kid could develop into a switch hitter if you taught him early enough."

In the middle of the Depression, baseball was the only way Mutt saw for Mickey to escape the cycle that had gripped him, as it had most young men from similar backgrounds in northeast Oklahoma: a near poverty existence and a lifetime of either being chained to the mines or farms of the area. This was a time in America in which, unlike a generation later, the only two sports through which youngsters could seriously dream of rising out of meager circumstances were baseball and boxing. Mutt's second brother Eugene had shown some signs of pugilistic promise and was nicknamed Tunney after world heavyweight champion Gene Tunney. Eugene once put out a man's eye, though not with his fists but with a shovel. A fight had broken out at a dance in Spavinaw in which Mutt, Eugene, and other Mantle family members found themselves outnumbered. In defending himself, Eugene apparently picked up a shovel and struck one of his assailants. The Mantle men would always boast of never having lost a fight, including that one. Baseball, however, was the real passion for all the Mantle men. Many of them spent their weekends playing on semi-pro teams in Mayes County. Even after Mutt moved to Commerce, he returned to Spavinaw every weekend to play with the local team.

Baseball was also a bond between Mickey's father and mother. Over the years, Lovell Mantle developed a love of her own for the game. Mantle friend Nick Ferguson remembered visiting and seeing Mickey's mother doing her housework while listening to radio broadcasts of St. Louis Cardinals' games. With Mutt away at work during the day, Lovell would jot down notes about the games in a kind of makeshift scorecard that she would later use to recount the games for Mutt, the family, and friends over dinner. "She'd tell you how this happened and that happened—she had it right in front of her," Ferguson told one early biographer, "and she made it sound exciting, too. And everybody had to know what went on. They'd keep asking for more and more, and she'd just keep telling them like she had actually been at the game herself."

Just how knowledgeable Lovell Mantle was about baseball, however, is debatable. Mantle was to later describe his mother as having been a fan, though hardly with the baseball knowledge and insight of his father. Nick Ferguson, on the other hand, has been quoted as claiming that Lovell Mantle—and not Mutt—had been the parent with the true "inside" perspective on the game, especially in what she would reportedly tell Mickey about his own play. "She'd never raise her voice," Ferguson said in one interview. "You'd barely hear her. But she'd sort of whisper to Mickey about what he had done in games she saw. She'd say, 'You know, in that situation, if you bunted, you woulda done this or that. If you backed a little bit at second, you'd have more room to take a ball. Or on this hitter or that hitter, you should maybe move over a little more.' She knew the game, and she could always get him to think about what he was doing."

Mantle himself remembers that his mother was most demonstrative as a basketball fan when he was playing on the Commerce High basketball team. "Mom used to rant and rave at those games," said Mantle. "If she objected to a referee's decision, you could hear her voice travel across the gym: 'Where are your glasses, you bum!' Believe me, if the referee called anything against Commerce, she'd cuss him out like a sailor. It unnerved my father. He'd cover his head with his hands and sit a few rows behind her to get away from the shouting."

Although his name was so closely linked to Commerce—the "Commerce Comet," they called him—Mickey himself later became surprisingly unsentimental about his adopted hometown. He would go so far as to tell friends in his later years that, as a youth, he had always felt like an outsider there. There were things in Mickey's childhood, things he would never reveal until many years later, that made it an unhappy one, and there was a level of dysfunction in the family that planted the seeds for addictive personalities throughout most of the family. Alcoholism ran through much of Lovell Mantle's side of the family. Her brothers were all alcoholics. It was a problem that also later afflicted Lovell's two children by her first husband. Mickey's half-sister Anna Bea married young, left home, worked as a barmaid, and died in her 20s. "Hers," said Merlyn Mantle, "was a short, sad life." Theodore, Mickey's half-brother, was also an alcoholic, though with a heart of gold. When he was discharged from the army, Theodore used most of his discharge pay to help Mickey buy Merlyn's wedding ring.

Mickey later would describe his father as "a light drinker who bought a half-pint on Saturday and sipped it for days. He would have whipped my fanny if he caught me taking a drink . . . Every night when he came home from working eight hours at the Eagle-Picher Zinc and Lead [mine], he'd head for the icebox and take a swig of whiskey. Dad would get drunk once in a while, like when he went to a barn dance and he might have five or six drinks. Hell, for me five or six drinks wouldn't have been a full cocktail party!" Mickey's pal Nick Ferguson, however, suggests that Mutt's drinking may have been more than what Mantle has indicated in his autobiographies and interviews. "I'm sure he didn't chase around with women," Ferguson said in one interview, "but Mutt drank, and he used to take Mick and us kids into the bars with him when we weren't even old enough to drink." What is known for certain about Mutt Mantle is that he did have one known addiction. He was a chain-smoker. Mickey excused it as something all the miners did, miners who "didn't see how nicotine could do any more damage to their lungs than the dust they inhaled every day." As a Yankee, Mickey would later endorse Camel cigarettes. Every week he was provided with a free carton of Camels, which he mailed home to his father, who would exchange the carton at a Commerce store for his favorite brand, Lucky Strike. With Mickey the hottest name in baseball, the Commerce grocer would often boast to his customers, "See these Camels? They came straight from Mickey."

Even as an adult, however, Mickey did not hold the fondest of memories for Commerce. In 1956, during the Christmas after his greatest season when he won baseball's Triple Crown, Mickey and Merlyn were visiting family when Mickey decided to go see some old pals at Mendenhall's bar on Main Street. The only problem was that he was supposed to be babysitting Mickey Jr., who was then three, and he took him along to Mendenhall's with him. A fight broke out when Mickey tried defending the bartender against a drunk. Sitting on a bar watching his father roll around on the floor, Mickey Jr. picked up his father's beer and took his first swig just as his grandfather, Giles Johnson, came in the door looking for them. The grandfather scooped Mickey Jr. off the bar into his arms and, on his way out, kicked his famous son-in-law in the side of the head, warning him: "Don't ever let me catch you with this kid in here again."

In later life, Mickey looked back on Commerce with many reasons to have mixed feelings about his life there. Former Commerce postmaster Bill Brumley remembered that when the Civic Pride Committee tried to start a Mantle museum in Commerce in the 1980s, Mantle's lawyer had threatened a lawsuit. Some townspeople harbored hard feelings against Mantle even after his death at the way he had often slighted Commerce, among them Mayor Jack Young, a 74-year-old native.

"Mickey Mantle didn't even show up when they dedicated Mickey Mantle Boulevard," he said. "People got down on him for stuff like that."

However, there also were others, especially among the younger generation in Commerce, for whom Mantle remained a source of local pride and admiration. To this date, Mickey is the biggest thing that ever happened to Commerce, Oklahoma. In 1993, two local men, Brian Brassfield and Todd McClain, buddies since Little League, bought Mantle's boyhood home. Over the next few years, they used their savings to begin restoration of the dilapidated house in hopes of turning it into a Mickey Mantle museum. Said Brassfield: "We've even talked about the tin barn and letting kids bat against it, just like he did." They envisioned life-size bronze statues of a young Mantle and his father, posed as hitter and pitcher the way they did every afternoon from the time he started school.

If he could, Mickey might tell them about another day, when he was 10 and playing as an undersized catcher with 12-year-olds on the Douthat team in the peewee division of the Gabby Street League. Overmatched against an outstanding right-handed pitcher, Mickey had struck out three times batting left-handed. Discouraged trying, Mickey decided on his own to try batting against the overpowering pitcher from his natural right-hand side. However, as soon as Mickey took his stance in the right-handed batter's box, a deep, booming voice stopped the game.

"Go on home!" Mutt Mantle shouted from the far edge of the baseball field. "Go on home! And don't you ever put on that baseball uniform until you switch-hit like I taught you."

Feeling punished and humiliated, Mickey hurried home. That night, after dinner, Mickey apologized to his father and promised not to do that again.

"He never drove me to play baseball, for no one ever had to do that," Mickey would later write in *The Education of a Baseball Player*, his 1967 autobiography. "But he worked hard to help me improve and he gave me good advice to follow and played with me when he had the chance. It wasn't the thought of riches or fame that drove me. I didn't think about those things. I had no desire to leave home or to get very far from Commerce and the towns around us. What did keep me driving hard, from the time that I was ten, to hit the ball better and farther was first of all my own love for the game and then my love for my father. I knew from the time I was small that every small victory I won, and every solid hit I made or prize I was awarded, brought real joy to my father's heart."

CHAPTER EIGHT

The Dark Side of Baseball

I was not in on it, would not have gone into it under any circumstances and did not bet a cent on the (World) Series after I found out what was under way.

—ARNOLD ROTHSTEIN,
GRAND JURY TESTIMONY ON THE 1919 WORLD SERIES

NO MATTER THAT HE HAD BEEN TO GRAND CENTRAL TERMINAL BEFORE, Mickey Mantle still marveled like a newcomer to New York at the sight outside where hundreds of red-capped porters scurried about helping passengers with their luggage. Many of the passengers, especially those dressed stylishly, which to Mickey seemed like almost everyone in New York, looked like movie stars and celebrities. But in April 1951, he was a raw rookie in more ways than on the baseball field and almost every aspect of the city was a new experience to a 19-year-old from Oklahoma. When he hopped into the Checker Cab with two fellow rookies in front of the Concourse Hotel in the Bronx where the team had housed them, Mickey had announced to the cabbie, "Grand Central Station, 15 Vanderbilt Avenue." The cabbie eyed him and gave him a piece of smart advice.

"Son," he said, "there *are* places in New York where the name alone is enough."

Inside Grand Central, Mickey struck the pose of a newly arrived sightseer, awestruck by the extravagant interior with its marble floors, Corinthian-style columns, stained-glass windows, a marble fireplace, and a restaurant. Once inside the concourse, he stopped for a moment to stare at the 125-foot ceiling vault painted with constellations. Mickey had described it to his mother as looking like an Italian cathedral, to which his mother had teasingly remarked, "Mickey, how would you know what an Italian cathedral looks like?" In fact, the concourse, which, when it opened, was hailed as the finest example of Beaux-Arts architecture in America, looked as though it could have been transported from 1870s France. Atop the symmetrical main facade was a large clock and sculptures of an American eagle and Roman deities.

It was what passed through the concourse every day, however, that gave Grand Central its buzz and always brought Mickey down to the earth of where he was: "It's a place everyday New Yorkers pass through, whether they are taking a train or not," John Belle, the architect in charge of a lavish restoration in the late 1900s, would later observe. "Grand Central is our town square." Each day drew upwards of a million people, some by subway, some on suburban commuter trains, others simply walking through the building to get somewhere else, but most at that time arriving or leaving on the railroads that in 1951 were still the heart of long-distance transportation in the country. In the 1940s and the 1950s, a popular NBC radio show closed each program with the line: "Grand Central Station—crossroads of a million private lives, a gigantic stage on which are played a thousand dramas daily."

Among those dramas unfolding from the spring through fall of each year were the New York Yankees baseball team, which would depart Grand Central, or Penn Station, for some of its out-of-town trips, to Boston to play the Red Sox, to Chicago for a series with the White Sox, to Detroit for the Tigers, to Cleveland to face the Indians, to Philadelphia to take on the Athletics, to St. Louis for the lowly Browns, and to Washington, DC, as they were this afternoon for their Opening Day of the season the next day against the Senators where President Harry S. Truman would throw out the first pitch.

Another New Yorker hurrying through Grand Central Station that day was an unusually devout Yankee fan, an Italian American who had closely followed Joe DiMaggio's fabulous career and now wanted to see in Washington the first game of what would be the Yankee Clipper's final season. Matthew Ianniello was a 30-year-old decorated World War II veteran who had received a Purple Heart and Bronze Star for combat as an Army artillery gunner in the Philippines. Two years earlier he had become partners with his uncle in his own restaurant, Matty's Towncrest Restaurant in Midtown. Ianniello himself had once been a young ballplayer with some promise as a hitter and had earned an unforgettable nickname, "Matty The Horse." However, it wasn't for his swing with a bat. In a youth baseball game, an opposing pitcher threw a high fastball that struck a teammate of Ianniello's squarely in the face. The teams' benches cleared, and Ianniello charged the mound knocking down the pitcher, surprising because the youngster was older and taller than Matty. Someone who witnessed the brawl couldn't help but say about Ianniello: "That boy is as strong as a horse."

Matty "The Horse" Ianniello would become one of New York's most notorious mobsters, a made man in the Vito Genovese crime family whose sponsor was future mob boss Frank Tieri. Years later, he would be convicted of skimming $2 million from an assortment of Manhattan restaurants and food suppliers—including one that provided the hot dogs for Yankee Stadium. In 1951, however, Matty "The Horse," the former kid ballplayer from Manhattan's Little Italy, was just a fan who wanted to catch the start of the farewell season of the Favorite Son of all Italian Americans. As a fan he was especially drawn to Italian ballplayers, particularly DiMaggio and Yankee catcher Yogi Berra. He often sent invitations to the Yankee clubhouse, hoping he could get DiMaggio or any of his teammates to stop by his restaurant. Occasionally some of the Yankees did go eat at Matty's place, but their loyalty was to the Stage Deli. When Ianniello learned this, he started dropping in at the Stage Deli as well as Danny's Hideaway where he knew Mafiosi often hung out. It was through those connections that Ianniello had met Alan Savitt, who tried to interest him in buying an interest he had in a deal to represent the Yankees' hot rookie, Mickey Mantle.

"He was a hustler and not a very good one," Ianniello said in a rare interview years later. "It was a long time ago. Who wouldn't know who Mickey Mantle was even then? That's all the papers wrote about. And this hustler was claiming he had his claws into Mantle. Maybe he did. Maybe he conned the kid. But it wasn't gonna go anywhere. And Savitt . . . how could you believe anything coming out of that man's mouth? There's an

Italian expression: *Bocca di miele, cuore di fiele.* A tongue of honey, a heart of gall."

Could there have been more, though, to an old rumor among mobsters that in 1951, Matty "The Horse" Ianniello had quietly owned a part of the young Mickey Mantle through that ill-fated scam of Alan Savitt's, even though there reportedly hadn't been any takers besides Holly Brooke? Ianniello's former partner in the Mob's silent underworld ownership of several New York bars thought so.

"Matty used to brag that he had owned a piece of Mickey Mantle back in the early 1950s, before he was a big star," said Paul Gelb, a survivor of World War II Nazi concentration camps who for years was the king of organized crime's strip joint operations in New York. "I don't know if he ever got any money from Mickey. He just said he had bought a piece of him from a guy he knew, and, of course, Matty knew a lot of people and he had a way of worming his way into a piece of any action he wanted. That's what he did with me."

In the mid-1960s, Gelb took his savings built from almost 20 years in the garment and jewelry businesses and bought a Manhattan Midtown topless bar from a man named Philly whom Paul knew had organized crime connections.

"What I didn't know," Gelb told me in a series of interviews, "was that Philly had been selling this club over and over again to people who would give Philly a down-payment, pay a few months' rent, then have to give him back the club when they went broke. Philly'd done this dozens of times. This was Philly's scam, until he sold it to me."

Gelb quickly turned his new topless bar into a surprising money-maker. Impressed, Philly became Gelb's new close pal. Gelb's success, however, quickly angered a competing topless bar impresario, none other than Matty "The Horse" Ianniello, who according to Gelb, retaliated with several unsuccessful attempts to run Paul out of business.

"He tried muscling me out," said Gelb, "but by this time Philly was my best friend and Philly was 'connected,' too. I said to Philly, 'Matty the Horse' is trying to put me out of business. What am I gonna do?' Philly made a call, and the next thing I know Matty is now trying to become my new good friend."

It didn't happen overnight, but by the late 1970s, Gelb and Ianniello were as thick as thieves. Gelb said that during baseball seasons Ianniello would often pine for the days of the great Yankee teams of DiMaggio and Mantle and on more than one occasion mentioned how he had for a brief period owned a piece of the great switch-hitting slugger. Gelb, according to government prosecutors, became a front man for both Ianniello and partner and fellow wiseguy Benjamin Cohen. Their operations included numerous topless bars and restaurants in Manhattan that by the early 1980s had attracted the attention of federal investigators. Gelb, according to court documents, became the Mob's mole through whom ownership in these bars and restaurants was hidden from federal and state authorities. A lengthy federal investigation that included extensive wiretaps and surveillance conclusively linked Gelb to an organized criminal conspiracy involving skimming bar and restaurant earnings, mail fraud, racketeering, and tax evasion. In 1985, Gelb was convicted on all 27 counts filed against him, as was Ianniello the following year. Both received six-year prison sentences.

In an interview, Ianniello, who died in 2012, said that he sometimes hung out at Danny's Hideaway in the 1950s, part of the group of mobsters who blended in with the nightly scene, and he said he often did see both Mantle and DiMaggio, usually separately, as they came to dine there. "You have to understand New York, the culture of New York, especially in that day," said Ianniello. "You could be sitting down to dinner with a princess, a real princess on one side of you, the mayor on the other side, and, yeah, DiMaggio or Mickey Mantle a table down. Whadaya make of that? Nothing, people eat, drink, live, and let live. Did I ever lay a bet after seeing them there? I can't say I didn't. DiMaggio? He was book. You could count on him in his day. Mickey Mantle? There were times, even when he was young and in his prime, you'd see him having a good time, maybe too good of a good time, and you'd think, 'No way. No way he can help the Yankees win tomorrow.' Then the next day, he goes 3-for-3 with a homer. Can you believe that, 3-for-3 and an upper deck jolt, and he's drunk on his ass, or pretty close to it cause it's a day game, and you saw him at one in the morning, and you knew you couldn't have even made it to work the next day in the condition he was in. I can't say

I didn't lay a bet against the Yanks when I'd seen him that way, and hell if I didn't get burned."

Gelb said that on a handful of occasions, he had picked up the checks at Danny's and Stage Deli for both DiMaggio and Mantle. "I would have done it more often except most times when you would tell a waiter that you wanted to pick up Mickey's tab, they'd say, 'Thanks, but it's taken care of.' I'm sure if he had wanted to, he could've had his tabs picked up by someone the rest of his life. Whadaya gonna say?

"It was Mickey Goddamn Mantle."

Mobsters might have said the same about Joe DiMaggio, who developed an association with Mafia boss Meyer Lansky, according to his daughter Sandra Lansky Lombardo. DiMaggio had made the connection through his friendship with Newark crime boss Ruggiero "Richie the Boot" Boiardo, the hidden owner of Vittorio's Castle restaurant in Newark where Joe began hanging out with Boiardo and Jerry Spatola, a funeral director who had also befriended the Yankee Clipper and eventually Joe's brother Dom. "Jerry the Spats," as Spatola was known among his cronies, had befriended Joe after hearing that he was a reclusive loner and far from his California home. Spatola caught up with DiMaggio outside the Yankee clubhouse after a game and invited him to his home for a home-style Italian dinner with his wife and family. The friendship soon grew so strong that Spatola and his wife and two daughters often sat behind the Yankee dugout at games as DiMaggio's guests. Meanwhile, Boiardo even provided Joe DiMaggio a driver, a small-time Jersey rackets guy named Jimmy "Peanuts" Ceres whose jobs included driving Joe's Cadillac to Florida so that he would have his own car during spring training. DiMaggio evidently even went so far as to accept from Boiardo the four-and-a-half-carat, emerald-cut diamond engagement ring that he gave to his first wife Dorothy Arnold, the actress he married at San Francisco's St. Peter and Paul Church on November 19, 1939.

However, the biggest contribution the Mob may have made to DiMaggio was finding and returning his favorite bat that had been stolen from the Yankee dugout between games of a doubleheader when Joe was trying to break George Sisler's hitting streak record in 1941. In the days that followed, Ceres spent the better part of a week tracking down the bat when he learned that the thief ran around Newark and had been bragging of having taken the bat, known as Betsy Ann. The story soon made the rounds that Ceres and Spatola had cornered the thief and used their collective muscle to convince him to return DiMaggio's bat.

Eventually, in Joe's mind probably, all those favors may have paled compared to what he asked years after his retirement. Unable to let go of Marilyn Monroe after their nine-month marriage ended in divorce in late 1954, DiMaggio sought repeatedly to reconcile but to no avail. Finally after Marilyn's subsequent marriage to playwright Arthur Miller ended in divorce in 1961, DiMaggio tearfully asked Meyer Lansky if he could use his influence to help reunite him with her. According to Lansky's daughter, her father assigned some of his men to tail Marilyn to get an idea of the possibility for a reconciliation. What he learned wasn't encouraging. Marilyn's life had spiraled out of control with illicit affairs with President John F. Kennedy and his brother, Attorney General Bobby Kennedy, and her growing dependence on prescription drugs.

Lansky told DiMaggio he didn't see how he could help achieve a reconciliation, but DiMaggio reportedly was unconvinced. Richard Ben Cramer insisted in his biography *The Hero's Life* that Marilyn had agreed to remarry before her death of a drug overdose in 1962.

"Who knows what the real story was," said Paul Gelb, who by the time of Marilyn's death was getting into bed with Matty "The Horse" Ianniello and the Mob. "There's always a story in New York, and the story in New York was that there was something fishy about Marilyn being a drug overdose. And poor Joe. He was beside himself, and the story in New York was that he had people, very powerful people, trying to get some answers and, more important, street justice if that was possible.

"And what happened next? All hell broke loose. John Kennedy is assassinated. Bobby Kennedy never becomes president. Teddy Kennedy kills a girl. Camelot's light goes out. As they say on the street: Karma. Ain't it a bitch."

CHAPTER NINE

The Theft of a Hall of Famer

A ball player has to be kept hungry to become a big leaguer. That's why no boy from a rich family has ever made the big leagues.

—JOE DiMAGGIO

WHEN MICKEY MANTLE ARRIVED AT SPRING TRAINING IN 1951, THE Yankee players and reporters covering the team were amazed not only at the incredible talent they saw on display but also at how cheaply the team had gotten him. Only a year earlier, the camp had been abuzz at another prize prospect, Jackie Jensen, many thought might eventually become Joe DiMaggio's successor in center field. Jensen, an All-American in two sports at the University of California, was a college golden boy with a national reputation. He had pitched and hit his Golden Bears team to the 1947 College World Series championship. Then he had led his football team to a perfect 10-0 season in 1948, finishing fourth in the Heisman Trophy balloting. He had given up his senior year to sign a $40,000 contract that made him a baseball bonus baby. As such, under baseball rules, Jensen had to be kept on the major-league roster, though he had proven to be a disappointment in 1950.

If Jackie Jensen, who looked like he would be a bust, at least for the Yankees, could command 40 grand, the thinking was, what kind of bonus did the ballclub have to put out to sign a phenom like Mickey Mantle? When other ballplayers heard that Mantle had been signed for a mere $1,500 bonus, most thought they had misheard. For Mickey Mantle, the kid Stengel and others were already raving about? For the next Ruth and DiMaggio? $1,500? Not $15,000? Joe DiMaggio, for one, found it hard to believe.

"I thought they were joking, to be honest," DiMaggio would say. "I couldn't believe it. I figure he either was a rich kid who didn't need the money or some kid off the farm who had no idea of what he was worth. Oh, my, what he had to learn. And can you imagine, if I'd had another few years, what kind of bargaining unit we could have been? We would have owned the Yankees."

Tom Greenwade would later say that signing Mantle had been the crown jewel of his scouting career. Signing Mickey Mantle, in fact, had been the culmination of a well-designed plan that had been in the works for the better part of two years. Greenwade had first laid eyes on Mantle in 1948 when he went to scout a teammate of Mickey's on the Whiz Kids team on which he was playing while still in high school. Of course, a baseball scout needs to be a consummate poker player, rarely letting on his true feelings about a prospect. It was to Greenwade's advantage to downplay Mickey's potential as a future professional player when he spoke to Mutt Mantle, who used this as motivational fodder for his son. Mickey, consequently, came to believe what Greenwade had said to his father—that he had not been overly impressed in his first view of what would ultimately become his prize signing. Mickey was still slight of build and was known as "Little Mickey" by some of his teammates. Mantle, however, had hit two home runs the first day Greenwade saw him, one from each side of the plate.

"When I first saw him," Greenwade eventually admitted, "I knew he was going to be one of the all-time greats." On another occasion Greenwade would say: "The first time I saw Mantle I knew how [Yankee scout] Paul Krichell felt when he first saw Lou Gehrig. He knew that as a scout he'd never have another moment like it."

Moreover, glimpses of Mickey's prodigious power were already in evidence. The Whiz Kids' home field in nearby Baxter Springs, Kansas, that manager and coach Barney Barnett had personally built, including a $3,500 expenditure for lights for night games, was bordered in right and center field by the Spring River that was some 400 feet to dead center field from home plate and some 500 feet from home to right field. As a 16-year-old in 1948, Mantle was routinely hitting balls near those distances. In one game in late summer, with 250 to 300 people looking on,

Mickey hit three home runs—two right-handed and one left-handed—that wound up in the Spring River. In the frenzy that erupted in the crowd, someone in the bleachers behind home plate passed a hat around to reward their slugger. After the game, Mickey was presented with $53 in small change that soon became a small headache for the Mantles. Someone reported the incident to the Oklahoma State Athletic Commission, which regulated high school sports. That commission determined that since Mickey had accepted the money, he had lost his amateur status and could not compete in high school sports at Commerce High his senior year. Mutt challenged the ruling, going to Oklahoma City personally to make the appeal. The ruling was reversed and Mickey's amateur status reinstated on the condition that he return the money. Mantle would later say he had to work odd jobs to earn back and repay the $53, which he had already spent. It is uncertain, however, whether that actually happened, since that fall Mickey was busy playing football after school. According to at least one version, Mickey repaid Barnett with a $53 check that was never cashed.

Mickey's power at that age, along with his foot speed, gives further credibility to the story that Greenwade, in fact, had been so impressed when he first saw Mantle that he wanted to sign him on the spot before learning he was only a 16-year-old high school student. Greenwade's own admission of having reacted to first seeing Mantle the way the scout who signed Gehrig undoubtedly felt suggests that Greenwade must have been torn, at the least, in having found his prize jewel at a time when big signing bonuses were becoming part of the business of the sport.

Learning that Mickey was only 16 must have also impressed Greenwade, who had more than a passing knowledge of Barney Barnett and his Whiz Kids team. The Whiz Kids were a highly competitive semi-pro team with the best players from Kansas, Oklahoma, and Missouri. The team played in the Ban Johnson League that operated in the tri-state area and had produced several major leaguers. At 16 Mickey was the youngest player and an obvious phenom. The team was composed mostly of 18-year-olds and played a schedule against other Ban Johnson League teams made up of players 18 to 21 years of age and on which players younger than 18 were a rarity. "On the Whiz Kids, Mickey was ahead of his years," said Ivan Shouse, Mantle's childhood friend. "Everyone knew it. He was a boy playing with men, and he was better than all of them."

The signing of Mantle for only $1,500 is all the more incredible when you consider that around the same time, in Broken Bow, Oklahoma, another young phenom—Jim Baumer, a promising power-hitting shortstop who was half a year older than Mickey—was signing with the Chicago White Sox for a $50,000 bonus. Baumer would go directly to the majors, then become a journeyman minor leaguer for the entire 1950s before playing briefly with the Cincinnati Reds in 1960. Eventually Baumer himself became a scout whose signings included Hall of Famer Robin Yount. In an interview, Baumer boasted of how on his high school graduation night his parents' living room had been filled with scouts, including Greenwade—who seemed confident he had Mickey Mantle safely in his pocket.

"That amount *is* a pittance even by the standards of that day," says Kevin Kerrane, author of the classic *Dollar Sign on the Muscle: The World of Baseball Scouting*, of the Mantle signing for $1,500. "It's amazing when you think that he was signed for so little."

The signing of Mickey Mantle was actually far more complex and involved than even Mantle fully realized, although over time he came to understand that all had not been as the Yankees and Greenwade made it out to be. Signing Mickey, in fact, would be a steal, not only in the incredibly unfair deal the Yankees made with the Mantles but also in that the Yankees appear to have violated baseball's rules against dealing with youngsters still in high school.

In the spring of 1949, Cleveland Indians scout Hugh Alexander had heard from a friend about an outstanding teenage baseball player in Commerce, Oklahoma. Meticulous about checking out tips, Alexander noted the name on a piece of paper. He had become a baseball scout at age 20 in 1937, and the first player he signed was pitcher Allie Reynolds, who won 182 games over 13 seasons with the Indians and the Yankees. Known as Uncle Hughie, Alexander became one of baseball's best-known scouts and went on to sign dozens of future major leaguers in a career that spanned six decades and countless miles on the back roads of America. A few weeks after getting the tip on Mantle, he drove from his home in

Oklahoma City to Commerce and went directly to the local high school. When Alexander inquired about the promising prospect named Mickey Mantle, the school principal Bentley Baker did something curiously out of character for a small-town educator. He lied. He told Alexander that the school did not have a baseball team and that the young man he was interested in had been hurt playing football and had developed arthritis in his legs. "It's hard enough to make the majors if you're healthy, and when I got back to my car, I took the piece of paper and threw it away," Alexander said of the incident. "I can still see it blowing across the parking lot."

The signing of Mickey Mantle was always recounted, even by Mantle himself, with a twist of homespun heroic adventure. On the night of his graduation, the school principal excused Mickey from commencement exercises so that he could play baseball in front of a New York Yankee scout who signed him immediately after the game. According to Mickey, it was Tom Greenwade who "got me excused from the commencement exercises."

Hugh Alexander would later suggest, and the facts certainly would support, that the Yankees effectively monopolized what should have been a healthy competitive bidding for Mickey, with the help of his high school principal who, for reasons he took to his grave, was scaring off Greenwade's scouting competitors. The shrewd and resourceful Greenwade, a former Internal Revenue Service tax collector, had obviously ingratiated himself with Mickey's principal as much as he had with his father.

Mantle insisted throughout his lifetime that Greenwade signed him on May 16, 1949, the night of his graduation, in Greenwade's 1949 Chrysler, having arranged with Principal Baker for Mickey to be excused from his commencement exercises to play a game with his prized travel team, the Whiz Kids. Mantle said that after the game Greenwade approached his father to tell him things didn't look promising for his son because of his size and his erratic play at shortstop—but that he was willing to gamble by offering a contract for a modest signing bonus.

Greenwade was lying, but Mutt Mantle did not dare call Greenwade on his lie. Mutt was anxious to get his son a professional baseball contract and too inexperienced to do justice to any negotiations on Mickey's behalf. When Mickey had turned 16, Mutt had gone so far as to take him to St. Louis trying to get him a tryout with the Browns, who had shown no interest. Mutt was disappointed, failing to understand that Mickey was still too young to impress the scouts as he soon would. Mickey was also just starting to pack on muscle and weight. In his senior year in high school, however, other scouts began showing an interest but were possibly more mindful of the major leagues' high school tampering rule. Runt Marr, a Cardinals' scout who was well known in the area, visited the Mantle home one day to express interest in Mickey and asked that he not sign with anyone else until St. Louis could make an offer. Mantle said that he gave up hope that the Cardinals would make an offer after days passed without hearing from their representative. The Mantles, however, apparently didn't fully understand that major-league teams were prohibited from even making *contact* with Mickey until he had graduated, much less making a signing offer.

Mutt's impatience about getting his son signed to a professional contract is troubling unless one understands that Mutt Mantle had been molded by the Great Depression. Although he was filled with optimism about Mickey's potential, a cold wind sometimes blew through the back of his mind—the knowledge that the world could collapse. Even as Mutt managed to overcome obstacles, the 1930s of his young adulthood whistled thinly through his memory. Those bleak years gave him an ambience of expectation about life and its pitfalls. Not too surprisingly, the Mantles used almost all of Mickey's signing bonus to pay off the mortgage on the family home. It is understandable how Mutt may have been extremely anxious to get Mickey playing professional baseball as soon as possible that summer; nevertheless, Mutt's decision to have Mickey sign so soon after becoming eligible to even talk to the pros appears to have been ill-advised at best. At the time, Mickey was one of the area's most talented amateur athletes. The University of Oklahoma tried to recruit him for its football program. Bill Mosely, who quarterbacked Mickey's high school football team at Commerce, received a college football scholarship when they graduated and went on to play at Pittsburg State Teachers College in Kansas.

Undoubtedly, Mutt could have used the college football offers as negotiating leverage with the Yankees. As Al Campanis, the late Dodger baseball executive and himself a former scout, would later say in reflecting on Mantle's signing: "[Baseball's] rule against signing someone before he graduates from high school doesn't mean that on the day you graduate you have to sign a contract. That just marks the start of the race. Mantle was just coming into his own then. The only reasons I can see for him signing so quick would be if there'd been a big bonus—and there wasn't—or if there'd been a contract that put him on the Major League team roster—and there wasn't that either. Mantle could've played [amateur] ball that summer and built up his value the more he was seen and scouted. There's no telling what he could've signed for."

In fact, the Yankees had authorized Greenwade to pay up to $25,000, if he needed to. Yankee general manager George Weiss later told friends that he had authorized Greenwade to offer that much—the same bonus Moose Skowron would receive—to sign Mantle and the Baumer youngster in nearby Broken Bow. Once Baumer signed with another team, Greenwade had all the money to use on Mantle. Weiss, a brilliant businessman who had been with the Yankees since 1932, had been the architect of the organization's farm system, which he had shrewdly built by signing a lot of Depression-era players cheaply and often making incredible profits when he sold some of them to other teams. After one of those deals, then Yankee general manager Ed Barrow asked Weiss: "George, doesn't your conscience bother you?"

After the war, Weiss was trying to rebuild his sagging Yankees with whatever it took, including signing bonuses to promising players. The 1947 Yankees had won the pennant and the World Series, but the 1948 Yankees faded to third place. The 1949 Yankees had started the season inauspiciously after losing Joe DiMaggio in the spring to an unexpected second operation to remove bone spurs from his right heel. The Yankees had entered the bonus baby market, and Greenwade was aware that he had a blank check to sign a prospect like Mantle. If anything, Greenwade appears to have been baffled that, unlike Baumer's father, Mutt had not even so much as hinted at what kind of signing deal he wanted for Mickey. Mutt, in fact, seemed to be more concerned with where his son would be assigned after turning professional. He was insistent on Mickey playing somewhere close to home that summer, preferably at the Yankees' Class

D team at Independence, Kansas, 75 miles from Commerce. Greenwade had also gotten Mutt to promise that he would give him the chance to match any offers. Greenwade, though, knew what no other scout in the area knew—that Mantle wasn't the damaged prospect with bum legs that Hugh Alexander and other scouts were being told he was by Mickey's own high school principal.

Ultimately, the signing of Mickey Mantle would became part of Americana and heroic fable, fitting of a *Saturday Evening Post* cover by Norman Rockwell. As author David Halberstam would later put it: "The myth of Tom Greenwade, the greatest scout of his age, blended with Mantle's myth to create a classic illustration of the American Dream: For every American of talent, no matter how poor or simple his or her background, there is always a Tom Greenwade out there searching to discover that person and help him or her find a rightful place among the stars."

For Tom Greenwade, Mickey Mantle would become the showpiece in the parade of 1950s and 1960s Yankee stars and mainstays that he signed, among them Mantle friend and roommate Hank Bauer, as well as Ralph Terry and Bobby Murcer. Greenwade had scoured America's heartland looking for his prized signing who would validate his life as a scout and the Yankees' decision to hire him. Mantle's signing also forever cement Greenwade's place with the Yankees and in baseball. Greenwade would remain with the organization for 40 years, retiring in 1985, a year before his death. Throughout his life, Greenwade would deny violating the high school tampering rule. Although he admitted to being worried about other scouts moving in on Mickey, he claimed to have waited patiently until the Sunday after Mickey's graduation from high school before offering him a contract that was ironed out in 15 minutes of negotiations between himself and Mutt. Mickey was signed for a total of $1,500—$400 for the remainder of the season with the Independence, Kansas, team of the Kansas-Oklahoma-Missouri League, and a $1,100 bonus. Altogether, Mickey would sign for a tenth of the money Elston Howard received from the Yankees a year later.

But then, the life of the baseball scout, neither then nor later, was hardly a gentleman's game. According to Kerrane, all was fair in fighting other scouts for the signature of a promising prospect. The passage of money under the table was not unheard of, especially when it came to attempting to keep competing scouts away from a prized player. Occasionally, said Kerrane, there were suspicions and allegations of scouts and their teams circumventing the rules on bonus babies. A player signed to a high bonus such as Jim Baumer was required under baseball's rules to be placed on the major-league team for a period of time, which would create havoc with the team's 25-player roster. To get around this, some teams were suspected of paying part of the bonus to a new signee under the table in cash, leaving the roster of the major-league team unaffected.

Of course, the job of a scout was made considerably easier when the family of a prized prospect like Mickey jumped at the first offer, and even then mismanaged the negotiations.

"I asked Mutt what they wanted to sign?" Greenwade said he told Mickey's father.

"Well, you'll have to give him as much as he'd make around here all summer, working in the mine and playing ball on Sunday," said Mutt, effectively missing an opportunity to ask for top dollar and instead asking for parity for working the mines and playing local semi-pro baseball. "His pay in the mine is eighty-seven and a half cents an hour, and he can get fifteen dollars on a Sunday playing ball."

"We wrote down how much he could make working with his father up in the mines in Picher and how much he'd be making playing semipro weekends in Spavinaw on the same team as his father," Greenwade told the *New York Herald Tribune*'s Harold Rosenthal a decade later. "Then we added up how much he'd make in three months in the minors and subtracted that from the first figure. It came to $1,150. That's what I could get for him to sign."

In another life, Greenwade with that flat, ridge-runner accent that made him sound so convincing, might also have been a used car salesman because he kept manipulating the numbers. Finally, at one point he threw out to Mutt a monthly salary of $140 that Mickey would earn playing with Joplin for almost three months for the rest of that summer.

"That's around four hundred dollars," he told Mutt. "Suppose we make up the difference and give you $1,100? That's about $1,500, right?"

The result would be one of the biggest signing coups ever made by a professional sports team and, unfortunately for the Mantles, a horrendous negotiating blunder that would cost the family tens of thousands of dollars. But this was to be only the first of numerous business deals during his career and after retirement in which Mickey would wind up on the short end of the stick.

"It was not until the signing was announced in the paper and I read Tom Greenwade's prediction that I would probably set records with the Yankees, equaling Ruth's and DiMaggio's, that I began to wonder if my father and I had been outslicked," Mickey said years later. "Greenwade, by *his* account, had just been going through Oklahoma on his way to look over a *real* prospect, when he stopped to talk to us. I never did find out who that *real* prospect was."

In his autobiography *The Mick*, Mantle recognized that it had all been a negotiating ploy by Greenwade. "When I read the announcement about my signing," wrote Mickey, "it quoted Greenwade as saying I would probably set records with the Yankees. Stuff like that. He did tell me later that I was the best prospect he had ever seen."

CHAPTER TEN

Twilight of the Hero

He should lead the league in everything. With his combination of speed and power he should win the triple batting crown every year. In fact, he should do anything he wants to do.

—CASEY STENGEL ON MANTLE

JOE DIMAGGIO WAS NEVER KNOWN AS A SENTIMENTAL MAN, BUT HE looked back at the start of the 1951 season with a longing hopefulness similar to his first season in the majors. The Yankees had an unusually large group of young rookies who were expected to help the aging team, and one in particular that many were comparing to him when he had been young. Joe had set his mind on wanting to win another World Series with which to end his career, and for selfish reasons he wanted Mickey Mantle to succeed, no matter how the writers had twisted their stories into creating a resentment that didn't exist.

"I resented Mickey and wanted my own teammate to fail, which would only hurt our chances to win the pennant? What utter hogwash!" DiMaggio would say to his friends in Reno's bar years later whenever anyone would raise a story that some new writer might have rehashed from old clippings or from an interview from some former teammate fostering some lingering resentment of his own.

As the 1951 season was about to begin, Mickey himself did not know if he would even play, just as he had been uncertain whether he would make the trip to Washington, DC, for the scheduled season opener or instead be sent off to one of the Yankees' minor-league teams. Mantle, however, had just completed an incredible spring training that had left some of the old-timers breathless with his unbelievable speed, which seemed more on display when he was running out ground balls, though Mickey hitting ground balls that spring was a rare sight. Instead, most of his hits had been amazingly hard-hit line drives and towering home runs. Though management had insisted their prize rookie needed more seasoning and that a year or two in the minors could be beneficial, one of the old-timers had disagreed—and he was no ordinary old-timer.

Casey Stengel, the manager of the Yankees, had bucked the bosses all spring, insisting Mantle was ready and that he needed the youngster, believing he had made a speedy conversion from being a shortstop to playing right field. "I want Mantles at the right hand of the Dago," Stengel had said to Yankee management. Playing right field, Mickey would actually be to the left of DiMaggio, unless you were looking at them, which may have been what Stengel meant. Who, after all, could ever exactly figure out Stengelese? He called Mickey "Mantles," and few could recall him ever calling the great Joe DiMaggio anything but "the Dago," except, of course, to DiMaggio's face.

This was to be DiMaggio's final season, he had revealed March 2, having spent the winter after the 1950 World Series considering his future. The announcement had stunned the Yankees and a disbelieving press corps following the team in spring training. Even more surprising was the fact that DiMaggio even after all these years remained a virtual stranger to most of his teammates and Stengel, who had become the skipper in 1949. In those two seasons, the Yankees had won back-to-back World Series championships. DiMaggio had been but a shell of his Hall of Fame form in 1949, suffering from various injuries he had kept hidden, but he rebounded in 1950 with 32 home runs, 122 runs batted in and a .301 average. However, he was in constant pain, keeping it from the writers especially, but unable to fool Stengel. The Yankee manager had coyly protected his star center fielder by positioning his right fielders a step or two closer to DiMaggio than they would have played in the past, all to make up for the speed and quickness he had lost. Now, with Mantle, who many thought was the fastest man they had ever seen on the baseball diamond, Stengel thought he could protect DiMaggio even more.

DiMaggio thought so, too, and the financial incentive had been so great that he thought he could get another season out of the body that was betraying the player who had been the envy and hero of men for longer than a decade. His Olympian feat of getting a hit in each of 56 games in a row in 1941 would be a record that would stand unbroken for well into the next century, and possibly even forever. During his previous dozen seasons, the Yankees had won nine American League pennants and eight World Series titles. In 1949, the Yankees had rewarded him with a record contract that made him the first baseball player to break $100,000 in annual earnings.

"Joe figured a hundred grand was a hundred grand, not that he needed it, but he was Joe fucking DiMaggio, America's hero, of course he was going to suck it up and give it another go," Reno Barsocchini, DiMaggio's longtime friend and business partner in San Francisco, told me years later. "But Joe was nobody's fool. He knew Casey had been shading his other two outfielders to take some of the pressure off him. Joe hadn't liked it at first. Nothing had been said, but he could tell you in his sleep where every position player was on the field at any one time. Joe thought his experience, his instincts, his knowledge of every hitter were enough to compensate for the step he had lost. So in '51, he was looking forward to having the kid Mantle playing on one side of him. Joe had said, 'He's no shortstop, but he's faster than the wind.' And he thought, 'Well, with that kid in right, the old man [Stengel] won't have to cheat the right fielder over to center and leave the [right field] line open to an extra base hit.' So DiMaggio was thrilled. He just didn't show it. Didn't talk about it. But he liked the kid. Hell, he loved the kid. In Joe's mind, since they were Yankees and all that meant—Joe was the Yankee legend at his end, Mantle was the Yankee legend at the beginning, they were like blood brothers, born of the same cloth, with all that that meant. He had to protect his successor because, in a sense, that was his own legacy.

"'Everything Mantle is and everything he was going to be, that was me at one point,' Joe once told me. 'People who say I didn't like the kid didn't understand. He's everything I was, everything I am. He was me.'"

In 1950 Mickey had given the Yankees a sneak preview of what to expect. That spring training, Mickey had spent most of the time with other minor leaguers away from the attention of Casey Stengel. Without the benefit of the pre–spring training instructional camp for rookies that would begin the following year, Stengel could mostly only hear of the promising youngster from other coaches. In the sprints, Mantle had timed the fastest in the entire camp. It was Mickey's switch-hitting, however, that brought attention to the freckle-faced kid who was a virtual unknown. In an intrasquad game on the fourth day of camp, Mantle slugged home runs from both sides of the plate—shots farther than anyone could remember balls hit in spring training. The first time most of the rookies in camp even saw Stengel was after Mantle's second blast when the impressed, aging manager ran out on the field, waving a fungo bat as he chased after Mickey circling first base, asking other coaches, "What'sis name? Mantle?"

Then Mantle was utterly amazing that 1951 spring training season.

Speed has always been an intangible quality in sports. Even in the sports where speed is not usually considered the most important of attributes, raw, natural swiftness afoot can be impressive. Stengel and his coaches at the team's instructional camp were immediately awestruck by Mantle's speed. In the early footraces, Mickey outran other players by such margins that Stengel at first thought he was cheating with head starts. Stengel and the coaches had Mantle running sprints against everyone at the camp, including some of the roster players who were there under the guise of being "instructors" so as to not violate the restriction against major leaguers coming to camp before March 1. Mantle outran everyone. He was clocked running from home plate to first base, and his times were 3.1 seconds from the right-handed hitter's side of the plate and 3.0 seconds from the left-hander's side. No one in the major leagues was that fast.

That was also when Stengel began calling Mickey "Mantles." Some in camp believed the origin may have been in Stengel believing he had two Mantles because of his switch-hitting talent, which by itself was a rarity. At the time of Mantle's arrival, the American League featured just one regular switch hitter, Dave Philley of the Athletics. Moreover, switch-hitting was seen as a device employed by hitters who were lacking other weapons. Of the switch hitters that had preceded Mantle—among them Frankie Frisch, Red Schoendienst, and Max Carey were the best—nearly all were disdainful of the long ball. In 1951, the career leader in home runs by a switch hitter was Rip Collins with 135. The idea of tape-measure power from both sides of the plate was enough to get anyone's attention.

As a switch hitter, slugging home runs from both sides of the plate, Mantle quickly began to impress the other Yankees as well. Beyond running faster than any player Stengel had ever seen, his hitting talent and potential were prodigious. Only his defensive skills underwhelmed. Mickey had a tremendous arm, but he was no major-league shortstop. The Yankees had left him at the position he had played in high school, but at Joplin in his first full minor-league season, he had committed 55 errors, unusually high for a shortstop. Nevertheless, Stengel had plans for Mickey. The thinking among Yankees' farm system director Lee MacPhail and others had been that Mantle might ultimately be converted into an outfielder. Once an outfielder himself, Stengel wanted to shift Mantle. Within days of Mantle's arrival at the instructional camp, Stengel made Mickey his own project, personally trying to teach him the new position and then retaining Tommy Henrich, the Yankee right fielder who had retired, to coach his young protégé. Stengel could barely contain himself and, in a burst of enthusiasm, invited the sportswriters at the camp to come watch.

"Mantles," Stengel told the writers, "is a shortstop and he ain't much of a shortstop, either. But he sure can switch-hit hard, and run as fast as anybody I ever saw. I've seen some pretty good runners and ol' Case was a pretty fair runner himself. You fellers be out here tomorrow and you might see this Mantle at a place that could surprise you."

Although they dismissed Stengel's comments as more Stengelese, the sportswriters who came by early the next morning caught Mantle taking outfield practice under Henrich's tutelage. The Yankees were determined to turn Mickey into a major leaguer, and Mickey was soon to learn that there was little room for sentiment. Yankee coach Frank Crosetti worked with all the infielders, and the first thing he noticed about Mickey was his glove.

"Where'd ya get this piece of . . . ?" the former Yankee great asked.

Mickey didn't hear exactly what Crosetti said about the glove and perhaps didn't want to hear. Neither could he bring himself to tell him just how special the glove was. It was a Marty Marion autograph model, designed for infielders and endorsed by the shortstop on the great St. Louis Cardinals teams Mantle and his father had rooted for. The glove had been a Christmas present that his father had given him when he was 16 and which Mickey had used throughout high school and his two seasons in the minors. "I knew exactly what it cost, for I had yearned after it for a long time," Mickey said of that special Christmas gift. "It was $22, about one-third of my father's weekly salary. And I knew, as all poor boys do, exactly what that amount of money meant in a family like ours. Of course, I doted on the glove with an unholy passion, loving even the smell of it, and I caressed and cared for it through the winter as if it had been a holy relic. But most of all, my heart was bursting with the realization of what a sacrifice like this said about my father's love for me and about his pride in my ability."

Crosetti never knew the story and might not have cared. The next morning he presented Mantle with an expensive, professional-model glove that Mickey suspected Crosetti had even bought with his own money. Mickey put the glove his father had given him away, one of the first of many steps he would take over the next few years in attempting to break the unusually close bond with Mutt, both as father and coach. Of course, plans to convert Mickey into an outfielder were already in the works. Although Mickey didn't realize it at first, the glove Crosetti bought him was a slightly bigger model designed especially for outfielders. Crosetti may also have been sending Mantle a subtle message: Perhaps it was time for Mickey to understand that his father had not known all there was to know about playing the game. That same day, Mickey used that glove in the intrasquad game that followed his outfield practice session with Tommy Henrich. He played center field where he made one putout and acquitted himself without committing any mistakes. It was at the plate, however, that Mickey made the writers take notice. He lined a triple to center field in his first at-bat, then drove a home run over the right field fence in his second time up.

"In Mickey Mantle," many of the sportswriters began reporting in their spring training updates, "the Yankees are grooming the successor to Joe DiMaggio."

That spring Mickey hit .402 in the Yankees' exhibition games with nine home runs and 31 RBIs, and reporters talked of him being the most exciting young player since Jackie Robinson, who four years earlier had broken baseball's color barrier with the Brooklyn Dodgers. In his first few exhibition games in Arizona, where the Yankees were training that spring, Mickey hit around .400 before the Yankees moved to California for a series of 11 games. Against the Pittsburgh Pirates, Mantle hit home runs from each side of the plate. Branch Rickey, the man who had signed Jackie Robinson for the Dodgers, was the general manager of the Pirates in 1951. Rickey could hardly contain himself after watching Mickey and at the game did something that was highly uncharacteristic of his conservative nature with money. He tore a blank check from his checkbook, signed his name and handed it to Yankee co-owner Dan Topping, who happened to be sitting next to him. "Fill in the figures you want for that boy," said Rickey, "and it's a deal." Topping smiled politely but left the check untouched.

The late author-journalist Dick Schaap remembered that "Mantle was so incredibly good on the field that even the men who praised him wondered, at times, whether they were maintaining their sanity." Jack Orr, who was then covering the Yankees for the *New York Compass*, reflected the general attitude among sportswriters in a column toward the end of spring training: "Some of us were kicking it around in a compartment on the Yankee train speeding through Texas. We worked over a couple of subjects, but, as always, we got back to the same old one. It was bed time when somebody said: 'Cripes, we've been going for three hours and we've talked about nothing but Mickey Mantle.'" Pitching coach Jim Turner said he never saw anybody who could excite another ballplayer the way Mantle had already done. "When he gets up to hit," he said, "the guys get off the bench and elbow each other out of the way to get a better look. And take a look at the other bench sometimes. I saw [Pittsburgh Pirates slugger] Ralph Kiner's eyes pop when he first got a look at the kid. [Cleveland Indian] Luke Easter was studying him the other day, and so was [fellow Indian player] Larry Doby . . . Here's one sure tip-off on how great he is. Watch DiMag when Mantle's hitting. He never takes his eyes off the kid."

That spring, though, DiMaggio remained his typically stoic self in talking about the rookie who was being groomed to replace him. "He's a big-league hitter right now," DiMaggio told one reporter. "Who does he remind me of? Well, there just haven't been many kids like him. Maybe he has something to learn about catching a fly ball, but that's all. He can do everything else." In San Francisco, Joe's hometown where the Yankees played an exhibition that spring, DiMaggio was asked if he resented Mantle moving in on his center field position. "Hell, no," said DiMaggio. "Why should I resent him? If he's good enough to take my job in center, I can always move over to right or left. I haven't helped him much—Henrich takes care of that—but if there is anything I can do to help him, I'm only too willing. Remember what I said back in Phoenix about those Yankee kids and how great they were? Well, the more I see of the ones we have now, the more convinced I am the Yankees won't even miss me."

"Mickey," said fellow rookie Gil McDougald, "had a spring training like a god."

Johnny Hopp, who would later be one of Mantle's roommates in New York, had the locker next to Mickey that spring and took to calling him "The Champ" because of his incredible streak of power hitting.

"You're going to make a million dollars out of this game, the Lord behold," Hopp said to Mickey after one spring game.

Mantle simply laughed. He was still unconvinced that he was doing anything special on the field. When he arrived at Grand Central Station that April day, Mickey still had no idea if he would be starting the season with the Yankees or be sent down to the minors along with a number of other rookies. Despite all the hype about Mantle, there were also the skeptics. One of them was Stan Isaacs, Orr's fellow staff writer on the *New York Compass*, who was also critical of all the media hoopla being made over Mantle. He wrote: "Since the start of spring training, the typewriter keys out of the training camps have been pounding out one name to the people back home. No matter what paper you read, or what day, you'll get Mickey Mantle, more Mickey Mantle, and still more Mickey Mantle. Never in the history of baseball has the game known the wonder to equal this Yankee rookie. Every day there's some other glorious phrase as the baseball writers outdo themselves in attempts to describe the antics of this wonder: 'He's faster than Cobb . . . he hits with power from both sides of the plate the way Frankie Frisch used to . . . he takes all the publicity in stride, an unspoiled kid . . . sure to go down as one of the real greats of baseball . . . another Mel Ott.'"

The train the Yankees were taking to Washington that day was still typical of baseball travel in the early 1950s. Baseball and train rides were part of the fabric of the American culture. For teams, the train rides from city to city were the extension of the clubhouse. Players passed the time on long train rides through open fields with card games and baseball banter. The main diner with its art deco lights and etched glass dividers made an immediate impression on Mickey, who was still getting used to walking normally through a speeding train as he followed Casey Stengel from car to car toward the bullet-shaped smoking lounge. He practically forced himself to ask, "Casey, can you tell me something? Am I going to play at [minor league] Beaumont this year?"

Stengel winked. "I think you'll stay with us. When we get back there, just be quiet, and I'll do the talking." In the smoking lounge, Stengel told general manager George Weiss that Mantle was ready to play with the Yankees. Weiss shook his head. He thought Mickey was too young.

"I don't care if he's in diapers," Stengel insisted. "If he's good enough to play for us on a regular basis, I want to keep him."

Yankee co-owner Del Webb and Topping both agreed with their manager.

"George," began Webb, "they've been writing so much stuff about Mickey, I feel we have to keep him."

"The thing is, George," said Topping, "we're not opening in New York. We're opening in Washington. After two or three games under his belt, I think he'll be all right."

Mickey swallowed hard, trying to hide his excitement. He was going to be a Yankee. The contract talk that followed was like an afterthought for Mickey that, at the time, didn't seem to matter. Stengel himself negotiated Mickey's contract with Weiss, a contract of course structured to the Yankees' best interests. Under Mickey's rookie contract, he would get $7,500 for the season—which was $2,500 above the minimum but still a bargain for the player being touted as the successor to Ruth and

DiMaggio. However, the Yankees' apparent generosity had a catch: If Mickey floundered and was sent to the minors, the Yankees would only be on the hook for the minimum.

Mickey returned to his train seat in a fog. He had just signed his first big-league contract. He had achieved his dream of making it to the majors. He had achieved his father's dream. He thought about his father Mutt, about his sacrifices not only on the long afternoons when he and his grandfather Charles pitched batting practice to him but about how his father doted on him—down to saving a piece of his cupcake every day and bringing it home to Mickey in his lunch bucket after working a hard day in the coal mines. He looked out at the rain that was falling as the train sped toward Washington, DC, and tears welled in his eyes as he thought about life back home.

CHAPTER ELEVEN

The Eternal Glory of Youth

You guys got to see this kid we have in camp. Out of class C ball, hits 'em both ways—five-hundred feet both ways! You've got to see him.
—BILL DICKEY ON MANTLE

WHEN THE OPENING SERIES AGAINST THE SENATORS WAS RAINED OUT, the Yankees returned to New York, where the opener would also be Mantle's major-league debut. After Mickey's sensational spring, Stengel was indeed beginning to look like another John McGraw, the legendary manager of the New York Giants who was known for sometimes taking chances on unproven players. The opening day lineup Casey posted in the dugout had Mantle playing right field and batting third behind left fielder Jackie Jensen and shortstop Phil Rizzuto and ahead of DiMaggio who was batting in the cleanup slot. Catcher Yogi Berra was batting fifth, first baseman Johnny Mize sixth, followed by third baseman Billy Johnson, second baseman Jerry Coleman, and starting pitcher Vic Raschi.

When he arrived in New York as a 19-year-old major leaguer, Mickey Mantle was the embodiment of what springtime in baseball can evoke, a symbol of innocence and hope. For the America then—and the America that nostalgia subsequently captured in the national conscience—Mickey was the eternal glory of youth. He was a country boy, innocent of the temptations of an urban jungle that was already becoming a predominant feature of American life. To be sure, that was the New Yorker's perspective, because seen through the eyes of his fellow Oklahomans, Mantle's arrival in New York was seen as that of a hero venturing forth from the world of common life into a region of glamorous splendor and fabulous forces. Mantle's ability as a baseball player was as innate as his essential goodness. Yet he had long been warned by his watchful father that he couldn't rely solely on his gift alone, or he would fail.

Mickey himself would later say that when he arrived in New York his view of the world wasn't much wider than the strike zone. "My childhood was part of what made me popular with the fans in New York and elsewhere," he said. "I was a classic country bumpkin, who came to the big city carrying a cardboard suitcase and with a wardrobe of two pairs of slacks and a pastel-colored sports coat."

"I remember my impression of him the first time I met him," Yankee pitcher Whitey Ford later said. "I thought, 'What a hayseed.'"

Yogi Berra had a similar recollection: "I remember he was a big, scared kid who we already knew could hit the ball out of sight. You know something else I remember? Even when he was a kid, we already knew he was a helluva guy."

On Opening Day at Yankee Stadium, Mickey was flabbergasted at the sight of the towering triple-deck stands already filling up. He had already been to Yankee Stadium before, when he joined the team for the final two weeks of the previous season. Mickey was ineligible for the World Series roster. However, at general manager George Weiss's invitation, he had attended the first two games of the Yankees' 1950 World Series against the Philadelphia Phillies. Mantle was joined in New York for that game by his mother and father, his twin brothers Roy and Ray, and his girlfriend Merlyn in what Mantle was to remember as "a visit to paradise." But on Opening Day of the 1951 season, Mickey now stared around the stadium for the first time from the playing field. As he studied the famous Yankee Stadium facade above the upper deck, Yogi Berra came up behind him. "Hey, what kind of an opening day crowd is this? There's no people here." Mickey had quickly come to realize that the Yankee catcher didn't say things so much as growl them out. He stared at Yogi, then understood he was joking. Jim Turner, one of the coaches, came up to them.

"How many people watched you play at Joplin last year?" he asked Mickey.

"I'd say about 55,000 all season," he answered.

"Well, take a good look," said Turner. "We got about 45,000 here today for one game—almost as many people as saw you in Joplin all year."

Mantle gulped. "No!" he muttered.

"Yes," said Turner, trying to put Mickey at ease. "And most of them came to see what you look like."

An hour and a half before the game, sportswriter Red Smith recalled watching Mantle looking nervously into the stands from the top step of the Yankees' dugout. From the bench, Stengel could only see Mickey from the chest down but he noticed that the sole of one of his baseball cleats had torn loose. The Yankee skipper got up to talk to Mickey and then returned shaking his head. "He don't care much about the big leagues, does he?" Stengel said. "He's gonna play in them shoes."

"Who is he?" asked a visitor in the dugout who hadn't seen Mantle that spring.

"Why, he's that kid of mine," said Stengel.

"That's Mantle?"

"Yeah. I asked him didn't he have any better shoes, and he said he had a new pair but they're a little too big."

The visitor chuckled along with Stengel. "He's waiting for an important occasion to wear the new ones."

Stengel was also trying not to show his apprehension, not about how Mantle would do but about this team he was patching up with Band-Aids, mirrors, and smoke. Pitcher Whitey Ford and infielder Billy Martin had been drafted and were lost to the team for this season at least. DiMaggio was ailing, and aging as well. All of the team's starting pitchers—Allie Reynolds, Vic Raschi, Eddie Lopat, and Tommy Byrne—were all in their 30s. If this Yankees team were to compete for the pennant again, Stengel knew it would have to be with the help of at least two or three prized rookies. Gil McDougald looked ready to take over one spot in the infield. Mantle appeared set to play in the outfield. Then there was another highly touted youngster, Jackie Jensen, to whom the Yankees had given a $40,000 signing bonus. A year earlier Jensen, who had starred in the 1949 Rose Bowl for the University of California, had been the spring training Golden Boy thought to be DiMaggio's successor. However, Jensen had trouble hitting major-league pitching. In the 1951 spring training, Stengel tried to convert Jensen into a pitcher. That experiment failed, and now his hopes were that Jensen might hit just well enough to stay with the Yankees.

As he waited to take the field at Yankee Stadium for the first time in his career, Mickey couldn't keep his eyes off Ted Williams in the Boston Red Sox visitor's dugout. DiMaggio had been Mantle's hero growing up, but it was Williams who was now still at his prime and would continue to be throughout the 1950s. Military service had taken away a couple of seasons in the 1940s, and would again during the Korean War. Williams was also coming off an ill-fated 1950 season when he broke his left elbow in the All-Star Game and played only 89 games. At age 32, Williams was already being acknowledged among his peers as the game's consummate hitter. Achieving that reputation was what Williams lived for. As a rookie in 1939, when Mickey was not even eight years old, Williams had laid out what he wanted his epitaph to be. "All I want out of life," he had said, "is that when I walk down the street folks will say, 'There goes the greatest hitter who ever lived.'" This is the line that Bernard Malamud would appropriate and change ever so slightly—"Sometimes when I walk down the street I bet people will say there goes Roy Hobbs, the best there ever was in the game"—for the mythical slugger in *The Natural*, which would be published in 1952. The 1951 season would mark the 10th anniversary of Williams becoming the last major leaguer to hit .400. Williams had already won Triple Crowns in 1942 and 1947, and would go on to hit 521 home runs and finish with a .344 average.

The first time Mantle actually saw Williams play in person had been in September of 1950, when he had been brought up for two weeks after the end of his season at Joplin. "I saw Ted hit two home runs off Vic Raschi," said Mickey, "and I became convinced he was the greatest hitter I'd ever seen." Mantle had another reason that Opening Day for not being able to take his eyes off Williams. Three players had been in the spotlight that spring: DiMaggio for what would be his last season, Mantle for his magnificent exhibition season, and Williams for his adamant refusal to play in exhibitions. During spring training just a few weeks earlier, Williams had set off one of the many controversies in his career by publicly criticizing the spirit of the Boston Red Sox fans, while praising that of the Yankees. Now, here at Yankee Stadium, Williams was the object of stares and admiration from fans and players alike.

There was a telling incident just before the game began. Williams came over to the Yankee dugout to greet DiMaggio, with Mickey standing by his side, awed and nervous. Williams quickly acquainted himself: "You must be Mick."

As Mantle watched Williams and DiMaggio talk, nearby a couple of sportswriters were talking to Bill Dickey, the former Yankee catcher and manager who was now one of Stengel's coaches. They all turned to look at Mantle and one of the writers said, "Gosh, I envy him. Nineteen years old and starting out as a Yankee!"

"He's green," said Dickey, "but he's got to be great. All that power, a switch hitter, and he runs like a striped ape. If he drags a bunt past the pitcher, he's on base. I think he's the fastest man I ever saw with the Yankees. But he's green in the outfield. He was at shortstop last year."

"Gosh, Bill," said the writer, "do you realize you were in the big leagues before he was born?"

"He was born in 1932," said Dickey, misstating Mickey's birth year by a year, "and that was the year I played my first World Series."

Half an hour later, after the traditional Opening Day speeches at home plate, Whitey Ford walked out to the mound wearing his army uniform—he was still in the service—and threw out the first pitch.

Mantle's big-league debut began with the Red Sox's Dom DiMaggio hitting a single to right field that Mickey fielded cleanly and returned to second base. At the plate, Mantle broke his bat on the first major-league pitch he saw and almost beat the throw on his infield grounder. He popped up in his second at-bat and came to the plate for the third time in the sixth inning with the Yankees leading, 2–0, with nobody out and runners at first and third. Waiting on deck, DiMaggio called Mantle aside and spoke to him. Mantle nodded, stepped to the plate, and got his first major-league hit. Batting right-handed, Mickey hit a fastball off of lefty Bill Wright past the outstretched glove of shortstop Johnny Pesky into left field, driving in the runner from third base.

As he scooted back to first base from the wide turn toward second, Mantle momentarily caught a glimpse of DiMaggio looking at him, a small smile across his face, nodding in Mickey's direction, and giving his heir apparent a sign of acceptance.

"I would have given anything for his approval," said Mantle. "And I'd gotten it."

Chapter Twelve

A Death in the Family

I can't explain it. All I know is that my timing is off. There is abso-
lutely nothing wrong with me physically. I had a great spring. I'm
in perfect condition. My weight is just right. I suppose I need more
batting practice.

—Joe DiMaggio

In the early weeks of the 1951 season, Joe DiMaggio was experiencing one of the most difficult years of his career. He had shoulder and
neck injuries that sidelined him in April, then pulled a muscle that kept
him out of the lineup again in early June. One by one his injuries had
taken a toll on his body. In 1947, doctors had operated on DiMaggio's left
heel and removed a three-inch bone spur. Then they found a new bone
spur in his right foot. His injured right shoulder had turned him into
a below average–throwing center fielder. It would pop out of its socket
without warning and leave him in agonizing pain. All the while, Joe continued to suffer from chronic ulcers that he compounded by drinking pots
of coffee. DiMaggio was also in the throes of mounting personal troubles.
To top that off, the relationship between DiMaggio and Stengel, which
had never been good, worsened to the point that the Yankees' biggest star
stopped talking to Stengel or anyone else on the team.

Few were aware of the bad blood between DiMaggio and Stengel,
least of all the rookies. In 1950, as DiMaggio was going through the worst
slump of his career, Stengel dropped him down in the batting order from
the cleanup spot that he had held since 1939. DiMaggio never forgave his
manager. Their chilly relationship worsened further when Stengel finally

benched DiMaggio, and it reached its lowest point when the Yankee manager tried to turn Joe into a first baseman. Years later it was the same position change the Yankees tried with Mantle near the end of his career. With both Yankee legends, the attempt to make them first basemen—in an era before designated hitters—met with disaster. "He's worried all over," Tommy Henrich said of trying to make DiMaggio a first baseman. "He's afraid of making a dumb play because he's not familiar with first base. It would have killed him to make a stupid play." DiMaggio, though, managed to survive the humiliation that came with playing first base. In one game, he stumbled and fell on what should have been a routine play. The incident was captured by photographers and saved for posterity in the next day's newspapers.

From even spring training, DiMaggio had also been dealing with the private anguish that his mother Rosalie was dying. His father Giuseppe had died during the 1949 season, and Rosalie soon became very ill as well. Diagnosed with cancer, she spent much of 1950 and 1951 hospitalized or bedridden at home. A dutiful son, DiMaggio tried to be by his mother's side in San Francisco as much as possible. A teacher in her homeland, Rosalie was often credited by Dom for having been the force behind her family, for instance urging the move from Martinez to San Francisco that greatly improved the opportunities for her children. She also was the moral compass for her family, telling her children biblical stories and demanding a high standard of conduct. Later, it was also Rosalie and not Giuseppe who would occasionally take the train across the country to see Joe play in New York and Dom in Boston. In 1951, DiMaggio spent many of his evenings of the early season talking long-distance to his mother and to his family for updates. Sadly, though, she deteriorated quickly, and DiMaggio left the team in late June to be with his mother when she fell into a coma.

"It was not a good time for Joe," said pal Reno Barsocchini. "He wanted to reconcile with [first wife] Dorothy. He still loved her. He wanted her back, but nothing was coming easy for Joe any more."

In the summer of 1937, already the toast of New York as he was having an even better season than his rookie campaign, DiMaggio had been given a cameo in a film being shot in the city, *Manhattan Merry Go Round*.

There he met actress Dorothy Arnold with whom he fell head over heels in love. At the end of Joe's 1939 season, they married in San Francisco as a throng of onlookers surrounded the church. On their wedding day, November 19, 1939, Joe was six days from his 25th birthday, and Dorothy turned 22 years old two days after walking down the aisle. They appeared happy and DiMaggio topped his incredible 56-game hitting streak record in 1941 by becoming a father. Joe DiMaggio III, the Yankee Clipper's first and only child, was born on October 23, 1941, three months after his father's defining moment in baseball. After his parents divorced three years later, young Joe—who was often mistakenly called "Joe Jr."—spent much of his early life in summer camps and military schools, including the now-defunct Black Foxe Military Institute, a few blocks west of Paramount Studios in Hollywood and known as the school of choice for the sons of Hollywood celebrities.

In 1951, just days before DiMaggio learned that his mother had lapsed into a coma, Dorothy and their nine-year-old son arrived in New York City to visit. It was an awkward moment all the way around. DiMaggio wanted Dorothy and Joe Jr. to return to California with him, while Dorothy refused to make another flight across the country. Their divorce in 1944 had estranged her from the DiMaggio family, and Dorothy didn't want to throw Joe Jr. into what she feared could be a traumatic experience seeing his grandmother's death and a sad funeral.

In little more than a year's time, DiMaggio had lost both his father and his mother during the same period when it became increasingly apparent that he had lost his skills and gifts on the field. Thus the DiMaggio that Mickey saw during his rookie season was barely a shell of the DiMaggio he had grown up hearing and reading about in Commerce. Slowed and bothered by age and injuries, DiMaggio would go on to play in only 116 of the Yankees' 154 games in what became his worst season. He would hit a humiliating .263, four points lower than Mickey's average that year, and he hit only 12 home runs and drove in 71 runs. DiMaggio's season was made even worse by Stengel's insensitivity to his decline. Once, after a first-inning rout of the Yankees, Stengel immediately pulled several of his veterans. In a move that could have been handled better, the Yankee skipper substituted Jackie Jensen for DiMaggio by dispatching

Jensen out to center field where DiMaggio was already standing. Visibly unhappy, DiMaggio had even more reason to have a strained relationship with Stengel. That day *New York Times* sportswriter John Drebinger wrote: "This has been DiMaggio's mood for a long time. In fact, he rarely talks to his teammates or manager, let alone anyone remotely associated with the press. On a recent train ride following a night game in Philadelphia, DiMaggio, in the Yanks' special diner, sat by himself at a table set for four. It's a queer set-up, but almost everyone traveling with the Bombers is leaving the Clipper severely alone."

"I hardly knew the man," Mickey himself said of DiMaggio in the 1951 season. "He was a loner, always restrained, often secretive. If you weren't family or a very close friend, you didn't dare probe into his personal life. He'd shut you off in a minute. Shy as I was, I never went to him seeking advice. Too scared. It was a simple hello and goodbye. Press me further and I'll also admit that DiMaggio never said to me, 'Come on, kid, let's have a beer and talk.'"

That wasn't exactly true, as Holly Brooke and others would recall. But it was typical Mantle, never wanting to intrude into DiMaggio's space. "I didn't know how to handle talking about Joe," he acknowledged. "I've never wanted to say that we've been more than we were. But you're right. We were teammates, and it's easy to forget what comes to pass. It's not, like you say, that I was there taking notes that Joe said this to me or that Joe did this or that."

That season, when he didn't have other things to do, Mantle admitted often having his eyes glued on the man he was too shy to talk to. He especially kept a close watch on DiMaggio during batting practice where he studied Joe's trademark wide stance, long stride, and classic smooth swing. Above all, DiMaggio was the consummate professional, never giving any indication in public that he was often in excruciating pain from bone spurs on a bad heel. Mantle and all the other Yankees, as well as the rest of the sports world, would read the daily newspaper stories about DiMaggio's aching heel—and that was about all they knew of Joe's condition.

Mantle's own earliest recollection of DiMaggio was the first day the Yankee star arrived in camp that spring. Mickey was involved in a game of pepper, hitting and fielding short but sharply hit ground balls. As

DiMaggio walked behind him, Mickey missed a ground ball that nicked Joe's ankle and skidded away. "He swiveled his head in my direction," said Mickey, "staring bullets. I felt sure I'd be gone that night."

Unfortunately for Mantle, in the final year of his career DiMaggio was only going through the motions and no longer cared to exert the kind of influence over the clubhouse that he had over the past few seasons. Although he was known to be aloof to most of his teammates, DiMaggio also could be the consummate team player when he chose to be. His dedication to the game was unquestioned, and he expected the same in his teammates. In the late 1940s, as the senior member of the team, DiMaggio had established himself as the clubhouse conscience of the Yankees. His presence demanded an all-out effort by his Yankee teammates. When presence was not enough, Joe didn't hesitate to berate someone in untypical DiMaggio fashion. Once, after coming into the Yankee clubhouse exhausted from a doubleheader and limping from the incessant pain caused by bone spurs in his right heel, he found Yogi Berra joking around nearby.

DiMaggio, however, wasn't amused, because the Yankees' young, promising catcher had begged off catching the second game. Resentful, DiMaggio blew up.

"You're twenty-three years old," he said to Berra, "and you can't catch a double-header? My ass!"

Berra quickly came around, even though there were other awkward moments in the presence of the Yankee Clipper. Yogi Berra, who also played the outfield, later remembered that DiMaggio had one rule for the players beside him in the outfield: "'If you call for it, it's yours. If you don't say anything, it's mine.'"

"One day, I said, 'I got it,' and he just stopped. The ball was nowhere near me," Berra said of a ball that dropped between them. "He just gave me the look. He didn't even have to say a word. As a kid coming from the hills of St. Louis, I watched everything he did. He was such a great ballplayer. He never made a mistake on the field. I never saw him dive for a ball. You'd see him head for second and you'd wonder where he's going, but he always made it. He never, ever walked off the field. You've got to admire a guy like that. He's got to be like Babe Ruth. They are the two greatest."

Yet DiMaggio could be extremely protective of what he felt was his territory. He later told friends he didn't resent Mantle or his being groomed to succeed him, but that he disliked the fact that many who had once been so close to him seemingly had figuratively buried him. He told Reno Barsocchini that was the reason it upset him to see pictures in the papers that spring of his longtime friend Toots Shor with his arm around his newest pal, Mickey himself. DiMaggio had personally bailed out Shor on a couple of occasions when he had been cash poor and needed money to make payroll or repairs to his place. "If it hadn't been for Joe, Toots Shor would have had to hit up loan sharks from the Mob for a quick fix on money," said Barsocchini.

DiMaggio also suspected Shor of having committed the ultimate betrayal by talking to the press about him. That spring, *Look* magazine published a story on DiMaggio's personal life, including the woes of his marital breakup with his first wife Dorothy, along with anonymous quotes that Joe knew had come from Toots Shor. DiMaggio would remember and never forgive. Years later, when Toots was old and lost his bar, Mantle, Whitey, Yogi, and others sent Shor money. DiMaggio, however, refused. When he was recovering from a stroke, Toots showed up in the Yankee clubhouse to see his old pals at an Old Timers' Day game at the Stadium. He got a big reception from all the players except DiMaggio. When he saw Toots struggle using canes to walk across the clubhouse floor toward his corner, Joe turned and hurried away, into the trainer's room.

In a way, DiMaggio wasn't just competitive, both on and off the field. He was ruthless, even with old high school friends. Former major leaguer Dario Lodigiana, Joe's lifelong friend who played high school baseball with him at Lowell High in San Francisco, remembered an incident when DiMaggio slid into him spikes-high, the way Ty Cobb did in his time.

"We were playing the Yankees when I was with Philadelphia and it was just a normal day, not a big game or anything," Lodigiana told San Francisco area writer Ed Attanasio. "And I was playing second base when Joe came sliding in real hard, knocking me ass-over-teacups. Then, he got up, brushed his pants off a couple of times, and never said doo, hello, squat, or nothing—he just ran off to the dugout. He had a real hard look on his face and was just staring straight ahead. You would never have known that we grew up together by the way he was acting."

In 1951 Mantle did not see this side of the ever-stoic DiMaggio. But if DiMaggio didn't show his resentment, his fans did. A few times in his rookie season Mickey got the treatment at Yankee Stadium, nothing like the deafening booing of future years, that always began with a smattering of catcalls and boos, which prompted Hank Bauer to tell Mickey: "In New York, most of the fans here are DiMaggio fans, so you're surely gonna get booed for being the guy who's gonna take his place. It's just a New York thing."

"I don't care who you are, you hear those boos," Mickey said once. "I well understood that my being made into a rival of Joe DiMaggio turned plenty of fans against me. But I was not ready for the dirty names or the screaming profanity or the tireless abuse [of the New York fans]."

Worse, Mantle feared that his own actions around DiMaggio did little to endear him to the Yankee great. Once, Stengel called to Mickey on the bench to pinch-hit. Mantle quickly tore off his Yankee jacket and flung it behind him as he hurried to the bat rack. Suddenly he heard a muffled yell from the bench and looked around. The jacket had landed in DiMaggio's face and was covering his head like a hood.

"He's a rockhead," DiMaggio told his newspaper pal Lou Effrat.

From DiMaggio's point of view, in these instances he was simply giving the young phenom much the same treatment he had been given by Ruth when he had been a rookie with the Yankees. "Joe met Ruth well after the Bambino's playing career, and their relationship was formal," said DiMaggio biographer Richard Ben Cramer. "Joe remembered well how Ruth dismissed him as a rookie and said he hadn't proved yet that he could play in the big leagues. In Gehrig's case, Joe and he were teammates for more than two years before Lou took sick and left the lineup, but both Gehrig and Joe were silent souls who came to the clubhouse, dressed, did their business, and left without a word beyond simple greetings . . . Joe was certainly responsible for the chill between him and Mantle in Mickey's rookie year. In 1951, when Mantle arrived, he was so shy he couldn't say a word to DiMaggio unless the big guy spoke to him first."

Mourning his mother's death, DiMaggio did his best to put Stengel's slights aside. Stengel had a long reputation of being the clown of baseball, while Joe had the experience of having played for one of the game's coaching legends—Joe McCarthy—who had stitched together two great Yankee eras. McCarthy had become the Yankees manager in 1931, after being fired by the Chicago Cubs at the end of the 1930 season. Babe Ruth and Lou Gehrig were baseball's biggest stars, but their end was in sight. The Yankees released Ruth after the 1934 season and Gehrig retired in 1939. By then, the Yankees had become DiMaggio's team. He had a tremendous rookie season in 1936, the first of four consecutive championship seasons for McCarthy and the Yankees. They won World Series titles again in 1941 and 1943. McCarthy became the first manager to win pennants with both National and American League teams, taking nine league titles overall and seven World Series championships—a record that has been tied only by Stengel. However, World War II upset baseball's pecking order as it did much of the world, and McCarthy resigned as the Yankees manager in the spring of 1946. DiMaggio returned from his tour in the military to lead the Yankees to another championship in 1947, winning the last of his three Most Valuable Player awards as well. However, by 1949 when Stengel took over as manager, DiMaggio was only a shadow of his greatness. He was 34 years old, past his prime in those days, and playing for a manager who could not have been more different than Joe McCarthy.

Nevertheless, that 1949 season with his most dramatic moments would show the mettle of DiMaggio's greatness despite his nagging injuries and deterioration of his skills. He had been sidelined by bone spurs on his right heel and did not play until June 26 when he flew to Boston to join the team in Fenway Park, hit a single and home run in his first two at-bats, hit two more home runs the next day, and another the day after that. Then, as the Yankees entered the final two days of that season trailing the Red Sox by one game, they had to sweep two games in Yankee Stadium to win the pennant. In the first game, with a rowdy crowd of 69,551 fans attending for a Joe DiMaggio Day, DiMaggio was almost too weak to play because of a severe viral infection. However, Joe still played, hitting a single and double before removing himself from center field on wobbly legs, and inspiring the Yankees to win the second game. Although limited to playing only 76 games that season, DiMaggio still hit .346 and was a big reason for Casey Stengel winning a World Series in his first year at the Yankee helm. Joe bounced back in 1950 to hit 32 homers and drive in 122 runs while batting .301. The Yankees also won back-to-back World Series crowns in those years. DiMaggio seriously considered retiring but was wooed by the Yankees and another offer of $100,000. In 1949, he had become the first baseball player to sign a six-digit contract that made him the highest paid athlete in the world.

In 1951, though, it wasn't as if Stengel was alone in knowing that the player with the fabled number 5 on the back of his uniform jersey was no longer the Joe DiMaggio who had once terrorized the American League. The scouting report on DiMaggio that circulated throughout the league made its way to Brooklyn scout Andy High when the Dodgers began looking ahead to possibly playing the Yankees in the World Series and late that season into *Life* magazine. DiMaggio "could not stop quickly and throw hard," making him a defensive liability that meant that baserunners "can taken an extra base on him . . . He can't run. . . ." Of his once majestic swing, the report said: "His reflexes are very slow and he can't pull a good fastball at all. The fastball is better thrown high, but that is not too important as long as it is fast. Throw him nothing but good fastballs and fast curveballs. Don't slow up on him."

The report did the Dodgers little good. The New York Giants overtook them in the final month and won a playoff to take the National League pennant and a spot in the World Series. However, there was no hiding just how far DiMaggio had slipped. His weakened arm strength was especially obvious. On balls hit deep to the outfield that DiMaggio caught or fielded, shortstop Phil Rizzuto or second baseman Jerry Coleman had to sprint almost halfway to the fence to take cutoff throws from Joe.

Among the veterans, the feud between DiMaggio and Stengel took its toll, with most of them quietly siding with their manager. What choice did they really have? Stengel made out the lineup. He determined who would come off the bench and for how long. His notorious platooning method already meant that some starters were playing only part of the time. Besides, it wasn't as if DiMaggio had ever made himself part of the players group who would usually go off to dinner and drinks while Joe retreated to his hotel and ordered room service.

Meanwhile, Mantle's strong start to his rookie season had stolen much of the thunder from DiMaggio's struggles. Mickey's father had already seen some of his games with the Yankees, but it was not until the Yankees traveled to St. Louis to play the Browns that his mother was able to attend a game. At Sportsman's Park that day were Mickey's mother, his girlfriend Merlyn, and her mother. A reporter even approached Merlyn after the game and asked her what she thought of Mickey having hit a home run. "I expected it," she said. "He promised me he'd do it."

As he had in spring training, Mantle impressed everyone with his speed. In a game against Detroit, Mickey was sacrificed from first base to second on a bunt. But when the Tigers' first baseman turned to check on Mickey at second base after the force-out, he found that Mickey was already streaking to third base. Mickey slid in safely ahead of the throw, and in the dugout Stengel jumped up from the bench, boasting to all around, "He went from first to third on a bunt!" Against Cleveland, Mantle lined a hit into left-center field that Indians center fielder Larry Doby quickly gathered in. When he looked up to throw the ball toward second base, Doby was shocked to see Mantle sliding into second. Mickey had never slowed down as he circled first and turned a routine single into a double.

"You ain't seen nothing yet," Stengel told the writers traveling with the team. "The kid doesn't run—he flies. He's positively the fastest man on the bases I've ever seen."

It was his speed that also helped Mantle make a quantum leap in his play in the outfield. Even when he was getting a late jump, Mickey was able to simply run down fly balls. He could cover incredible amounts of territory for a right fielder, especially in the cavernous expanse of the Yankee Stadium outfield. With DiMaggio slowed by age and injuries, Stengel would eventually pull Mantle aside and quietly ask that he take balls that might ordinarily be fielded by the center fielder. "You can run faster than any other outfielder in the business," Stengel told Mantle, "but one never would know that from watching you out there. Put on a show.

Run hard for the ball. Haul off. Throw a foot high into the air when you heave the ball. Don't be afraid to throw."

As much as Stengel may have taken pride in Mantle's improved defensive play, the real credit belonged to Yankee outfielder-turned-outfield-coach Tommy Henrich. That spring Henrich had spent long days with Mantle teaching him how to catch the ball and get rid of it, all in one motion. Mantle was especially attentive to Henrich for two reasons. One, Mickey was the first to acknowledge that he knew little about playing the outfield, particularly the techniques Henrich was teaching him. The second was that it had nothing to do with hitting and with changing anything that his father might have taught him. Over the years Mantle would earn the reputation of being a poor learner, especially from Stengel, but it was almost always a hitting lesson that Mickey would completely tune out. The telling incident on just how well Mantle had learned his lessons from Henrich came early that rookie season against the Chicago White Sox. Jim Busby of the White Sox was at third base tagging up on a fly ball to Mickey in right field. Mantle caught the ball at the same instant that he planted his right foot the way Henrich had taught him. In almost the same motion, Mantle fired a strike to the plate so fast that Busby was forced to stop halfway home and retreat to third. The Yankees in the dugout came to their feet, and Henrich walked over to Stengel. "That's the best throw I've ever seen anyone make," Henrich said. "I don't think I have anything else to teach him. He's got it down pretty good."

Chapter Thirteen

Down from Olympus

Holly was the most beautiful woman I'd ever seen. She could have been Miss America, that's how beautiful and wonderful she was.
—Mickey Mantle

In 1948, the Miss America officials in New Jersey faced a crisis they learned about only after one of their state's beauty pageants had already awarded the Miss New Jersey local qualifying title to a beautiful redhead who had beaten the competition but whose presence now threatened the integrity of their program. The pageant's 23-year-old winner had confirmed to them the distressing rumor that had come into their office. She had been previously married, a violation of the pageant's rules. Worse, for a pageant built on presenting the image of a beautiful, chaste, unmarried symbol of young womanhood in America, the woman was the mother of a young son. Never in her wildest dreams had Marie Huylebroeck of Bayonne, New Jersey, thought she would ever come close to winning even a preliminary Miss New Jersey title, she said years later.

"I knew I was beautiful and had talent and I guess I just wanted to see how I kind of stacked up against other beautiful, talented women," she said. "And if anyone in the pageant had said to me, 'Young lady, you're going to win,' I would have dropped out or not even entered. I wouldn't have wanted to put myself in that kind of predicament. Who would?"

Much to the relief of pageant officials, Huylebroeck agreed to quietly relinquish her newly won crown. A cover story was immediately put together, and the new Miss New Jersey quickly introduced, almost as if nothing had happened.

Even in quiet disgrace, though, for Marie Huylebroeck the experience was a validation in the belief she had for herself, a Jersey girl with grand dreams and great expectations but an unusual name of Belgian and French origin. The Americanized pronunciation was Holly Brook, and as a teen that was the artistic name she chose, spelling it Holly Brooke. She continued to use it when shortly after high school she moved to Manhattan, where she decided she wanted to become an actress. Those dreams, though, became sidelined when she married in 1945 and had a son two years later.

By 1951, Holly Brooke was back in Manhattan. She had appeared in several small parts in off-Broadway productions and bit roles in films. By early summer, she was effectively living with Mickey Mantle and spending every off-the-field moment with him when the Yankees were home. Mantle was 19. Holly was 26, about to be 27, and had a son in the first grade. His Yankees teammates, those who knew of the relationship, feared she was a femme fatale who would ruin Mickey. Mantle would call her his first and great love. All was well as long as Mantle played well and continued to hit the way he had in the early weeks of the season. Mickey, however, had begun drinking heavily and had no control, especially since he could always find someone to pay for his drinks or buy the booze he would take home.

"He moved from the Concourse Hotel to 53rd near the Stage Delicatessen—I think they were on the fourth floor—and he wanted me there all the time," Holly told me in one of a series of interviews, "and I couldn't because I had to work as an actress and model. I would come there after my work, and sometimes I'd work on a movie until ten or eleven at night. One night I came home late, and he had started drinking and was so sick that I had to stay there with him all night, rubbing his back and helping him to the bathroom because he was so sick he kept throwing up. I felt bad that I hadn't been home earlier, and I kept telling him, 'Mick, you can't keep doing this. This isn't good for you.'"

Was Mickey Mantle a 19-year-old kid unable to hold his liquor or was he already hooked, already an alcoholic, something he would finally admit to years later but which in his rookie season was quickly becoming a problem? To his credit, though, he didn't wake up wanting a drink, something Holly said she wouldn't have stood for, especially as Mantle grew closer to her family.

"I remember the first weekend the Yankees were home and me telling him I had to go home for the weekend, and Mickey begged me not to go," Holly recalled. "And I said, 'Mick, I've got to. I see my son on weekends.' I had already told him I was a working mom, and that my family kept my son during the week, and I'd go home on the weekends. He said, 'Well, okay, Holly, bring him up here, and we'll spend the weekend together.' I couldn't believe he'd said that, but I thought, 'Well, let's see.' And I brought my son Harlan up, and I swear Mickey took to him like he was his own."

It all continued to go well for Mantle for several weeks. He spent most of his free time with Holly, often at the wheel of her car driving around New York or sometimes just parked while they listened to music, hoping to hear their favorite song, Rosemary Clooney's "Come On-A My House." On the baseball field, Mickey was striking out more often than Stengel liked, but he was leading or near the top of the team's statistics in several categories. In early July, Mantle was leading the Yankees with 45 RBIs and had slugged seven home runs. However, his batting average had slipped to .260, and was rapidly falling. By the second week of July, Mickey was beaten, adrift in a slump that had humbled him as never before.

Yankee pitcher Allie Reynolds, who often spent time that season trying to instruct Mickey on the ways of the big leagues, later took the blame for inadvertently putting a jinx on Mantle that led to his rookie slide. An Oklahoma boy at heart, Mickey in those early days had attached himself in the dugout to veterans like Reynolds, a fellow Oklahoman. Reynolds was a favorite of Stengel's who had once called him "two ways great" because of his skills as a starter and a reliever for six Yankee World Series champions from 1947 through 1953. In the dugout one day, Mantle casually said to Reynolds, "Do you know that I'm leading the league in average, RBI and home runs?"

Reynolds knew that Mantle was saying this to him more in amazement than as a boast, so he tried to tease Mickey. "Did you ever stop to think what that can mean to you economically?" he asked Mantle.

"After that he lost twenty-five points off his batting average," Reynolds said. "I created the pressure."

Mantle sank into a slump that worsened as he began to press. For most rookies, this becomes a normal period of adjustment to better, smarter pitching than what they faced in the minors. Mickey stubbornly refused to change his approach to hitting after pitchers discovered that he was a sucker for high fastballs just above the letters. Mantle didn't have the discipline not to chase those pitches, nor the patience to drive outside pitches to the opposite field. Walt Masterson of the Washington Senators and Satchel Paige of the St. Louis Browns may have been the first pitchers to find Mickey's weakness and begin his downward spiral. "Man, he was striking out like crazy," said Yogi Berra. Soon word of how to pitch Mantle got around the league. What concerned Stengel most wasn't the slump but that Mickey wasn't even putting the ball in play consistently. Mantle's skid reached a low point in a doubleheader in Boston where he struck out three times in the first game and twice more in the second game, returning to the dugout in tears and throwing his bat in a fit of anger.

"Put someone in there who can hit the ball," he cried to Stengel. "I can't."

Stengel tried being patient and even fatherly in protecting Mickey from the press, especially the negative stories that pointed out how much he was striking out.

"Never mind that crap," he said to Mantle after the appearance of one critical story. "All you need is a couple of hits. It's only a slump. Everybody has 'em."

Stengel tried playing Mantle only against right-handers, believing he was a better hitter left-handed. But Mantle began having troubles that way, too. Stengel then tried batting Mickey in the leadoff spot, thinking he could capitalize on his great speed to get on base. Mantle, however, continued to strike out, chasing after the high fastballs that were his weakness. In Cleveland in mid-July, Bob Lemon struck him out three times. In the dugout, Mickey smashed two of his bats against a wall. At other times, he smashed his fists against walls after striking out. Stengel threatened to fine him, but Mantle's outbursts continued unchecked. At one point, Paige was seen laughing on the mound at Mickey's frustration. At his wit's end, Mantle tried to lay down a two-strike bunt with a runner in scoring position in the bottom of the ninth inning, but fouled the bunt attempt for an out to end the game. Stengel was furious. "Nice going, son," he said to Mickey in front of his locker. "You sure fooled us. Next time I want you to bunt, I'll give you the sign."

For a while in the spring, Stengel had given Mantle the same liberty he gave to some of his veterans—allowing them to hit with a count of two balls and no strikes. Mantle was now chasing such bad pitches on 2-0 counts that Stengel withdrew the veterans' privilege from his rookie, and began giving him the take sign on those counts. When he saw that Mickey's confidence eroded further, Reynolds pulled him aside and tried to explain the manager's decision.

"If you can stand up there and swing at good pitches, hitting them isn't the point," he told Mantle. "You're going to miss some because you swing so hard, and you go for the long ball. But you have to swing at good pitches, and if the count is 2-0 and you swing at a pitch over your head, the pitcher has an advantage, and Casey has to take the advantage away from him."

Mickey's temper didn't help him any. After striking out, he would often attack water coolers in the dugout and then take his brooding out into the field where his defensive play suffered. Once when he blew an outfield play while Lopat was on the mound, the veteran pitcher threatened to beat the crap out of him. The temper tantrums didn't amuse the Yankees, who were trying to calm down the furor that had erupted over Mickey's military draft status. Mantle's draft board in Oklahoma had ruled him 4-F, unfit physically for military service because of a bone disease, osteomyelitis, that had stricken him as a teenager. Mickey's wondrous baseball exploits in the wake of the Korean War had raised new questions among some of why he wasn't draft eligible. Mantle had undergone a second preinduction physical and failed that as well, but he remained the target of hecklers. In a game against the White Sox in Chicago, fans threw firecrackers at Mickey, and Stengel threatened to pull the Yankees from the field before authorities intervened.

It all ate away at Mantle, all those expectations of greatness that he wished had not been placed on him.

"When I came up, Casey told the writers that I was going to be the next Babe Ruth, Lou Gehrig and Joe DiMaggio all rolled up in one," Mantle would later say. "Casey kept bragging on me and the newspapers kept writing it and, of course, I wasn't what Casey said I was. I don't mind admitting that there was incredible pressure on me because of what Casey was saying, and the fans were expecting so much, which I wasn't able to deliver."

CHAPTER FOURTEEN

A Hometown Sweetheart

When he stopped hitting home runs, the only time he had any self-esteem was after a drink or two.

—MERLYN MANTLE

THE RELATIONSHIP BETWEEN MICKEY AND MERLYN WOULD BE A CURI-ous one from beginning to end. In Mantle's books and in some of the magazine articles of the 1950s, their relationship was portrayed as young love between hometown sweethearts that was severely tested in the big city. The description, however, does not tell the full account which, as with all relationships and marriages, was far more complex and convoluted than the small-town fairytale cover story. Love was certainly a large part of it. Mickey's letters to Merlyn, especially during his minor-league season and his rookie year, are filled with his expressions of love and endearments. At various times through his life, Mantle also talked or wrote about his love for and devotion to his wife, though usually in the context of her being the mother of his sons. Thus, a major aspect of their relationship was also duty: duty to Merlyn, especially later in their lives, but perhaps more importantly, duty to his father.

Mickey first saw Merlyn Johnson at a high school football game at neighboring Picher High School not far from his Oklahoma hometown. It did not begin as love at first sight, although the night he had first seen Merlyn he had returned home and said to his mother, "I met the cutest little thing in Picher tonight. She twirls one of the batons for the Picher band. She's got freckles, reddish hair and is no taller than that." Mantle's childhood friend Ivan Shouse was dating Merlyn's sister Pat, and both were majorettes at Picher High. A few days later Ivan arranged a triple date in which Mickey was paired off with yet another majorette, Lavanda Whipkey, and Merlyn went out with another of Mickey's friends, Preston Christman. Mickey was disappointed.

Fortunately for Mickey, things soon worked out in his favor. When Lavanda was unable to go on a date they had tentatively planned, Mickey approached Preston to ask if he would mind if he asked Merlyn out on a date. Christman told him to go ahead. Even then, however, Mickey still had to ask Ivan Shouse to arrange a double date this time. The story goes that when Shouse called Merlyn to ask if she would go out with Mickey, her response was: "Who's Mickey Mantle?" Mickey quickly made up for not having made much of a first impression. After the third date, he asked Merlyn to go steady. She agreed, and from then on was known as Mickey's girlfriend in the Commerce-Picher area.

"I developed an instant crush on Mickey Mantle," Merlyn said in her memoir, "and by our second or third date, I was in love with him and always would be."

Merlyn's mother was among those amazed at their relationship. She knew how quiet her daughter was, and she was also aware of how shy Mickey appeared to be. "I don't know how Merlyn and Mickey ever got acquainted," she would say later. "Neither of them ever says a word."

Merlyn was the daughter of a highly respected family in Picher. Her father, like her grandfather, had been a deacon in the Baptist church. He also was a member of the local school board. Merlyn's grandfather had founded the Johnson Lumber Company, which annually sponsored a team in the area's summer baseball leagues. Her father Giles had worked in the local mines until he suffered a head injury in an accident. Unfortunately, a subsequent operation to remove a blood clot left him with epilepsy, and he was forced to take an office job in the family lumberyard. Merlyn herself grew up in a loving family in which she was encouraged to excel in her studies as well as in her singing. She once entertained the troops at nearby Camp Crowder during World War II and another time won a music contest in which she sang an aria in Italian. During her senior year in high school, Merlyn won a scholarship to Miami [Oklahoma] Junior College. She was also starstruck with the movies and Hollywood, secretly harboring a fantasy that one day she might find herself in the world of celebrities and recording stars. Once she fell in love with Mickey, however, Merlyn gave up her dreams of college or a career. Mickey was her focus, and she ultimately became one of those women for whom life involves living in both the glory and the shadow of their famous husbands. By her own admission, being Mrs. Mickey Mantle "was all I had really wanted since the second or third time I had seen him."

Merlyn would ultimately admit that she was as addicted to Mickey as she later became to alcohol. She wrote in *A Hero All His Life* that she "loved Mickey Mantle so much that I wanted to crawl inside him and underneath his skin. I wanted to control everything he did." Few who grew up knowing Merlyn would ever have suspected her to be capable of harboring not only such strong emotions but also feelings that, by her own account, would become unhealthy and contribute to destroying their love.

Years later I would personally witness the pressures Merlyn Mantle lived with. It was on the same day I met Mickey over lunch in the Turtle Creek area of Dallas. He ended up so drunk that evening that he was in no condition to drive home. That task fell upon me, and I found myself behind the wheel, though having a difficult time locating his house. I finally had to pull into a service station, near a payphone booth, to call the city desk at my newspaper, the *Dallas Times Herald*, to ask for Mickey Mantle's home address. It was a strange experience driving your childhood hero home in a drunken state, something that would happen often in the coming months. That first night was typical of what it was like getting him home. He slumped against the window in the passenger side of my car but thankfully never passed out. I'm not sure what I would have done if that had happened. He would have been too heavy to carry from the car to his house. From my experience it was also best to leave a sleeping drunken man alone, lest you get an inadvertent but damaging wild swing thrown your way. With Mickey, I got the impression that part of him was always awake through the drunken stupor. It led me to believe those baseball stories of how Mantle, hung over and possibly still drunk, came off the bench to slug pinch-hit home runs. This apparently happened more than once. In one story, Mantle complained that he was seeing three baseballs coming out of the pitcher's hand, leading a team-mate to ask how he had known which ball to hit.

"I just hit the one in the middle," Mantle is reported to have said.

In another instance, a hung-over Mantle had been pretending to watch the game on the bench, not realizing he was no longer on the disabled list and was being called upon to pinch-hit. Told by his manager that he had been placed on the active list that day, Mantle struggled to the plate, unable to see straight. Former teammate Hank Bauer was then a coach for the opposing team, the Baltimore Orioles, and knew Mickey was both rusty and hung over. Calling a timeout, Bauer went to the mound to tell the pitcher that Mantle would never be able to get his bat around on a fastball. Mantle then swung at the first pitch, a fastball, and hit it out of the park. He circled the bases with Bauer looking on from the Orioles' dugout in stunned silence. Once back in the Yankee dugout, Mickey slumped down on the bench next to teammate Whitey Ford.

"Kid, great hit," said Whitey. "I dunno how you hit that."

"Hell, hitting the ball was easy," Mickey shot back. "Running around the bases was the tough part."

I could imagine Mickey doing all that. Even when drunk, there was a part of him that appeared completely normal unless you knew him. I learned that the first time I drove him home. I made sure he got inside his house where his wife Merlyn took one look at him and turned up her eyes in disgust. She had a drill for whoever brought Mickey home on nights like that. She wanted to know where Mickey had left his car, where his car keys were, and if he had his wallet with him. She didn't seem to care about any of the money in the wallet. It was Mickey's identification that concerned her.

"It is just so much trouble for Mickey to get his driver's license replaced," Merlyn said. "He has to do it himself and once they know it's Mickey Mantle, there's a long line of people that builds up wanting his autograph. He winds up staying there for hours."

This, of course, was before the memorabilia boom that hit a decade later. There were no baseball card shows, to speak of, in 1970. Few people knew the value that would later be attached to Mantle's cards, especially those of his rookie season that would eventually sell as high as $100,000, which equaled his salary with the Yankees at the height of his career.

Merlyn never worried if Mickey left his El Dorado at the Preston Trail Golf Club in far North Dallas. It was the exclusive new course designed by golf legend Byron Nelson where Mickey played two or three times a week. At other times, Merlyn insisted on personally retrieving Mickey's car, usually having a girlfriend drive her there. On a few occasions, I drove her myself and was surprised to learn how much she loved country music. Once in your car, Merlyn took control of the stereo and would pull out of her purse eight-track tapes with Willie Nelson and Waylon Jennings music that she would accompany as you drove. She had a nice voice, and she was a beautiful woman who had built her entire life around Mickey. In her late 30s, Merlyn was at a period when her life had begun changing from what she had known it to be for almost two decades. The children were in their teens or preteens. Mickey Jr. was in high school; David and Billy were 14 and 12 years of age, respectively; Danny, the baby of the family, had just turned 10. They had their own sets of friends and their own lives.

"The only child I have to take care of now is Mickey," Merlyn said to me on one of those drives to pick up his car when he had been too intoxicated to drive home. She didn't say that sadly, so much as matter-of-fact.

One time I asked Merlyn what it was like having Mickey home during the summer, which had never happened until he retired the previous year.

"Well, we're still getting to know each other again!" she said. "We've never had this much time to ourselves."

Merlyn would later write in her own book about life with Mickey that these had been among the most difficult years of her life. She would develop a drinking problem herself, she wrote, in part from trying to be close to her husband. In 1970, Merlyn showed no sign, to me at least, of having a drinking problem yet. She appeared sober but concerned whenever I brought Mickey home. Sometimes she would be angry, especially if he had forgotten that they had plans for that evening. In our time together, Mickey rarely spoke of her, not that he necessarily should have. When he did, it was usually something about "Merlyn and the boys." I suspected this is how he had come to think of her, as the mother of his children. For all his reputation as a womanizer, I also never saw Mickey attempt to pick up any women; and there were numerous opportunities in the clubhouses at the golf courses where we played or at restaurants where we ate. There was some expected flirting with waitresses and women who brought their sons to our table seeking autographs. There were also numerous instances of women, either alone or with friends, catching Mickey's eye and possibly expecting him to get up from the table and walk over to meet them. But he didn't. The only affection I ever saw from him toward a woman, both while sober and drunk, was toward Merlyn who still had a shock of blonde hair and the beauty of the cheerleader she had been at Picher High School in Oklahoma in the late 1940s.

Merlyn was not unlike the women of her time, especially the wives of successful men. Her existence was so closely interwoven with that of her husband that she had never developed a life of her own. She was Mrs. Mickey Mantle. Her life, as she had more or less put it, was taking care of Mickey and his legacy. When she finally got around one day to ask me what I did for a living, she was stunned and mortified to learn that I was a journalist.

"A reporter?" she asked, astonished. "Does Mickey know that?"

I told her the story of how I had called him and how we met.

"Are you going to write about us?" I'm sure she was wondering why she had been so open with me.

"No, ma'm," I said. "My editor didn't have any interest."

She looked disappointed when I said that. She couldn't understand either why there would be no immediate interest at a Dallas newspaper about Mickey.

"Well, if you ever do," she said. "I would just ask that you be kind and wait until we're dead and buried."

In the weeks ahead, I came to understand a little of what Merlyn was dealing with in living with Mickey Mantle in retirement. I learned that it was advisable to get Mickey talking about golf and as little about baseball as possible. He had just recovered from his most embarrassing injury as a Yankee, and it upset him to dwell on it. While trying to get into his suite that spring, he had put his hand through a glass door at the St. Moritz

Hotel in New York and needed stitches. The injury also put an end to the idea that he could coach first base for the Yankees that season, which had been a public relations disaster from the start. "I wasn't naïve. I put extra people in the stands, that's all," Mantle said of his days as a Yankee coach. "There I was, pacing back and forth in the [first base coaching] box, and saying, 'Let's get it going now!' and feeling like a fool when Bobby Murcer drew a leadoff walk in the fourth inning, called time and asked me what the signs were. I said, 'Mine look good. I'm a Libra.' I was nothing more than a public relations gimmick."

In Dallas, Mantle now lived in virtual anonymity.

"It was like Mickey Mantle had died," he said about life after retirement. "It was weird. I'm thinking, 'Geeze, what did I do?' It seemed nobody cared what I was doing."

Well, some of the people at the Preston Trail Golf Club with its exclusive membership of Dallas's elite cared. They knew Mickey as a fun-loving guy who sometimes gave them some unexpected awkward moments. Mickey, for instance, had a tendency to walk into the club's restaurant to order a drink completely naked. Mantle had also on occasion shocked members of a nearby country club by going skinny-dipping in the club's pool. At Preston Trail, Mickey's naked antics led the membership committee to finally institute what became known as "The Mickey Mantle Rule," prohibiting anyone nude from entering or lounging in the club's restaurant.

"The problem with people in Texas," Mickey said, "is that they're so busy trying to be taken seriously they've forgotten how to have fun."

I suppose that made me the perfect choir member. Finding a wide-eyed young reporter who wanted to talk to him about golf was just what Mickey needed at the moment. It was a bonus that I could also play a decent game of golf and could take off early a lot of afternoons to get in nine or 18 holes. More importantly, I had the moxie to play for money without folding under the pressure. But then it also wasn't my money. Mickey loved to gamble—on the round, on holes, on putts, regardless of whether they were his or mine. If a putt was six feet or shorter, he was betting.

"Hey, Waco." He continued to call me Waco, and I would answer to it. "You wanna keep playin' with me, ya be sure to make those putts."

I blew a four-footer once, and he didn't talk to me for two holes.

"Waco, I was thinkin'. Blow another putt like that," he said. "Then be damn sure you make the next one."

"Mick, I won't miss another one," I assured him.

"Nah, miss the next one."

I didn't understand, but I intentionally missed the next short putt, and he lost a bet. Then on the next short putt I faced, it all made sense. Mickey upped the stakes, tripling the bet, and cleaned up when I sank a seven-footer. And, of course, he kept betting.

"It's a lot more fun playing," he said, "when you're gambling with other people's money, ain't it, Waco?"

It was the first time I ever thought of Mickey Mantle as a philosopher.

In her book, Merlyn described Mickey as having suffered from extreme insecurity all his life. She believed Mickey had emotional problems stemming from his unresolved relationship with his father: Mutt's exceptionally high expectations and Mickey's fears of failing to meet them. Merlyn would later say that an entire book could be written about Mantle's relationship with his father. Mantle, however, neither as a young man nor later in life, wanted to deal with it. In 1989, screenwriter Angelo Pizzo, who wrote the highly regarded basketball film *Hoosiers*, met with Mantle to discuss a possible motion picture based on Mickey's life. "When I started probing below the surface of his life," said Pizzo, "he got uncomfortable and angry, especially about his father." As much mutual love as existed between father and son, it was never shown. Even when Mickey returned home after being away during his 1949 and 1950 minor-league seasons, Mutt always greeted him not with a hug but a handshake. Merlyn felt that the early pressure on Mantle to play baseball along with his own drive to be the best contributed, in part, to the bed-wetting problem he had, even through high school. Mantle apparently corrected the problem himself, through sheer willpower, after signing his professional contract and being sent to play his first minor-league season at Independence, Kansas. Mantle also had unresolved emotions from the sexual abuse his older half-sister and her friends had inflicted upon him as a young boy. He never talked about it until he confided to Merlyn in his later years. Mantle never forgot the image of his half-sister and her friends laughing at him, and being made fun of was one of the few things he could not tolerate. Mantle couldn't deal with humiliation, either personally off the field or professionally on the field.

"Mickey's very proud," Merlyn said in a 1970 interview. "There's some things he forgets sometimes, but he never forgets who he is. He doesn't forget he's Mickey Mantle."

CHAPTER FIFTEEN

Mind Games

I'm just a ballplayer with one ambition, and that is to give all I've got to help my ball club win. I've never played any other way.
—Joe DiMaggio

SOME MIGHT ARGUE THAT THE BIGGEST PROBLEM FACING AN ATHLETE is controlling one's emotions. Mantle's temper, it was becoming evident that rookie season, was every bit as big and raw as his talent. If Mutt Mantle is to be faulted for anything in the way he raised Mickey, perhaps it is in not having enforced more discipline on his son's temperament. Mantle's legendary temper and childish attitude would become a source of embarrassment and unforgivable displays of boorish behavior throughout his career and for almost all of his personal life. There are no stories or accounts of Mutt ever having disciplined Mickey when he had thrown temper tantrums as a young ballplayer.

"The feeling between Mutt Mantle and his son," Merlyn Mantle said, "was more than love. Mick was his work of art, just as much as if his father had created him out of clay. He spent every minute he could with him, coaching, teaching, shaping him, and pointing him toward the destiny he knew was out there. Baseball consumed Mickey. He talked, when he talked, of little else. It was the number one priority in his life and, in a way, always would be."

Mickey himself claimed that his outbursts did not become a problem until he joined the Yankees, possibly because they were a release of pent-up pressures from the great expectations placed upon him. In those early Yankee years, Casey Stengel never firmly disciplined his young star when he kicked water coolers, flung bats, and took out his anger on fans.

"You can see him take the heat," Casey told a group of writers late in May 1956 when Mantle was taking batting practice.

Always the clown, Stengel sometimes would imitate Mickey after the switch hitter struck out. "He comes in and walks along the steps until he gets to the post," Stengel would tell writers. "He gives it a big whack with his hand. Nobody says anything. He goes to the end of the dugout and leans carefully against the wall. Everybody is watching him. All of a sudden he straightens up and yells at the pitcher, 'Put something on the fuckin' ball.' Then he looks around for something to kick."

In June that season, after striking out six times in a doubleheader, he took his frustration out on water coolers, destroying the cooler in the visitors' dugout in St. Louis while playing the Browns. Yogi Berra tried to make light of it.

"Why are you so nervous?" he asked Mickey who mumbled that he wasn't. "Then how come you're wearing your jock strap outside of your uniform?"

Yogi said it jokingly, but he got Mantle to look down to see if it was true.

There was an isolated incident that Mantle once told about himself involving a Yankee fan he knew only as Mrs. Blackburn, who owned season tickets in a box next to the Yankee dugout. In that rookie season, the woman used to dote on Mickey, often giving him candy and chewing gum as he waited on the on-deck circle. But she grew increasingly disappointed with Mantle's cursing and obscenity-laced tirades after striking out and slowly withdrew her encouragement. There came a day when she finally had had her fill listening to Mickey's foul mouth as he returned to the dugout after striking out yet another time.

"Stop that talk," she screamed at Mickey, who was momentarily dumbstruck but whose anger was not about to subside.

"Shut your goddamn mouth!" Mantle shot back.

Mickey thought she would never speak to him again, but she did a few games later when she called him over to her.

"Any more outbursts like that," Mrs. Blackburn told him icily, "and I'm going to make a personal protest to Mr. Topping."

By mid-July, however, Mantle's slump and temper were the least of Stengel's problems. His chilly relationship with DiMaggio had become a public relations nightmare for the Yankees, who had had to publicly issue a clarification on the apparent slight of the Yankee Clipper when Stengel had benched him in the middle of an inning. It occurred in a game against Boston at Yankee Stadium after the Red Sox had taken an early 6–1 lead, largely because of a ball DiMaggio misplayed. Furious, Stengel stopped play and decided to substitute for DiMaggio, sending the recently acquired Johnny Hopp to center field.

"I'll tell Casey when I come out!" Joe told Hopp, waving the veteran National Leaguer back to the dugout. DiMaggio was livid and unforgiving.

"When that inning was over DiMaggio came back to the bench and went right past Stengel into the clubhouse without a word," said Phil Rizzuto. "I don't think they ever talked again. From then on, things got worse. Casey couldn't wait for DiMaggio to quit."

The sportswriters who had always been skeptical of Stengel having been named manager in the first place now rallied in support of DiMaggio and again questioned Stengel's handling of the team as well as the Yankees' direction under general manager George Weiss. *New York Times* beat writer John Drebinger was especially critical of Stengel, writing in midseason: "Probably for the first time since taking over the Yankee management, Casey isn't finding the shifting of his talent easy. For no matter how he maneuvers things, weak spots continue to pop up, while his alternating hitters do not seem to fit so well defensively as in other years."

The legendary sportswriter Jimmy Cannon was even more direct in addressing how Stengel and the Yankees had stupidly insulted the symbol of baseball. "There has only been one truly great baseball player in this generation," Cannon wrote. "Someone should remind Casey Stengel the man's name is Joe DiMaggio . . . It was a mean little decision. It was a thoughtless act of panic and insensitivity. It was nasty and petty and follows the pattern of cheapness, which has assumed shape since Lonesome

George Weiss, the friendless general manager took charge. The prestige of the Yankees diminishes rapidly."

Clearly, it had not been a good year for Stengel in making personnel decisions. As the manager of the American League All-Star team, he had come under criticism in his selection of pitchers, especially after his squad lost to the National League All-Stars. A day after Stengel had chosen Bob Lemon of the Cleveland Indians over teammate Bob Feller, Feller pitched the third no-hitter of his career. Stengel had also picked the Yankees' Ed Lopat over Reynolds for the All-Star team. Two days after the game, Reynolds threw the first of his two no-hitters that season.

Understandably, Mantle's failure to immediately establish himself as the next Yankee star only frustrated Stengel further. Along with Weiss, he was being second-guessed by the writers as well as some among the Yankees' brass for having invested so much of the team's hopes on a 19-year-old rookie straight out of Class C baseball batting third in the lineup. For his part, Stengel was desperately trying to communicate with the 19-year-old prodigy, but he was getting the impression that Mantle was bored, skeptical, and unimpressed with much of what he had to tell him. Mantle himself was equally at a loss on how to deal with his manager, except to sense that all Stengel was concerned about was how well he performed. "You couldn't fool Casey because he'd pulled every stunt that was ever thought up," said Mantle. "He didn't mind it too much either, so long as you didn't start to lose it on the ball field. That's where it all came out, on the field. You could run around like some of the guys, or you could travel with the club looking like DiMaggio in those beautiful blue suits and Countess Mara ties. Either way you did it, if you played like DiMaggio, you'd keep Casey off your back."

Unfortunately for Mantle, in 1951 he was playing like DiMaggio was at the end of his career, although arguably better. By the middle of July, when his average had dropped to .260, Mantle had driven in 45 runs. The 45 RBIs would project to over 90 runs batted in over a 154-game schedule. By midseason, Mantle had 14 more RBIs than New York Giants' rookie rival Willie Mays, as well as 16 more hits and 14 more runs scored. Mays's only edge was his batting average, which was 13 points higher than Mantle's at that point. Rookies with 45 RBI by the All-Star break are usually in the midseason classic, not on their way back to the minor leagues. By comparison Gil McDougald would go on to win the 1951 Rookie of the Year honors with 63 runs batted in, two fewer than Mantle wound up with for the season despite playing in 35 fewer games. Even the number of Mantle's strikeouts that raised concern for Stengel and the Yankees is not that alarming after considering Mickey's run production. By midseason he had struck out 52 times in less than 250 at-bats, which would project to 104 for the full season. The following season, Mantle would strike out 111 times, and he would strike out over 100 times in eight seasons over his career.

For all the connections that have traditionally been made between Mantle and Stengel, a much stronger argument exists that Stengel was anything but the ideal manager for Mantle, especially during his rookie year. Although Stengel had hoped that Mickey would be the monument he would leave to baseball, the Yankees' colorful manager did not have the temperament necessary to nurture and develop young talent. Stengel often preferred to fill out his roster with veterans to support the core that George Weiss assembled. In the 1950s, a series of promising rookies came up through the Yankee ranks and, under Stengel, none developed into major stars with the exception of Mantle and Whitey Ford. For all the great Yankee teams of that era, the only Hall of Famers developed by Stengel were Ford and Mantle. Even then, Ford's greatest seasons came under manager Ralph Houk, and Mantle never wavered in crediting his own father for making him the player he became.

Throughout his career with the Yankees, Stengel proved that he was an outstanding manager at getting the most out of journeymen players who had already been developed, and that he lacked patience with those who were young or inexperienced. His platoon system of using right-handed hitters when a lefty pitched and vice versa was designed as a short-term solution that never allowed for right-handed hitters to develop themselves batting against right-handed pitchers nor for left-handed hitters to improve themselves against lefties. Players caught up in Stengel's platoon system resented him for it and for what it ultimately did to their careers. Among them was Gene Woodling, an outfielder and left-handed hitter who had a .300 batting average five times in a career that spanned 15 seasons. He was among eight players who appeared in every victorious Yankee World Series from 1949 to 1953. However, Woodling was never secure in a full-time outfield position and was often platooned by Stengel. "I liked Stengel, but I did a lot of fussing with him," said Woodling long after his playing days. "And I didn't care for the platoon system. I always felt that I could hit any pitcher."

With Mantle in 1951, Stengel was prepared to deal with his temperamental phenom when he succeeded but found that he had little use for a struggling rookie whose slump threatened his own success. Arguably, it appears that an inordinate amount of the blame for the Yankees' sluggishness was being placed on Mantle. By mid-July, the Yankees had fallen to third place, behind the Red Sox and the White Sox and only a game ahead of the fourth-place Indians. Mantle, however, was not alone in his struggles. Bauer, for instance, was mired in an 0-for-17 batting slump. Jerry Coleman had fallen off from the previous year's form. DiMaggio was having the worst season of his career.

During the 1951 summer slide, righthander Vic Raschi, known as the "Springfield Rifle" in honor of his hometown and his fastball, had failed in three straight starts to win his 13th game of the season. Raschi, a native of West Springfield, Massachusetts, was the keystone of one of the most acclaimed pitching staffs in the history of major league baseball. The Big Three of Allie Reynolds, Raschi, and Eddie Lopat combined for 53 victories in 1949, 55 in 1950, and 59 in 1951. Raschi's five World Series victories, which put him in eighth place on the major league list, included such notable performances as his two-hit shutout of the Philadelphia Phillies in the first game of the 1950 Series. However, Yankee pitching, which had been largely responsible for carrying the team to championships in 1949 and 1950, had faltered throughout the first half of the season. Stengel could not allow an opportunity for a third straight pennant to get away from him, and he and Weiss began toying with their options. With his team languishing in third place, Stengel felt that the Yankees could overtake the Red Sox and hold off anyone else in the pennant race by improving their pitching. So desperate for pitching were the Yankees that on July 12, the Yankees gave the Dodgers two minor-league pitching prospects plus cash in exchange for left-hander Art Schallock, a minor-league sensation who, at not even five feet nine inches tall, was considered by many scouts to be too small to succeed in the big leagues. That same afternoon, Reynolds and Feller engaged in one of the great pitching duels of the decade. Reynolds no-hit the Indians, while Feller carried a no-hitter against the Yankees into the sixth inning, when Mantle doubled for the first hit of the game. The Yankees won the game 1–0 on Gene Woodling's solo home run in the seventh. In the next day's *Times,* Drebinger wrote ominously, "when Schallock reports, one player on the New York team will have to be sent to Kansas City."

The Yankees' pitching broke down over the next two days, giving up 19 runs to the Indians, with Mantle going 1-for-5 in the first game, and being benched in favor of Jackie Jensen in the second game. The Yankees' decision on who would be sent down to make room for Schallock had already been made. With the team struggling and criticism mounting, Stengel needed a scapegoat. Stengel had developed a pattern of how he took out his frustrations. Author Leonard Koppett wrote in *The Man in the Dugout: Baseball's Top Managers and How They Got That Way*: "He was hardest on the best talents, like Mickey Mantle, driven by what he saw as unrealized potential even beyond Mantle's accomplishments, yet quite tolerant toward those with lesser ability. . . ."

On July 15, three days after Allie Reynolds pitched a no-hitter against Cleveland, Mantle was called aside by the clubhouse man at Briggs Stadium in Detroit, who told him Stengel wanted to see him. Mickey knew what was coming and walked into the manager's office to find Casey with tears in his eyes. "This is gonna hurt me more than you," he began.

"No, skip, it's my fault." Mickey struggled to hold back his own tears.

"Aww . . . it ain't nobody's fault. You're nineteen, that's all. Mickey, you're getting a little nervous and tight at the plate, swinging at too many bad pitches. You're going to develop into a big-league star one of these years. But maybe a change of scenery might do you a lot of good. I want you to get your confidence back, so I'm shipping you down to Kansas City."

Mantle was crushed. Stengel later said that it was one of the most difficult things he ever had to do in his life. Stengel would never openly admit that he had rushed Mantle. In fact, he could with good cause convince himself that Mickey needed him as much as he needed Mantle. Stengel was aware that Mickey's talent, especially his ability to hit from both sides of the plate, had been developed and honed by Mutt Mantle's dedication to his son. He even joked to some of his coaches that spring that maybe he should add Mickey's father to the Yankee coaching staff. But Stengel knew that Mantle, if he were to ever realize his potential at the major-league level, now needed the nurturing and tutelage that only someone such as he could provide.

Casey Stengel, meanwhile, had no inkling of the emotional tailspin the demotion would create for Mickey. As the DiMaggio fiasco had shown, the Yankee manager's uncanny intuitive sense about baseball did not extend to people, especially the superstars who often required special handling. At times, Stengel may have been a player's manager, but he was not a star's manager. As Yogi Berra later put it: "When Casey took over as manager in 1949, he didn't want stars—he wanted to be the star of the team." He admired the stars he had seen in the game: Ott, Gehrig, Williams, even DiMaggio. But he was not emotionally equipped to pamper and cater to the sensitive egos of the game's premier players.

If Stengel could treat the legendary DiMaggio the way he did in the three years he managed him, there was no reason to believe he could or would be any more understanding of what Mantle was going through his rookie season. For Mantle, unfortunately, Stengel was not Leo Durocher, the manager of the New York Giants whose stormy personality did not prevent him from developing a nurturing, close bond with his own temperamental rookie, Willie Mays. After Mays went 1-for-25 in his first six games with the Giants that year, the rookie collapsed in tears by his locker. Durocher put his arm around the young center fielder and gave him a pep talk. Then he moved him down to eighth in the batting order, and Mays took off. He wound up National League Rookie of the Year, batting .274, with 20 home runs and 68 RBIs, and the Giants went to the World Series.

A Durocher-type pep talk is what Mantle desperately needed during his summer slump, which was not the worst on the Yankees, and no worse than some of the bad stretches Mays went through that same season. Stengel, however, did not have that kind of relationship with Mantle, nor would he ever. If he had, he would have recognized that underneath

Mantle's 19-year-old man-child frame was an insecure youth not that different from Mays. Both were high-strung perfectionists, given to tears, foul language, and temper tantrums when things went poorly for them. Mays was also prone to fainting spells and mysterious bouts of nervous exhaustion, for which he was twice hospitalized during his career.

Stengel, though, looked upon the young Mickey Mantle as a puzzle piece that he needed to help him fulfill what he believed to be his own destiny. A baseball man his entire life, Stengel sensed that he was on the verge of etching his name into a special place in baseball history. When he was named manager of the Yankees in 1949, it had not been without serious second-guessing throughout baseball, especially in New York. The doubting was justified. Stengel had managed the Brooklyn Dodgers and the Boston Braves without much success and a fair amount of second-division mediocrity. The back-to-back pennants and World Championships had gone a long way toward silencing the skeptics, but there were still some who argued that Stengel was little more than a pretentious baseball court jester who had the good fortune of stepping into a manager's dream job.

He had that in the New York Yankees team he inherited. DiMaggio, though at the end of his career, was still DiMaggio. Along with Henrich and Charlie Keller, DiMaggio formed one of baseball's most acclaimed outfields for the Yankees before and after World War II. The Yankees had an outstanding pitching rotation anchored by Allie Reynolds and Vic Raschi. Veteran Phil Rizzuto was arguably the best defensive shortstop in the league, and Yogi Berra had emerged as a valuable catcher who could both handle the Yankee pitchers and pose a dangerous offensive threat at the plate. Even with DiMaggio declaring that 1951 would be his final year, Stengel felt confident that with some retooling and tweaking, the Yankees could be contenders for the next few years.

Stengel made no secret that he had patterned his life, especially his teaching and managing in baseball, after the great John McGraw. The two most prominent names among baseball managers at this time were McGraw, for whom Stengel had played while with the Giants, and Joe McCarthy, whose managing stints included the great Yankee teams of the 1930s. In fact, the idea of Yankee skippers being "father" to the players, as

Stengel at times was prone to do, had originated with McCarthy. After McCarthy's resignation in 1946, Joe DiMaggio had even lamented his departure by saying, "he was like a father to most of us." McGraw had won four straight pennants, and McCarthy had gone one better by winning four straight pennants and four straight World Series.

However, it was John McGraw who was Stengel's hero. In 1921, when Stengel joined the Giants with whom McGraw was in his 20th season as manager, only the newly emergent Babe Ruth was a more dominant figure in baseball than McGraw. The Giants manager was arrogant, combative, temperamental, and extremely successful. He imposed his personality on the team and obviously on Stengel, who was to boast: "I learned more from McGraw than anybody." One thing he learned in watching McGraw is that, aside from winning championships, very little compares with molding and developing young baseball players, especially when they become some of the best players in the game. John McGraw had always taken great pride in his role in developing Hall of Famer Mel Ott, who as a 16-year-old had come to McGraw through one of his baseball friends.

McGraw refused to send young Ott to the minor leagues for fear that some manager down there would change or ruin the youngster's unorthodox swing, which would ultimately become Mel Ott's trademark. Ott had a distinctive batting style in which he lifted his front foot high off the ground in a kind of exaggerated stride that no batting coach would ever teach. McGraw kept Ott close to him on the bench for the first two seasons, nurturing him and his knowledge of the game before unleashing him. Ott became the National League's home-run king of his day, and his success has been heavily credited to McGraw's nurturing.

Cleveland Indians manager Al Lopez would say admiringly of Stengel: "He took chances with kids, and he won with them. McGraw was that way. He'd stick with a young guy and nurse him along. McGraw and Stengel were both very good with young kids. Casey would sit and talk to them by the hour. He never had any children of his own, so he had a lot to give them. Come to think of it, McGraw had no children of his own either. Just thirty years' worth of baseball teams."

In young Mantle, Stengel saw his own Mel Ott. In Mickey, he felt he had the next great ballplayer, maybe even the greatest who would ever play the game. And he would be taught by Stengel. "Can you imagine," he would ask a friend, "what McGraw would say if he saw this kid?"

Undoubtedly, he would have said the same thing other veteran baseball men were saying, unable to contain themselves. "This is the kind of kid a scout dreams of," said Bill Essick, the Yankee scout who signed DiMaggio. "You come up with one like this in your lifetime, you're lucky. I had that moment when I got DiMaggio."

Now, though, Stengel faced a similar challenge and dilemma to what McGraw had encountered with Ott. Stengel, though, was no John McGraw. He would not take the risk of sticking with his struggling young star.

"It's not the end of the world, Mickey," Stengel said to Mantle as he told him of his demotion to the minors. "In a couple of weeks you'll start hitting and then we'll bring you right back up again. I promise."

Understandably, Mantle took Stengel's assurance of returning to the Yankees as what he later described as "no more than a crude effort to take the curse off of the sentence he had just passed."

"Casey probably assumed that, as I had been ready to go to Beaumont in Double-A ball, it would be no serious jolt to find myself in Kansas City, which was Triple-A then," Mickey said years later. "But he might as well have told me he was shipping me back to Independence. I had been a Yankee, and now I was nothing. I was always one of those guys who took all the bad luck doubly hard, who saw disaster when there was just everyday trouble, and who took every slump as if it were a downhill slide to oblivion."

In the *New York Times* the following day, Drebinger called Mantle's demotion "startling."

"For in order to keep within the player limit," Drebinger wrote, "the Yanks had to lop off somebody and the fellow who drew the unlucky straw was Mickey Mantle, the highly touted youngster the Bombers had confidently expected to win the rookie-of-the-year accolade."

DiMaggio couldn't believe the news that it was Mantle who was being sent to the minors when he heard it.

"I thought they were trying to make Mick the goat for the team's troubles," he said in a particularly harsh interview in 1978 in which he was especially—though not surprisingly—critical of Stengel as a manager. "I wouldn't have sent him down. I don't know anyone else who thought it was a wise move, but who ever said you were going to find three wise men in baseball, much less one. You're going to tell me a kid like Mick was back then who was having some difficulty with major league pitching is going to figure it out against minor league pitching? He would have figured it out if he had just been given some patience and at-bats.

"I have to say that I wondered if Stengel, by sending Mickey down, wasn't just sending out a message. A lot of us weren't having very good years, and you had to figure he was saying, 'If I can send this great kid down, I can send anyone down.' Some people just have to play their games."

Chapter Sixteen

"Kansas City, Here I Come"

Somebody once asked me if I ever went up to the plate trying to hit a home run. I said, "Sure, every time."

—Mickey Mantle

In the time he was away at Kansas City that year, Mantle missed some of the drama involving DiMaggio and Stengel. On July 30, DiMaggio was photographed sharing cake with Stengel in a clubhouse celebration of the manager's 61st birthday, but that was the high point in their relationship. George Solotaire, a ticket broker who was his closest friend in New York, told me that DiMaggio detested Stengel and in 1951 often expressed second thoughts on whether he should have returned to play for the Yankees one last season.

"Stengel made life hell on earth for Joe that summer," said Solotaire in an interview. "He would come home from the stadium mentally and emotionally exhausted from dealing with Stengel or just putting up with his antics. Stengel would do little things like telling a player to get ready to go to the 'outfield' in the next inning. He wouldn't say left field or right field the way he usually would telling a player where he was going. He'd leave it as just the 'outfield,' and say it just loud enough for Joe to hear. And this was after Stengel had embarrassed Joe a couple of times by sending a player out to center while he was already out there, and Joe would have to wave 'em back to the dugout. He wasn't coming out."

DiMaggio lived in Solotaire's suite at the Elysee Hotel in Midtown close to Central Park, away from where most Yankee players lived in the Bronx or in New Jersey. The boutique hotel, though, fit in with DiMaggio's lifestyle of being close to the restaurants in Manhattan, while being virtually waited on hand and foot by Solotaire, who filled the role of a personal valet. He took care of DiMaggio's clothes, dry cleaning, and shopping. Often he would also pick up Joe's meals from restaurants and bring them to him so that he could rest in the suite. Publicist Ruth Cosgrove, who later married Milton Berle, told the story of having been invited to dinner with DiMaggio to complete a foursome. When she arrived at the table, she thought Solotaire had pulled out a chair for her only to quickly realize that he was doing the courtesy for DiMaggio.

"When you were around Joe DiMaggio," Cosgrove said, "no one had eyes for anyone else."

It was Solotaire who would get DiMaggio theater tickets through a show agency he managed. The most notable of the shows DiMaggio saw, the Broadway debut of Swedish playwright August Strindberg's *The Father* starring Raymond Massey in the winter of 1949, led to a romantic crush that Joe developed on a beautiful young actress destined for fame that would exceed even the Yankee Clipper's—Grace Kelly.

According to Reno Barsocchini, DiMaggio solicited the help of several of his friends attempting to arrange an introduction to the future Princess of Monaco, who at the time was only nineteen.

"Joe couldn't get her off his mind," said Barsocchini. "He was obsessed with her and wanted to meet her, but Joe had more pressing matters. He was in New York that November because doctors were checking out his heel again. He'd missed the first three months of the season because of the pain, and it looked like he might go under the knife again, which he didn't want to. He'd had a good season, for the time he played, and the Yanks got into the series and won a championship. But Joe was dragging, man. He was in constant pain and had the worst World Series of his life. He barely hit a hundred in that series, and Joe was determined to get his heel right cause he didn't want to go through another year like that.

"I think Joe met Grace Kelly later when he was with Marilyn, but he didn't meet her that winter when he first saw her. Later we used to kid him about it. Any time when Joe was getting a bit full of himself, we'd put him in his place. 'Hey, Clipper. What'd she want with a Dago prince like you? She wanted a *real* prince!'"

"But George [Solotaire], if he could have arranged it, he would have gotten Joe in there with her. George would tell Joe, 'Hell, that guy [Rainier], he's only a prince. If she'd have gone with you, she'd have had a king.'"

By coincidence, Solotaire was with DiMaggio one night when he had dinner with Mickey and Holly at Danny's Hideaway just a few days before the Yankees went on their last road trip in which Mantle was sent to the minors. Solotaire remembered that Mickey was worried about his troubles at the plate, and that DiMaggio offered some advice. "It all starts with one hit, Mick," he said DiMaggio told Mantle. "Even now, at my age, I'm always reminding myself that I can't look beyond that moment that I'm in."

But even DiMaggio's advice couldn't save Mickey from being sent down to the minors, something that Joe never experienced. In coming years, as part of their ongoing one-upmanship, DiMaggio never missed an opportunity to make a dig about Mantle's demotion. Of course, for Mickey, there was no way around the fact that his demotion to the minor leagues, after his half-season with the Yankees, was a major public humiliation that perhaps only a professional athlete can appreciate. Even after Mantle's death, in talking about his place among the Yankee greats, DiMaggio praised Mickey but then went out of his way to note that, of course, Mantle also had to be sent down to the minors in his rookie season.

DiMaggio, Ruth, Gehrig—none of the Yankee greats and few of the legends of baseball—had been humbled in such a way as to have had their worthiness of being in the major leagues challenged. For Mantle, riding off to join the Kansas City Blues who were playing in Minneapolis, it might have been better if he had started the 1951 season in the minors. Stengel and George Weiss apparently were not aware of just how far Mantle's self-confidence had sunk. If they had been, they might have sent him down to the Yankees' Class AA team in Beaumont where Mantle might have felt more comfortable playing for Harry Craft, who had coached him his previous year in the minors.

The Yankees, however, thought they were doing their best by sending Mantle to learn patience at the plate from Kansas City manager George Selkirk, a former Yankee outfielder. In 1935 Selkirk had replaced

Babe Ruth in right field and was even issued Ruth's uniform number, the famous 3 that eventually would be retired on Babe Ruth Day in 1948, just weeks before he died. While he could not come close to Ruth's home-run output—he hit 21 homers at his best in 1939—Selkirk batted better than .300 in five of his first six seasons. A patient hitter, Selkirk had the distinction of having drawn two walks in an inning four different times, and he walked 103 times in 1939. In 1935, Selkirk had been the first to suggest that a cinder path six feet wide be installed in the outfield so that a player knew when he was nearing the wall—the modern-day warning track. In Selkirk, someone who had played with Ruth, Gehrig, and DiMaggio, the Yankees thought they had someone who might impart some badly needed wisdom to their presumed heir. In addition, Stengel had a fondness for Kansas City, and thought Mantle would be better off there than in an outpost of Texas. Stengel had been born and raised in Kansas City, and he had quit high school in 1910 just short of graduating to play baseball professionally with the Kansas City Blues.

When Mantle joined the Blues, it was with the same mixed fanfare that welcomes any major leaguer coming down to slum. The minors, from where only one of 14 ever makes it to the major leagues, are a world of underpaid, overworked players and coaches who do not look kindly on squandered talent and overblown press clippings. Mantle later described the Blues as a group of "malcontents" whose pitchers "carried pints of whiskey in their back pockets." For Mantle, there was also the torment of jealous teammates, who knew that Mickey was down in the minors with the understanding that he would get special treatment designed on getting him back to the majors. Mantle, in fact, was immediately inserted into the lineup with the expectations of a promising hot prospect. On his first at-bat he surprised everyone by beating out a drag bunt down the first base line, a hit he could use to boost his self-confidence and as a positive on which to build. Mantle also desperately needed a pat on the back or just a word of encouragement. Instead, when Mickey returned to the dugout at the end of the inning, he was confronted by Selkirk. "What's the matter with you?" he yelled at Mantle. "They didn't send you here to bunt. You're here to get some hits and get your confidence back."

"That finished me," said Mickey. "I felt like hell when I went out to my position, I could feel the tears of self-pity stinging my eyes. 'What did a guy have to do?' I asked myself."

From then on, Mickey could do little right. American Association pitching made him look even worse than the American League pitchers had. After the bunt single, he went hitless in his next 19 at-bats before the team returned to Kansas City. Worse, Mantle was practically friendless on the team and among the fans. He spent most of his free time alone by himself, often pouring over the Yankee box scores. He had learned from the newspapers that his replacement on the Yankee roster, Art Schallock, had bombed in his first start and would not be the solution to the Yankees' pitching problems. Harry Wells, the undertaker for whom Mickey had dug graves back in Commerce, visited Mantle during his minor-league stay and was stunned to find a stack of fan hate mail in a corner of his hotel room. Much of it, Wells said, was about Mantle's draft status. The Korean War was in full swing, and the "draft dodger" issue had followed him to Kansas City. None of his critics seemed to care that Mickey twice had been classified 4-F by preinduction doctors who concluded that the osteomyelitis that had hospitalized him as a youth posed too great a risk of returning if he were pressed into military service.

For Mantle, however, the personal war he was now fighting was no longer against opposing pitchers. It was instead against his own fear and foreboding at the prospect of failure. The real slump wasn't on the baseball diamond—it was in his head. Years later, a therapist working with Mantle and Merlyn had concluded that "Mickey is totally controlled by fear. He is filled with fear about everything." At the height of his slump, each time Mantle came to bat, he was overcome by sudden surges of overwhelming anxiety that came without warning and without any obvious reason. It was more intense than the feeling of being "stressed out" that most people experience.

Baseball slumps, according to Kevin Elko, adjunct professor to the Sports Medicine Fellows at the University of Pittsburgh School of Medicine, are largely fueled by panic. "The panic," said Elko, a consultant to several professional sports teams, "has become a condition. More than any other variable, panic is the malady." Selkirk and some of the other

Blues coaches had begun to suspect that Mantle's problem was a case of nerves—that maybe Mantle just didn't have it. However, it may have been something far more serious: a hint of possible panic disorder.

Later in his life, Mantle would exhibit similar symptoms that were perhaps too easily and prematurely attributed to his drinking. These panic or anxiety attacks became more frequent as Mantle traveled around the country for card shows. The most publicized of these attacks occurred aboard an airplane on a flight back to Dallas. Mantle began to hyperventilate and was first feared to have had a heart attack. Emergency paramedics met the plane at Dallas's Love Field. Mantle was checked out and diagnosed as having had a panic attack. In 1993, Mantle admitted that "depression was a regular part of my life. At times, I thought about killing myself." In 1951, at age 19, Mantle fit the profile for someone afflicted with panic disorder, a condition that usually appears during the teens or early adulthood. While the exact causes are unclear, doctors say there does seem to be a connection with major life transitions that are potentially stressful. In Mantle's case, having his dream—and his father's—of becoming a major-league baseball player go topsy-turvy into a nightmarish experience certainly qualified as a major life transition. Baseball, specifically being a major leaguer, was how Mantle identified himself and his self-worth. "When Mick retired," Merlyn later observed, "a big chunk of his self-esteem went out the window. I question whether he ever had much to begin with. . . ."

The only thing Mickey felt he had going for him that summer was Holly Brooke, with whom he was talking almost daily.

"I was calling him 'Mickey Mouse,' a pet name only his mother had used before," Holly said, repeating almost word for word what had appeared in a 1957 *Confidential* magazine exposé. "More than once, Mickey would ask me how I felt about marrying him, owning him 100 per cent . . . permanently. But he always answered his own question. 'No, I guess not,' he'd say. 'You'd never be happy in a little town like Commerce.' And he was right on that. Other towns were different though. For instance, I remember flying to Columbus [Ohio] to see him and buck up his spirits. I'd planned to stay one night but wound up staying three days. That was in 1951 when the big blow fell and the Yankees shipped him off to their Kansas City farm club. When he heard the news, Mickey broke down and bawled like a baby. He often called me from there and other minor league towns, asking me to fly out and spend a few days with him because he was so lonesome." Brooke also wound up with one of the few existing photos of Mantle in a Kansas City uniform, which he inscribed, "To Holly, with all my love and thoughts."

Soon, however, Holly was concerned enough to put her life in New York on hold and immediately join Mickey in Kansas City. "He called me and said he needed me," she told me. "But this was different than whenever he had said that before. He sounded desperate and helpless. When I got to Kansas City, he looked terrible. He had been drinking too much and sleeping too little. All I could really do was console him and to try assuring him things would get better. But he was at the lowest period of his life to that point and feeling sorry for himself."

With his career in a frightening free fall, Mantle decided to quit. He called his father and found him at the Eagle-Picher mines and over the phone told Mutt it was over. He couldn't hit even minor-league pitching and wanted to come home. The slump was no surprise to Mutt. He had been keeping up with Mickey in the newspapers, as had a good portion of the Commerce area that either knew the Mantles or had an interest in baseball. What Mutt had not expected to hear was the desperation in his son's voice. He had never heard this kind of panic and anxiety in Mickey's voice and quickly concluded he needed to see his son. Mutt rounded up his wife Lovell along with son Larry and daughter Barbara. He left almost immediately on the five-hour drive from Commerce to Kansas City where they found Mantle at the Aladdin Hotel. Merlyn was also along on the trip, and it would be the first time that she and Holly would cross paths.

"I was living there, and boy, was I glad to see him," Mantle said in recalling the incident. "I wanted him to pat me on the back and cheer me up and tell me how badly the Yankees had treated me and all that sort of stuff. I guess I was like a little boy, and I wanted him to comfort me."

"How are things going?" Mutt asked Mickey.

"Awful. The Yankees sent me down to learn not to strike out, but now I can't even hit."

"That so?"

"I'm not good enough to play in the major leagues," Mickey said. "And I'm not good enough to play here. I'll never make it. I think I'll quit and go home with you."

"I guess I wanted him to say, 'Oh, don't be silly, you're just in a little slump, you'll be all right, you're great,'" Mantle later said. "But he just looked at me for a second and then in a quiet voice that cut me in two he said, 'Well, Mick, if that's all the guts you have, I think you better quit. You might as well come home right now.'"

Mickey wanted to tell him that he had tried, but he knew better than to argue with his father when he was in the mood he now found him in.

"Mickey, you can't have it easy all your life. Baseball is no different than any other job. Things get tough once in a while, and you must learn how to take it—the sooner the better. It takes guts, not moaning, to make it. And if that's all the guts you have, I agree with you. You don't belong in baseball. Come on back to Commerce and grub out a living in the mines for the rest of your life."

Then Mutt said the words that tore into Mantle's heart:

"I thought I raised a man, not a coward!"

After saying hello to Mutt, whom she had met in New York, Holly had retreated to the bathroom while Mickey's mother, his brother, sister, and Merlyn had gone back out into the hallway. Merlyn later said she heard much of what Mutt had said to Mickey through the door, as did Holly in the bathroom. As for Holly and Merlyn, Holly said they exchanged tentative glances but didn't speak to one another.

Mickey would later say that Mutt's lecture that night "had been the greatest thing my father ever did for me. All the encouragement he had given me when I was small, all the sacrifices he made so I could play ball when other boys were working in the mines, all the painstaking instruction he had provided—all of these would have been thrown away if he had not been there that night to put the iron into my spine when it was needed most.

"I never felt as ashamed as I did then, to hear my father sound disappointed in me, ashamed of me," Mantle said. "I have wondered sometimes exactly what it was. I know that I wanted my father to comfort me. He didn't. He didn't give me any advice. He didn't show me how to swing the bat any different. He didn't give me any inspiring speeches. I think that what happened was that he had so much plain ordinary courage that it spilled over, and I could feel it. All he did was show me that I was acting scared, and that you can't live scared."

Indeed, throughout both his childhood and adult life, fear was the one emotion that ruled him and motivated him as both a boy and a man, as both a player and a husband. It began as a mixture of fear and respect for his father, much as it is for many youngsters who are pushed to succeed in any endeavor that is as meaningful to a parent as to the youngster, if not more so. But Mutt's influence over Mickey—Mutt's ability to motivate his son by the fear of disappointing him—would extend far beyond Mickey's childhood as well as beyond baseball. Mickey's marriage to Merlyn during the Christmas holidays that year would be an act possibly more out of love and fear of disappointing Mutt than out of love for Merlyn. In later years, Mickey would measure himself as a husband and father against his own father and, of course, pale in the comparison because anything short of perfection would have failed his father.

That evening, with his father watching from the grandstands, Mantle broke out of his extended slump with two prodigious home runs. Mickey returned to being as hot as he had been in spring training. Over the next 41 games, Mickey hit .361 with 11 home runs, 50 RBIs, three triples, and nine doubles. Mantle suddenly was the darling, if not of Broadway, then at least of Kansas City. The Blues rode Mickey's success into an American Association championship chase that effectively ended the day he was recalled back to the Yankees. Years later, writer and Kansas City native Calvin Trillin would compose an essay lamenting his own disenchantment with baseball and dating it back to when the Yankees took Mantle back from his beloved Blues. "I hate the Yankees," he wrote. "They called Mickey Mantle up from Kansas City right in the middle of a hot pennant race with the Indianapolis Indians." If Mickey did this for the intelligentsia of Kansas City, imagine what he must have done for the fans in the cheap seats.

In mid-August, Stengel and the Yankees decided to bring Mantle back to the majors, only to learn that they would have to stand in line.

In what had become an ongoing soap opera lasting much of the year, the Selective Service had called Mantle back for yet another physical examination.

No one at the time dared boast that their son was classified 4-F, a military reject. However, the draft board in Mantle's Oklahoma county had already rejected Mickey for service because of the osteomyelitis when he was called for his preinduction physical examination. Mickey's medical records bore out that he had been hospitalized for extensive treatment of osteomyelitis in 1946 and again for a flare-up in 1947. Osteomyelitis happened to be one of the medical conditions that the government had decided was automatic grounds for denying entry into any of the branches of the military. Although the disease had been arrested, it could recur at any time. If that were to happen while in the service, the government would be liable for paying a disability pension for life—conceivably hundreds of thousands of dollars in pension payments and medical bills.

However, after his fabulous spring training, Mickey Mantle found that he was no longer simply the unassuming youngster from Oklahoma. At the end of Mantle's triumphant showing on the Yankees' exhibition swing to the West Coast, Mickey returned to the team's spring training facility in Phoenix to find a letter from his father and learn that his draft board wanted him to take another physical examination.

"My dad wrote . . . that a lot of people were asking why I wasn't soldiering in Korea," Mantle recalled years later. "To be candid, the war was the furthest thing from my mind. Certainly I knew about the mounting casualties, the talk going around that General MacArthur was planning an all-out fight against Communism, even thinking of dropping an atomic bomb on China. Well, I could understand how some people felt, especially those who resented seeing young, apparently healthy guys hitting baseballs while their own sons and husbands were being killed in battle."

In his biography of Casey Stengel, author Robert W. Creamer claims that the Yankee organization, seeking to quell growing criticism about Mickey's 4-F status, went so far as to ask the Oklahoma Draft Board to reexamine Mantle's case. Indeed, no one was more aware of the potential public backlash and harm over Mickey's draft status than the Yankee brass, especially general manager George Weiss, who soon enough would begin developing a protective attitude toward Mantle. Weiss had an aristocratic gentility about him, and he saw Mickey as a naïve, vulnerable country boy completely out of place in the big city. Unfortunately for Mantle in 1951, as the hailed successor to Ruth and DiMaggio and with the spring training exploits to prove it, he had become virtually a walking expression of the American culture's irrationality, as he would be throughout his career and even beyond. He was loved for what America thought he should be—a personification of the country's own aspirations; he was vilified for his human vulnerability that kept him from realizing those expectations.

Despite being rejected a second time for military service, Mantle continued receiving criticism questioning his courage for not fulfilling his "military obligation." In fact, it seemed that the hate mail and public taunts increased the more that the legitimacy of his draft exemption was mentioned, even throughout the rest of the decade. "Mantle began to receive vituperative hate mail and as the debate raged around him, the shy, uncommunicative boy shrunk deeper and deeper into his shell of silence," Yankee historian Peter Golenbock wrote in *Dynasty: The New York Yankees, 1949–1964*. So on August 23, 1951, Mickey underwent a third physical by Army doctors at Fort Sill, Oklahoma, and was once again classified 4-F because of the osteomyelitis.

The next day, the Yankees recalled Mantle to the majors.

When Mantle returned to New York, one of the first people he went to see was Yankee Stadium clubhouse man Pete Sheehy, to get his uniform. Sheehy was a man with an uncanny sense of destiny. For more than half a century, he had worked in virtual anonymity with the Yankees, except among the Yankee players and the Yankee family. He was a short, wispy man who later was memorialized when the home locker room at Yankee Stadium was named the "Pete Sheehy Clubhouse." Sheehy obviously recognized that there was a symmetry to the Yankees line of succession: Lou Gehrig had assumed the superstar role after Babe Ruth; DiMaggio's debut had come at the end of Gehrig's career; and now Mantle appeared headed to join the Yankees in DiMaggio's last season. Sheehy was known as one of the few people who could joke around with the somber, stoic DiMaggio, who was like an ice god emotionally. The story goes that DiMaggio once asked Sheehy to check out a red mark on his backside.

"Hey, Pete, take a look at this," Joe said. "Is there a bruise there?"

"Sure, there is, Joe," Sheehy replied in a matter-of-fact tone. "It's from all those people kissing your ass."

Among Sheehy's other duties was assigning new players uniforms and, in particular, a uniform number that was not already worn by a player or retired to honor players like Ruth, Gehrig, or other Yankee legends. It is a not too well known story that when DiMaggio joined the team in 1936, Sheehy issued him number 18, which had previously been worn by a tempestuous pitcher named Johnny Allen before he was traded to the Cleveland Indians. Later, sensing that DiMaggio would be the historical successor to the legacy of Ruth and Gehrig, Sheehy changed his uniform to number 5. Ruth, of course, had worn number 3, and Gehrig had been number 4. Perhaps Sheehy's perspective had been sharpened with anticipation or intuition because when Mickey arrived at the Yankee instructional camp, he issued him the only number that made historical sense—number 6. Mickey would wear this through his fabulous spring training and into the first few months of the season before history would take a different twist. "Around this club," Sheehy would say, "you always had the feeling that great things would happen. It started with Ruth and kept going on."

Sheehy was no less superstitious than any other veteran baseball man, which is to say that he was as superstitious as they come. He had issued Mantle uniform number 6 in the spring, and he now wondered if maybe that hadn't been a mistake. It had been Mickey's uniform number when he was sent down, and now Sheehy didn't want to take any chances. That, plus Mickey had pleaded with him to exchange his uniform for number 7. Sheehy hoped it would be a lucky number; and it would prove to be fortuitous, for in baseball Mantle would forever after be associated with number 7.

"To be honest," he later said, "I didn't put any stock in whether I was wearing number six or number seven. But after I had number seven on for a while, no one was gonna take it off my back."

CHAPTER SEVENTEEN

Broadway's Old and New

When baseball is no longer fun, it's no longer a game.
> —JOE DIMAGGIO

MICKEY'S RETURN TO NEW YORK THAT SUMMER MARKED THE BEGIN-
ning of his friendship with Billy Martin, the Yankees second baseman
who would become a central figure throughout his life. If Casey Stengel
saw in Mantle the son he never had, Billy Martin found in him the little
brother of his dreams. Mickey was the adoring kid brother who would
go along with anything Billy proposed doing, and who would never dare
to talk back. Mickey also marveled at Martin's unique friendship with
DiMaggio, of which Mickey could only be admiring and envious. Few
Yankee players could boast of anything but a passing acquaintance with
the team's star center fielder, who often could sit in the clubhouse for
hours without speaking to anyone. Martin, however, had managed to
endear himself to DiMaggio with his clubhouse pranks and joking manner that amused the stoic Yankee Clipper.

Somehow Martin, who was 23 and had only joined the Yankees
in 1950, had quickly become one of the few who could break through
DiMaggio's aloof exterior. Teammates were often stunned to see Billy
enter the clubhouse behind DiMaggio imitating his distinctive walk all
the way to their lockers, which were next to one another. Billy would then
continue to comically mirror each of the things DiMaggio did: ordering
coffee, taking off his pants, and hanging up his shirt and coat. It would
approach a Marx Brothers routine, with even DiMaggio having to laugh.
"You fresh little bastard," DiMaggio would say to him. No one could

explain why DiMaggio took to Martin, except perhaps that both were Italian. In the past DiMaggio had opened up a part of himself to players from Italian backgrounds. With Martin, he often spent hours in the clubhouse after games, nursing a beer and talking baseball. They eventually became after-game dinner companions. Martin's candid, unpretentious manner put the formal DiMaggio at ease.

"I think the reason they became friends," said Phil Rizzuto, "was because Billy would do anything DiMaggio wanted, any time. You had to want to do anything Joe wanted to do and, you know, that's hard to do. But Billy was the type who wasn't bothered by that, and Billy loved Joe. He idolized him."

But another secret to why the Martin-DiMaggio friendship clicked may have been that he always treated Joe not like a star but like any other teammate. "Billy would say to me, 'He's just like anyone else,'" Whitey Ford said. "'All you have to do is open up when you're around him.' I'd tell him, 'I can't do that.'"

Mantle had similar recollections about the DiMaggio-Martin relationship he saw in that 1951 season. "Joe DiMaggio was my hero," said Mantle, "but Billy used to play jokes on him and hang around with him. Billy wasn't afraid of Joe, maybe because they both came from San Francisco. Besides, Billy was a fresh kid, and he even pulled some stunts on Joe. There was one in particular I'll never forget. Billy had one of those pens with disappearing ink. Well, Joe would always come to the ballpark in a shirt and tie and these expensive suits. Anyway, I just couldn't believe that Billy would do this, but he goes up to Joe and asks him for an autograph for a friend. And as he hands him the pen, he shoots ink all over Joe's nice-looking suit. Joe started getting angry, telling Billy, 'Damn it, how could you do that?' Well, Billy got a laugh and quickly explained that the ink would disappear. Billy could get away doing things like that with Joe and then going out to eat with him. I used to watch and ask Billy what Joe was like. And he'd say, 'Shit, he's just like anyone else. All you have to do is open up when you're around him.' And I'd say, 'Shit, I couldn't do that.'"

Billy took to Mickey as he had to no other player and helped smooth over Mantle's rookie year, especially after his return from Kansas City. On the road, the two became roommates. Back in New York, the pair behaved like the city's most eligible bachelors, despite the fact that Billy had a wife at home and Mickey had Holly whom he was seeing regularly. Mickey and Billy also were keeping postgame company with teammates Hank Bauer and Charlie Silvera, and their nightlife was a far cry from the small-town lights of Commerce. One of their regular spots was the Harwyn Club on the East Side, where on any night Mantle and his pals were rubbing elbows with celebrities and other sports stars. In 1951 that included Rocky Marciano celebrating the latest of his boxing championship defenses. Just as life on the town could be high, through pranks and hijinks it could also sink to lows. Once, at the same Harwyn Club, Mickey and Billy sneaked in a whoopee cushion that they slipped under the seat of a contractor friend as a practical joke that succeeded in erupting their side of the club into an uproar of laughter.

"That place—I was like a kid in a candy store," said Martin friend Jack Setzer, who had grown up with Billy in West Berkeley, California. "I met Joe DiMaggio, Leo Durocher, Charlie Dressen, some umpires—I don't know who—and I met Sid Caesar, Jo Stafford and her husband, Paul Whiting, Imogene Coca, Carl Reiner—the whole 'Show of Shows' cast . . . And then the other nights on my trip . . . I'm having dinner with Yogi Berra and Mickey Mantle and Billy."

Anyone looking inside the Yankees' clubhouse or in their dugout might not have believed the sight of Mickey and Billy as two merry pranksters, beginning late in the 1951 season and continuing for several years. They bought water pistols that they squirted each other with in the clubhouse. They sneaked Polaroid camera shots of one another on the toilet. They wrestled on the trains when the team traveled on road trips. Mickey had never known that baseball could be such fun.

For Mantle, the world had completely turned around in the less than six weeks' time he had spent in the minors. A day after his return to the Yankees, Mantle slugged a home run off Mike Garcia that helped New York beat the Indians, 7–3. A week later, against the Browns in St. Louis, with his family looking on, Mickey slugged another home run and drove in four runs. In the 37 games after his return to the majors, Mantle hit .283 and drove in 20 runs to help the Yankees win their third straight American League pennant. His strong comeback against American

League pitching in the homestretch of the pennant race had reaffirmed the Yankees' faith in him, and he was already looking ahead to the next year with anticipation.

Mutt had been pleased with the courage his son had shown in Kansas City and then with the Yankees after he had been recalled—so much so that he arranged to take time off at the mine to drive to New York to watch Mickey play in the subway series against the Giants. Mickey couldn't wait to show the New York he now knew to his father, or at least the New York he knew Mutt would approve of. Mutt was driving up from Commerce with two of his friends, which was going to make the Series a little easier for Mickey. He didn't know what he would have done had the entire Mantle family decided to come to New York and had brought Merlyn with them, as they had to St. Louis earlier in the season, especially since Holly would be at all the World Series games at Yankee Stadium.

All summer long Mickey had been vacillating in his emotions, torn between his feelings for Merlyn and the duty he felt to keep his promise to marry her and his newfound love for Holly. Mickey was engaged to Merlyn, but he was sleeping with Holly. He didn't know how he would ever explain Holly to Merlyn and was hoping he wouldn't have to. In fact, after seeing Holly in Mantle's hotel room in Kansas City, Merlyn had come to the realization of impending heartbreak and had decided not to pin her hopes around a future with Mickey, no matter how many assurances she kept getting from Mutt. At the end of September, as the baseball season was winding down, Merlyn had quit her job at a local bank in Commerce and relocated to Albuquerque, New Mexico, presumably to get a fresh start on life. She continued to wear the engagement ring Mickey had given her, though how much sentiment Mantle had invested was questionable. Merlyn's ring had been bought by Theodore Mantle, Mickey's half-brother, who had used most of his army discharge pay to help pay for it. Additionally, the fact that no wedding date had been set may have said even more about the solidity of Merlyn and Mickey's relationship.

Meanwhile, Holly had Mickey all to herself in Manhattan. She had helped him adjust to life in the big city, which had been part of the problem that had doomed Mantle midway through the season. However, he now felt he knew how to balance his life off the field with his responsibilities as a Yankee. Mickey was both in love and indebted to Holly and uncertain of what to do next. He wanted his father to get to know her better, and he was hoping that if he did, he would understand that he needed her in his life.

When it came to dealing with his father, however, Mantle would forever remain the child, always trying to please, rarely asserting himself, and never standing up to him on anything that was important to Mickey but with which Mutt might have disagreed. Mickey's relationship with Holly was perhaps not only the best example but also a potentially life-altering decision that Mantle would leave completely in his father's hands. The moment Mickey introduced Holly to him, he sensed that his father didn't approve.

"Mickey, you do the right thing and marry your own kind," Mutt said to Mickey after pulling his son aside.

Mantle tried to explain his relationship.

"Merlyn's a sweet girl," Mutt said, cutting him off, "and she's in love with you."

"Yeah, I know."

"The point is, she's good for you," said Mutt. "She's what you need to keep your head straight."

"I know."

"Well, then after the Series, you ought get on home and marry her."

However, Holly said that as the 1951 regular season drew to a close, the issue of Mickey's future with either Merlyn or her was far from decided. When Mutt was nearby, his influence over Mickey was extraordinary, beyond the usual father-son relationship. New York, though, had already changed Mickey, who had come to realize that the provincialism of Oklahoma had dated his father's beliefs and that they were each part of separate generations. Holly was also symbolic of that growing divide between father and son and their two generations.

"We didn't talk that much," Mickey said, talking about his father in an interview years later. "First of all, we didn't have a phone in Whitebird, Oklahoma, and that's where we was living at that time. We didn't talk a lot, but I knew he was watching the papers to see what I was doing or listening to the radio if he ever had the chance. I knew he was paying attention and watching what I was doing and everything, and I know it made him really proud that after he left [Kansas City] that I started doing a lot better."

Holly told me that at the height of the pennant chase, she was surprised by Mickey again talking about them marrying at the end of the season. Mantle figured that once the World Series was over and his father on his way back to Oklahoma, he and Holly would elope, possibly to Niagara Falls, which at the time was the place for honeymooners.

"Mickey said to me, 'I don't suppose you want to marry me?' That was his proposal," Holly remembered. "He really didn't want to marry [Merlyn]. He never, ever, really loved Merlyn, never."

Holly made the investment, but Mickey collected the dividends!

Mickey Mantle *(continued)*

SOME GIRLS HAVE MINKS, some own diamonds. I had to be different. I own one-fourth of the most gorgeous hunk of man in the major leagues, Mickey Mantle. And there have been times when he was mine—100%.

Don't get me wrong, I haven't a thing to do with the New York Yankees paycheck he brings home to his wife Merlyn. But any time Mickey endorses a product, steps before a TV camera or makes a personal appearance, I'm entitled to my slice of the profits.

Me, a Manhattan model, owning such a big chunk of one of baseball's immortals? Seems incredible — and that's the way it sounded to me, too, when the idea was first broached back in the spring of 1951.

I'd met a Broadway publicity man and personal agent and agreed to let him handle my press notices for a year. Over the drink or two we had to clinch the deal, he revealed that "The Mick" was also one of his clients.

He painted a gaudy enough picture of the possibilities in managing Mickey, but it was of no great interest to me until he suddenly came up with a proposition. He was short of cash to exploit his contract with Mantle and wanted me to loan him $1,500 for a few months. If he didn't pay the money back by January 10, 1952, I was then to become owner of one-quarter interest in Mickey.

How to Keep Tabs on Your Investment

To me, that was a lot of money but I had some extra cash and owning a piece of Mickey sounded like it just might be a gold mine. A girl ought to look over her investments *before* making 'em though—at least that's my motto—and I'd never even set eyes on Mantle. I talked with the agent about the deal but made no moves until he called one night and invited me to meet him—and Mickey —at a New York steak house, Danny's Hideaway.

I arrived with bells on and was mighty impressed with the prospective property. Mantle was shy, until he had carefully inspected my red hair and 37-25-37 figure. "I like you," he said over dinner. "Let's be buddies."

Actress Holly Brooke, Mickey's girlfriend his rookie season, dines with Mantle at Danny's Hideaway in Manhattan, 1951. THE MICKEY MANTLE MUSEUM, COOPERSTOWN, NY, AND TOM CATAL AND ANDREW VILACKY

Confidential magazine reported the story of Mickey Mantle's relationship with actress Holly Brooke during his 1951 rookie season. THE MICKEY MANTLE MUSEUM, COOPERSTOWN, NY, AND TOM CATAL AND ANDREW VILACKY

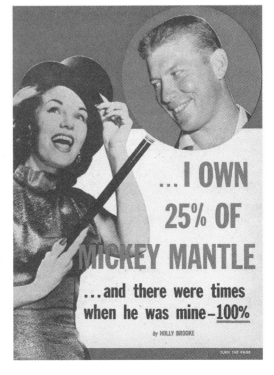

... I OWN
25% OF
MICKEY MANTLE
... and there were times
when he was mine—100%

by HOLLY BROOKE

TURN THE PAGE

The three DiMaggio brothers all played in the major leagues, though only Dom actually played with the Red Sox during his 13-year career. Vince DiMaggio, the oldest of the brothers, played for several teams, including the Cincinnati Reds (1939–1940), Pittsburgh Pirates (1940–1945), Philadelphia Phillies (1945–1946), and New York Giants (1946). Joe, of course, became a legend with the Yankees, playing his entire career in New York. In this 1946 photo, though, they are all wearing Red Sox uniforms for an exhibition in Boston—including Joe, apparently because his Yankees uniform had not yet arrived. THE MICKEY MANTLE MUSEUM, COOPERSTOWN, NY, AND TOM CATAL AND ANDREW VILACKY

The New York Yankees–Boston Red Sox rivalry was a family affair for the DiMaggios with Dom, nicknamed the Little Professor, becoming a seven-time all-star outfielder for the Red Sox while Joe endeared himself as the incomparable Yankee Clipper in his 13 seasons in New York. This is a photo of them in 1940, Dom's rookie season. THE MICKEY MANTLE MUSEUM, COOPERSTOWN, NY, AND TOM CATAL AND ANDREW VILACKY

Yankee legend Joe DiMaggio and rookie phenom Mickey Mantle are all smiles in the first weeks of their 1951 season. THE MICKEY MANTLE MUSEUM, COOPERSTOWN, NY, AND TOM CATAL AND ANDREW VILACKY

Mickey Mantle collapses with a knee injury as Joe DiMaggio catches New York Giants' rookie Willie Mays's fly ball in the second game of the 1951 World Series. THE MICKEY MANTLE MUSEUM, COOPERSTOWN, NY, AND TOM CATAL AND ANDREW VILACKY

Retired legend Joe DiMaggio and Mickey Mantle accompany Mick's mom, Mrs. Lovell Mantle, at ceremonies for Mickey Mantle Day at Yankee Stadium, 1965.
THE MICKEY MANTLE MUSEUM, COOPERSTOWN, NY, AND TOM CATAL AND ANDREW VILACKY

In one of the rare photos of Mickey in a Kansas City minor-league team uniform, Mick inscribed it to his girlfriend, Holly Brooke: "To Holly, With All My Love & Thoughts, Mickey Mantle" THE MICKEY MANTLE MUSEUM, COOPERSTOWN, NY, AND TOM CATAL AND ANDREW VILACKY

Merlyn and Mickey Mantle share wedding cake on their wedding day, December 23, 1951, in Commerce, Oklahoma. THE MICKEY MANTLE MUSEUM, COOPERSTOWN, NY, AND TOM CATAL AND ANDREW VILACKY

Manager Casey Stengel places on Mickey's head the crown emblematic of baseball's Triple Crown that Mantle won in 1956 when he led the American League in home runs, RBIs, and batting average. THE MICKEY MANTLE MUSEUM, COOPERSTOWN, NY, AND TOM CATAL AND ANDREW VILACKY

Joe DiMaggio and Mickey Mantle pose for photographers after Mick's return to the Yankees after his brief demotion to the minors. THE MICKEY MANTLE MUSEUM, COOPERSTOWN, NY, AND TOM CATAL AND ANDREW VILACKY

Joe DiMaggio, Mickey Mantle, and Ted Williams—three of baseball's all-time greats—strike a pose before a Red Sox–Yankees game in 1951, the only season all of them played in the majors at the same time. THE MICKEY MANTLE MUSEUM, COOPERSTOWN, NY, AND TOM CATAL AND ANDREW VILACKY

Left: New York Yankee rookie phenom Mickey Mantle greets high school sweetheart Merlyn Johnson, his younger brother Ray, and his dad and mom, Mutt and Lovell, before a 1951 exhibition game against the Boston Braves in Kansas City, Missouri. Right: Yankees scout Tom Greenwade visits Mickey Mantle, the prize signee of his career, during his rookie spring training season, 1951. BOTH: THE MICKEY MANTLE MUSEUM, COOPERSTOWN, NY, AND TOM CATAL AND ANDREW VILACKY

Mickey Mantle, Merlyn, and Hank Bauer are recognizable in a photo that also includes Charlene Bauer with Stage Deli partner Hymie Asnas and his wife to the left of Mickey and restaurant co-owner Max Asnas to the right of the Bauers. Mickey and Bauer shared an apartment above the deli in the 1951 season. THE ASNAS FAMILY PHOTO COLLECTION

Manhattan restaurateur Hymie Asnas befriended a number of New York Yankees during baseball's Golden Age, none bigger than Joe DiMaggio, shown here dining with him at the Stage Deli years after his retirement. THE ASNAS FAMILY PHOTO COLLECTION

Mickey Mantle, the 1951 rookie sensation, hangs out with restaurateur Hymie Asnas, the owner of the Stage Deli where Mick ate many of his meals while in New York. THE ASNAS FAMILY PHOTO COLLECTION

CHAPTER EIGHTEEN

Baseball and America

Now I've had everything except for the thrill of watching Babe Ruth play.

—JOE DIMAGGIO

THE UNIQUE RELATIONSHIP BETWEEN AMERICA AND BASEBALL MUST BE understood to fully appreciate Joe DiMaggio and Mickey Mantle's place in the equation. This was the age when baseball players were the princes of American sports, along with heavyweight boxers and Derby horses and the odd galloping ghost of a running back from down South or the occasional lanky basketball player in short shorts. Baseball players were the souls of their cities—Stan the Man in St. Louis; The Kid in Boston; Pee Wee, the Duke, Jackie, and Furillo in Brooklyn; and, of course, the incomparable Willie Mays for Giants fans. As 1950s historian Jacques Barzun was to aptly observe: "Whoever wants to know the heart and mind of America had better learn baseball. . . ."

Long before DiMaggio and Mantle, long before baseball became an industry of multinational owners and millionaire players, Walt Whitman wrote, "Well, it's our game. That's the chief fact in connection with it: America's game. It has the snap, go, fling of the American atmosphere. It belongs as much to our institutions, fits into them as significantly as our Constitution's laws, is just as important in the sum total of our historic life." Baseball is, to be sure, an American cultural declaration of independence. It has come to express the nation's character—perhaps never more so than during the intense, anti-Communist, post–World War II period, when a preoccupation with defining the national conscience might be expected, particularly defining the national self in a tradition that is so culturally middle of the road. As American Studies authority Gerald Early put it: "I think there are only three things America will be known for 2,000 years from now when they study this civilization—the Constitution, jazz music, and baseball. . . ."

By the middle of the 20th century, baseball as an unquestioned symbol and performance-ritual of the best qualities of something called Americanism was an entrenched truism. The fictional literary character Terence Mann perhaps stated it more succinctly in the Hollywood film *Field of Dreams* when he says to protagonist Ray Kinsella: "The one constant through all the years, Ray, has been baseball. America has rolled by like an army of steamrollers. It's been erased like a blackboard, rebuilt, and erased again. But baseball has marked the time. This field, this game, is a part of our past, Ray. It reminds us of all that once was good and it could be again."

America in the 1950s was also not so much a stage as a set piece for television, the new national phenomenon. It was a time when how things looked—and how we looked—mattered, a decade of design. From the painting-by-numbers fad to the public fascination with the First Lady's apparel to the television sensation of Elvis Presley to the sculptural refinement of the automobile, American life in the 1950s had a distinct style in material culture and in art history at eye level.

America in the 20th century, to be sure, needed heroes like DiMaggio and Mantle to transform from largely conventional baseball figures into pop-culture deities of entertainment, which is what the game ultimately became in the age of DiMaggio and Mantle and thereafter. In the 1950s, Mickey Mantle would become the cultural equivalent of Elvis, Marilyn, and James Dean. He was young, he was handsome, and he came to be seen on television in millions of homes in ways DiMaggio, for instance, never was. It should be no surprise that popular biography has reflected this conversion, or that the change parallels the way baseball has come to be viewed in the years after DiMaggio and Mantle arrived on the American scene. In a sense the image of all popular figures is a reflection of the public that follows them. But with a dead figure that reflective process grows exponentially—like the compounding effect of a series of mirrors.

As a cultural symbol whose life can now be made into anything with impunity, Mantle has become, in Elvis biographer Greil Marcus's words, "an anarchy of possibilities"—a reflection of the public's mass fears and aspirations and also a constant vehicle for discussing those sentiments. Thus Mantle, Elvis, and Marilyn alike have evolved into a collection of cultural deities—modern-day equivalents of the Greek gods, who were immortal while sharing the characteristics of the human beings who worshipped them.

"When I was playing," Mantle said looking back, "I used to feel like everything was happening to some other guy named Mickey Mantle, like I was just me and this guy called Mickey Mantle was another person."

Or as Mantle's close personal friend George Lois put it: "Mickey Mantle was the last American hero. He was a walking shrine to an age of innocence and a symbol of a time when all was right with the world."

Like DiMaggio, Mantle's career was storybook stuff, hewing more to our ideas of myth than any player since Babe Ruth. Mantle himself came to realize that Ruth and Joe DiMaggio represented a state of mind that never existed beyond the abstract. They were a mirage, just as he, too, would become an icon. A lesson to be reaffirmed, sportswriter Richard Hoffer once suggested about Mantle and perhaps heroes altogether, is that we don't mind our heroes flawed, or even doomed. In America, failure is forgiven of the big swingers, in whom even foolishness is flamboyant—and that the world will always belong to those who swing from the heels.

"I guess," Mantle once said, "you could say I'm what this country's all about."

DiMaggio would later explain how people like Ruth, Gehrig, Mantle, and himself were able to succeed in baseball in more simple terms. "A ballplayer," he said, "has to be kept hungry to become a big leaguer. That's why no boy from a rich family has ever made the big leagues."

In 1951, though, DiMaggio was playing largely on pride and experience. No one had to tell him he was no longer the same ballplayer of his prime, nowhere close to it. However, he had helped put the Yankees in position to win another pennant and possibly one more World Series championship. It was especially telling that the Yankees had done it almost as a reflection of their aging star. The team had no one with more than 30 home runs or 100 runs batted in, and only one player was batting above .300. The Yankees were fighting for the pennant using the dominant pitching of Vic Raschi, Ed Lopat, and Allie Reynolds, plus the hitting of catcher Yogi Berra who would go on to win the first of his three Most Valuable Player awards.

"I know what's the matter with me," DiMaggio told the *Boston Herald* that summer. "I'm not getting the old snap on my swing. I just don't seem to give it that old follow-through . . . I'm swinging late, but it's not because I'm biting at bad balls. I'll go for a bad one now and then. But most of the time, they're right down the middle. I see them coming, and I set myself. But when I swing, the ball shoots up at me."

As the season wore on, DiMaggio had to discard his favorite bat—a heavy 37-ouncer—for one two ounces lighter that made a world of difference to his swing. It was also a Babe Ruth model, and he disliked the handle so he sanded it down to make his swing even whippier. No one had to tell Joe that his batting average that season was 60 percentage points lower than his career average and that he had been leaving runners in scoring position more often than ever. DiMaggio knew that now, in September, was when the pennant would be decided, and he was determined to make a difference. And he vowed that to his fans and his legacy.

"I don't want them to remember me struggling," he said more than once that season.

For as Mickey Mantle would become America's first sports hero of the new television age, Joe DiMaggio had been the nation's consummate star of the radio era. "It is no coincidence that DiMaggio's fame was so lasting, and that he was the last great hero of the radio era," David Halberstam would write in his book, *Summer of '49*, about Joe and the 1949 American League pennant race.

"He was a guy who knew he was the greatest baseball player in America, and he was proud of it," said DiMaggio's former teammate Lefty Gomez. "He was always trying to live up to that image. That's why he couldn't be silly in public . . . or ever be caught without his shirt buttoned or his shoes shined. He knew he was Joe DiMaggio, and he knew what that meant to the country."

As it turned out, his final September would be a fitting month for DiMaggio's last hurrah. At one point Stengel dropped him from his usual cleanup spot in the lineup and moved Gil McDougald into that slot in the first game of a doubleheader. McDougald had a tremendous game, going 4-for-4 and driving in every runner in scoring position during his at-bats. The move, though, was short-lived, much to Stengel's chagrin. Between games, the Yankee brass ordered him to put DiMaggio back at cleanup. In the second game of that day's doubleheader, McDougald was dropped to eighth place in the lineup and DiMaggio was back batting fourth. But on September 16, DiMaggio was dropped back to the fifth spot, this time in favor of Yogi Berra, in a crucial game against the league-leading Indians whom the Yankees trailed by a game. It was a rare time when Mantle got to see at close range a glimpse of the old DiMaggio. With the Yankees trying to add to a 3–1 lead against Bob Feller, Mantle opened the fifth inning with a drag bunt single. Two outs later, Mantle was at second base when Cleveland decided to inflict one more insult on DiMaggio's farewell year. The Indians intentionally walked Berra to pitch to DiMaggio, something no one would have even considered doing when Joe had been at his prime.

DiMaggio, though, had been at critical junctures before. He had faced Feller many times since 1936, and his blazing fastball—sometimes still in the high 90 mph range—was something Joe's mind had memorized indelibly. On a one-ball, two-strike count, DiMaggio anticipated the heater and got the Babe Ruth model bat around as if he were the Bambino in his heyday. He scorched the pitch to the deepest part of Yankee Stadium, past center fielder Larry Doby, for a game-clinching triple that scored Mantle and Berra. The Yankees moved into a tie for the league lead, then went ahead of the Indians the next day on DiMaggio's game-winning run in the bottom of the ninth inning. Even that run, though, was an extraordinary display of Joltin' Joe of an earlier era. DiMaggio smashed a single by Indians' third baseman Al Rosen and advanced to second base on Gene Woodling's single. Then the Indians' Bob Lemon walked Bobby Brown to load the bases. From third base, DiMaggio broke for home on the pitch and scored the winning run on Phil Rizzuto's suicide squeeze bunt.

"I was going crazy because I didn't have to bat next," Mantle said of being on-deck as DiMaggio scored the winning run. "I think Casey would have me bunting, too."

DiMaggio scored standing up, and Mickey was the first teammate he grabbed to celebrate. From that point on, the Yankees were unstoppable, winning nine of the last 12 games and capturing the American League pennant by a comfortable five-game margin. They clinched the pennant in dramatic fashion on September 28, when Allie Reynolds pitched his second no-hitter of the season. The last pitcher to do that had been Johnny Vander Meer of the Cincinnati Reds in 1938, hurling them consecutively. Reynolds pitched his second no-hit gem against the Red Sox at Yankee Stadium, and almost had it ruined by a teammate. Representing the last batter between Reynolds and his no-hitter, Ted Williams popped a fly behind home plate for what seemed to be the final out. Yogi Berra, however, lost the ball, then his footing, and dropped the ball as he fell to the ground. Reynolds helped him up, then gave Berra an assuring pat on his butt.

Moments later, Williams popped up another pitch near the Yankee dugout that Berra chased down and caught for the pennant-clinching no-hitter. DiMaggio hit the last regular season home run of his career with a three-run dinger as Mantle, who was not in the lineup for that doubleheader, sat on the bench.

The regular season was over, and Mantle was headed to his first World Series, which would also be DiMaggio's last. Mickey, though, had mixed emotions about what should have been one of the most exciting moments of his rookie year. He didn't expect to start in the series, and he had his father coming to town to watch the games. The entire World Series would be played in New York, as the Yankees would face either the Dodgers or the Giants who had wound up in a tie and would play a best-of-three playoff series for the National League pennant. Trailing the Dodgers by 13½ games in the middle of August, the Giants won 37 of their last 44 games to finish in a tie with Brooklyn.

On October 3, with the playoff series tied at one win apiece, the Giants and Dodgers met in the deciding game of their pennant playoff at the Polo Grounds. Mantle's father Mutt had recently arrived in town along with Mickey's uncle Emmett and friends Turk Miller and Trucky Compton. Mickey was simply thankful that Merlyn hadn't come along, Holly remembered, because he already anticipated some kind of a scene with his father. In the days leading up to the World Series opener, there were signs of Mantle brooding and being unusually standoffish, not unlike DiMaggio's usual demeanor.

DiMaggio, however, was going through more than his usual pain from his various injuries, especially the heel from which he had never fully recovered, according to his friend Reno Barsocchini. "Joe was in insufferable pain at the end of '51, pain that would have sidelined anyone else," Barsocchini told me. "Any kind of pressure on that heel brought tears just looking at how he wanted to cry out. But he didn't. Joe didn't want anyone to feel sorry for him, and they wouldn't if they didn't know. He just wasn't gonna show that to anyone on the outside."

Fans, especially his legion of diehards, must have found it difficult to imagine that an injured heel could derail their hero. They had seen him rejoin the Yankees after the war, when he was 31, and struggle to regain his prewar stride. In 1946, for the first time in his baseball career his batting average was below .300 as he hit .290 in 132 games. That had been the start of the bone spur in his left heel bothering him, and the Yankees lost the American League pennant to the Boston Red Sox. Of course, there were baseball pundits who argued that the postwar DiMaggio never regained the stunning brilliance of the young Joe DiMaggio of the prewar years. However, he had surgery on the troublesome heel in 1947 and missed the first two weeks of the season before returning in heroic fashion. DiMaggio hit a home run in his first at-bat of the year, he went on to lead the Yankees in hitting with a batting average of .315, and he won his third Most Valuable Player award.

On November 15, 1948, DiMaggio underwent the surgery that effectively shortened his career. Performed at Johns Hopkins Hospital in Baltimore, the procedure removed a small bone spur from his right heel. Eighteen months earlier, surgeons had performed a similar procedure to remove a spur on Joe's left heel. However, the surgery on Joe's right heel apparently didn't go well. Joe continued to experience pain through the first two months of the 1949 season and missed the start of that season.

"There was considerable doubt that I'd ever play again," DiMaggio said at the time. "Many believed the bone spurs in my heels spelled the finish."

In the following years, questions would arise as to whether the surgeries on DiMaggio's heels may have been botched. "Not so long ago the surgery involved making a large incision around the heel, peeling off the skin and removing the bone spur," Dr. Alan Meyerberg, a Long Island specialist on heel surgery, later wrote. "Joltin' Joe DiMaggio had this done and it ended his career." In both procedures, as well, little if any of the padding that normally protects the bottom of the heel against pressure on the foot was left. That virtually guaranteed that DiMaggio's heels—the heels of a professional athlete—would be in constant pain from the bones being unprotected. DiMaggio also had a serious infection after the first surgery that required additional procedures, and there was controversy about how the surgeries were performed as well. In 1948, a young *Baltimore Sun* reporter found DiMaggio, resplendent in silk pajamas recovering from his second heel surgery, and asked, "Mr. DiMaggio, I guess the reason you're here is that when Dr. Sidney Gaynor, the Yankee physician, treated your heel last year, it was a failure?" Joe appeared surprised. "Yes, son," he told the reporter, "but we don't say that."

Nevertheless, for the rest of his life DiMaggio would carry hard feelings about what he considered failed surgeries that shortened his career. Years later, at the Presidio Country Club in San Francisco, Joe was approached in the golf locker room by *San Francisco Chronicle* columnist Arthur Hopp, who was a member of the club. "He was dressing as I limped past his locker," Hopp remembered. "I paused, gathered my courage and said, 'I have a bone spur in my heel.' He was instantly attentive. He chatted for a good five minutes. He even removed his socks to show me the scars on both his heels. The operations, he said with some bitterness, hadn't worked. 'Whatever you do,' he said, 'don't have surgery.'"

In 1951, knowing his playing days would soon be over, DiMaggio was just trying to mentally prepare for one final series.

CHAPTER NINETEEN

Test of the Prodigal

On two legs, Mickey Mantle would have been the greatest ballplayer who ever lived.

—NELLIE FOX

MICKEY MANTLE HADN'T EXPECTED TO START IN THE WORLD SERIES, still uncertain of where he fit in with the Yankees. But on the day that Bobby Thomson hit his dramatic home run off the Dodgers' Ralph Branca—the legendary "Shot Heard 'Round the World"—to win the National League pennant for the Giants, Mantle grabbed the evening papers at a newsstand and got a surprise. The sports page carried the Yankees' starting lineup for the first game of the series at Yankee Stadium, and his eyes opened wide. Leading off and playing right field for the Yankees would be the rookie, Mickey Mantle.

Mickey celebrated with his father, who was already in town, as they watched the game with most of the Yankee players, who all expected they would be playing the Dodgers in the World Series. "We were all sitting behind third base that day," Hank Bauer once said, "and until Thomson hit the homer, we thought we were going to play the Dodgers, but we were rooting for the Giants because the Polo Grounds was bigger than Ebbets Field. We'd make more money if the Giants won."

On deck when Thomson hit his home run had been Willie Mays. Like Mantle, he would be playing in his first World Series, and their paths would soon converge in a fateful play that would last with Mickey for the rest of his life. "Outside of Joe DiMaggio, Willie Mays is the greatest all-around baseball player of my time," Mickey said in a 1968

Esquire magazine joint interview with Willie. "Certainly he's been the most daring. Mays would steal home, a tough play, and one in which you've got a great chance to look bad. Willie didn't even think of that, he'd just go. Nine times out of ten, he'd make it." Of Mantle, Willie said: "Mickey used to get booed a lot at Yankee Stadium. I didn't have any problems like that until later when the Giants moved to San Francisco. Then I got booed. It wasn't so much what we were, it was more what we weren't. Neither of us was Joe DiMaggio."

Mantle and Mays met for the first time on October 4, 1951, horsing around for photographers before the first game of the World Series in what would be the beginning of their long friendship. Earlier that day in the Yankee clubhouse, Stengel had taken Mantle aside and instructed him to be especially aggressive from his right field position. "Take everything you can get over in center," Stengel told Mickey. "The Dago's heel is hurting pretty bad."

The Giants won the series' opening game, 5–1, as left-hander Dave Koslo, the Giants' number four starter, pitched a seven-hitter. The Giants' Monte Irvin stole home in the second inning, and Alvin Dark hit a three-run homer in the sixth inning that sewed up the game. Mantle was hitless but walked twice against Koslo. Determined to get a World Series hit, Mantle led off the third inning of the second game with a drag bunt single and scored his first series run on Gil McDougald's bloop single to right field.

For Mickey, the scene at Yankee Stadium that afternoon was like something out of a dream. He was playing in the World Series, in the Yankee outfield next to DiMaggio, with his father watching from the stands. Then, with Willie Mays leading off the top of the sixth inning, Mantle shaded over a couple of steps toward center field. Looking over at DiMaggio, it was still hard to imagine the great Joltin' Joe even a step slower than in his prime. He still moved so gracefully under fly balls and made every catch appear easy and effortless. A moment later Mays connected and drove a fly ball into short right-center field. There had once been a time when a fly ball like this one would have been routine for DiMaggio, who was notorious for selfishly guarding his territory in center. One time in 1949, then-rookie Hank Bauer had eased over into right-center to take a fly ball, much as Mickey had now been instructed to do. DiMaggio had stared at the young outfielder between innings in the Yankee dugout until Bauer asked him if he had done anything wrong. "No, you didn't do anything wrong," replied DiMaggio, "but you're the first son-of-a-bitch who ever invaded my territory."

Now in the sixth inning of Game 2 of the series, Mantle sensed that Mays's short fly ball was exactly the kind of play Stengel had asked him to make. "I knew there was no way DiMaggio could get to it," Mantle said, remembering the play, "so I hauled ass. Just as I arrived, I heard Joe say, 'I got it.' I looked over, and he was camped under the ball."

Mickey would later tell friends that as he saw DiMaggio, he thought, "Oh, shit! I'm gonna hit DiMaggio. I'll put him in the hospital. They'll never let me play again! That's when I slammed on the brakes. My spikes caught on the rubber cover of a drain hole buried in the outfield grass. Pop! There was a sound like a tire blowing out, and my right knee collapsed. I fell to the ground and stayed there, motionless. A bone was sticking out the side of my leg, [and] the pain squeezed like a vise around my right knee."

As he lay in agonizing pain, Mickey was convinced from the cracking sound he had heard that he had broken his leg and figured his career was suddenly over. His body was motionless on the outfield grass with his eyes closed, with fans and fellow players not sure what had happened to him. Yankees coach Tommy Henrich, who had helped Mickey make the transition from shortstop to the outfield, told writers after the game that he thought Mickey had passed out. "I thought maybe he had fainted," he said. "You know, the tension of these things can do some funny things to you—and he's only a kid." In that moment, Mickey wished to be a child again and wanted to pretend that this hadn't happened and that he would be jumping to his feet any second. Most of all, what Mickey felt like doing was crying, but he couldn't with a stadium filled with 66,018 fans looking at him—and his boyhood hero standing over him.

DiMaggio thought for a split second that Mickey might have been shot.

"I was afraid he was dead," DiMaggio later said. "I shouted, 'Mick! Mick!' And he never moved a muscle or batted an eye. Then I waved to our bench to send out a stretcher . . . After what seemed like a couple of minutes but probably wasn't that long, Mantle suddenly opened his eyes and burst out crying. He bawled like a baby. I don't know whether he thought maybe he had missed the ball or that he was seriously injured. I leaned over and told him, 'Don't move. They're bringing a stretcher.'"

Mantle was later quoted as saying, "I guess that was about as close as Joe and I had come to a conversation. I don't know what impressed me more, the injury or the sight of an aging DiMaggio still able to make a difficult catch look easy." However, considering they had had a season of conversations off the field, beginning with the Opening Day conversation before their CBS radio interview, Mickey's recollection was wrong or someone completely fabricated the quote.

DiMaggio biographer Richard Ben Cramer would question Mantle's memory as well, though his book about Joe seemed set in portraying him in the worst light possible. "In later years, among friends, the Mick was neither so stoic nor impressed by the Clipper," Cramer wrote. "The way Mantle figured, DiMaggio wouldn't call that ball until he was damn sure he could make it look easy. Joe had to look good . . . but Mickey would never play another game without pain."

Mutt Mantle had been seated not far behind the Yankee dugout, and his first thought was Mickey's mother. "I thought he was hurt bad, but I didn't know what to think," he said to Harold Kaese, of the *Boston Globe*. "I guess I thought about his mother back home listening to the game." Thirteen hundred miles away, Lovell Mantle listened intently as she heard the announcer tell her that her son was lying prone on the ground in right-center field. Mutt moved toward the field when he realized the seriousness of the injury, then made his way to the dugout where he saw Mickey being carried off on the stretcher.

In the trainer's room after the game, Yankee trainer Gus Mauch put splints on both sides of the leg and wrapped it up to protect the knee. Dr. Sidney Gaynor, the Yankees physician, told reporters that "the youngster had suffered a sprained right knee that would sideline him for the rest of the series." Gaynor also made arrangements for Mantle to go to Lenox Hill Hospital the next day, and a look of relief came over Mutt's face as he saw that Mickey started to dress in the clubhouse.

Mutt's relief was that the injury did not appear to be as potentially career threatening as the osteomyelitis that sidelined Mickey in high school. As a sophomore in 1946, Mickey pleaded with his father to allow him to play football, which Mutt was at first reluctant about. He had seen and heard of knee and shoulder injuries ruining promising baseball careers. All of Mickey's friends, however, were going out for football, and Mutt finally relented—a decision he was to regret. With his incredible speed, Mickey played halfback and appeared ready to earn a starting position in the Commerce High School lineup. In an early-season practice, a teammate accidentally kicked Mickey in the left shin, leaving what first appeared to be nothing more than a bruise. However, the pain worsened, and Mickey woke up the next morning to find the ankle swollen to twice its normal size with a frightening blue shade. Mutt rushed his son to a local hospital where a doctor diagnosed an infection but suggested that Mickey be taken to a hospital in nearby Picher, which was equipped with X-rays and other diagnostic equipment. There, doctors diagnosed something far more serious than a simple infection. Mickey, they said, had a serious disease called osteomyelitis. A disease that produces chronic inflammation of the bone, osteomyelitis can be arrested temporarily but can never be completely cured. In Mantle's case, it was never clear whether the injury to the leg caused the onset of osteomyelitis, or whether bacteria or fungus was responsible for the infection. Only two out of 10,000 people ever contract the disease, and Mantle happened to be one of the unlucky ones.

When Mickey heard about the gravity of his illness, his immediate thought was that he might never play sports again. Mantle's recollection: "When it finally dawned on me that possibly I would be forced to forget about baseball, football and any other sports, I thought I'd go crazy." Mutt had the same fear, but he reacted quickly. He drove his son to Oklahoma City where the latest medical facilities were available. For two solid weeks, Mickey remained at Crippled Children's Hospital in Oklahoma City. Every day, every three hours, he received penicillin injections. Between the shots, his ankle underwent heat treatments. At first, the disease refused to respond, and the attending doctors mentioned the possibility of amputation.

Worse, Mantle feared that he might die. His weight, which had been a little more than 130 pounds when he was injured, dropped dramatically. Mickey's pal Nick Ferguson remembered seeing him at the hospital and thinking that he may not have weighed even a hundred pounds. Alone at night in his hospital bed, he suffered hallucinations and sweating spells, partly from the fever that at one point got as high as 104 degrees, and partly from anxiety. In one nightmare, Mickey dreamed that he had awakened to find his leg already amputated. In another dream, he saw himself hitting a home run only to find that he was unable to run with a leg swollen to the size of a tree trunk.

Mantle's hospital stay was made more miserable because this was his first time away from home. Mickey also harbored a youngster's normal fears of hospitals, worsened by the fact that his only other time in a hospital had been to visit Grandpa Charlie when he was dying. To ease their son's fears, Lovell Mantle would stay with him during the day, and Mutt would be with him in the evenings.

"[Mickey] was really sad. He was depressed," said Ferguson, one of Mantle's regular visitors during his extended hospital stay. "He was always used to having his brothers and sister around. The people he saw most of the time [at the hospital] were doctors and nurses, and he wasn't getting any better, and he didn't know what was happening to him. He was scared, and he didn't know what was going on." Ferguson also remembers that soon Mickey began putting on weight almost as dramatically as he had lost it shortly after the injury. According to Ferguson, Mickey wondered if the doctors hadn't given him a steroid medication, claiming it was steroids that quickly pumped his body up to 160 pounds.

Mickey's cousin Max Mantle, whose father Tunney Mantle was to die of Hodgkin's disease a year later in 1947 at the age of 34, also remembered the family fearing the worst outcome. "They moved [Mickey] to Oklahoma City, and it was there that they told him he was going to have to cut his leg off," said Max in his recollection. "I don't know what his dad said, but his mom was the one who said no. His mom said there was no way in hell they were going to do that. She's the one who did that. She's a tough woman, yes, she is. Said, 'Ain't a-gonna take that leg off.' And then, after that, with all that penicillin, he had these boils all over him, had boils on his arms and legs and even his eyes. And they disappeared."

A few years earlier, Mantle, in fact, might have lost his leg. Osteomyelitis occurs when bacteria invade bone, grow, and cause damage and destruction. The blow to Mickey's leg had apparently punctured the leg all the way to the bone and exposed it to bacteria. Without penicillin, which although discovered in 1928 was not readily available in the United States until the 1940s, the outlook for saving Mantle's leg would not have been promising, and most likely it would have eventually developed gangrene and required surgery.

"The leg was abscessed, swollen to almost grotesque size and turning purple," Mantle said years later. "I had a fever of 104. But mom yanked me out of there when a doctor at the first hospital said they might have to amputate. At the next hospital they treated me with a new wonder drug, penicillin, and though I was in bed for weeks and lost thirty pounds, I recovered."

But finally, the swelling subsided and the pain eased. The osteomyelitis had been arrested. Late in September 1946, not yet 15 years old, Mickey was sent home on crutches. He was under doctors' orders not to exert himself.

Now, five years later, Mickey faced a similar crisis. Hours after the injury in the Yankee Stadium outfield, his knee began to swell to almost twice its size. This time, though, he was confident that being in New York he would have the best possible medical treatment available. In the clubhouse, as he was being treated by Dr. Gaynor, there had been talk of possibly needing surgery. Nothing was certain except that Mickey's first World Series was over, as was his rookie season. That night, Mickey took the bandages off to sleep and rewrapped the knee the next morning before heading off to the hospital with Mutt.

CHAPTER TWENTY

Joltin' Joe's Gone Away

There is always some kid who may be seeing me for the first or last time, I owe him my best.

—JOE DIMAGGIO

JOE DIMAGGIO'S SWAN SONG, HIS FINAL WORLD SERIES, WAS A MISER-able last hurrah for the first three games. He was hitless, and the image of the young Mickey Mantle sprawled on the outfield grass as they almost collided in Game 2 already had begun to haunt him. He was 0-for-12 in his first dozen at-bats, causing fans and writers to wince at the thought that this was the way the Yankee Clipper would end his marvelous career. Even Joe's longtime friend Lefty O'Doul couldn't help being critical, tell-ing one writer: "He looked terrible, really. He was doing all the things that he used to tell his brother Vince not to do, lunging, finishing up off balance, swinging too hard."

DiMaggio was getting advice from all quarters. The legendary Ty Cobb, by then 64 years old and baseball's hits king until Pete Rose sur-passed him in 1985, called Joe at Toots Shor's bar and suggested that he open his stance slightly by moving his right foot closer to the plate. Finally, in the fourth game, after striking out in the first inning against Sal Maglie, DiMaggio flared a two-out single to left field. The damage was minimal, though the Yankees managed to give Allie Reynolds a 2–1 lead that he nursed into the fifth inning. The Yankees had been listless since winning the second game, and they trailed the series, two games to one, with the Giants having a chance of winning it all if they could sweep Games 4 and 5 at the Polo Grounds.

Then in the fifth inning, with Yogi Berra on first base, DiMaggio slugged a pitch into the upper deck in the left field stands. "If someone had to hit a homer off me," Maglie said after the game, "I'm sure glad it was Joe DiMaggio. Joe's a great guy and has taken a lot of abuse. He means a lot to that ballclub." The Yankees went on to win the game, 6–2, and DiMaggio's hot hand continued in Game 5. He singled in the third inning to drive in Gene Woodling, then singled again in the fourth inning, and doubled in the seventh inning to score Woodling and Phil Rizzuto. Joe ended the day 3-for-5 at the plate with three runs batted in. Joltin' Joe's sudden hitting inspired the Yankees to win the next two games and the World Series championship, the ninth of DiMaggio's career. DiMaggio capped it off with a final at-bat in which he doubled into Yankee Stadium's right-center field off Larry Jansen. The Yankees were leading 4–1 at the time when Gil McDougald laid down a bunt that, unfortunately, led to DiMaggio being thrown out at third base. The only consolation was a thunderous ovation that went up from Yankee fans as DiMaggio dejectedly crossed the diamond in returning to the dugout. Years later when his lawyer Morris Engelberg, on meeting him, reminded Joe of the love that had been shown at Yankee Stadium as he walked off the field, DiMaggio snapped, "Mr. Engelberg, I did not *walk* off the diamond. I *ran* because I was embarrassed."

In Game 6, DiMaggio broke a major-league record that, like his 56-game hitting streak, would stand the test of time. He appeared in his 51st World Series game, breaking St. Louis Cardinals manager-player Frankie Frisch's record of 50 that had stood since 1934. In that sixth game of the 1951 World Series, Mantle's replacement in right field, Hank Bauer, rid himself of a career-long World Series slump that had totaled five hits in 32 at-bats with a two-out, three-run triple off left-hander Dave Koslo in the sixth inning. "He had me struck out with a knuckleball that I took," Bauer said, "but the umpire called it a ball for three-and-two, then I hit the next pitch over Monte Irvin's head in left field. He didn't know that when the wind was blowing in, it really was blowing out because it would hit the stands in right field and swirl around."

Bauer's triple broke open a 1–1 tie and sent the Yankees to a 4–3 victory, sealed when Bauer made a sensational series-ending catch of Sal

Yvars's line drive with the tying run in scoring position. "Nobody could tell me where to play Yvars because he hardly ever played," Bauer said. "I anchored myself on that drain pipe that Mickey tore up his knee on and when Yvars hit that liner, I saw it, then I didn't see it, then I dove for it and it stuck in the webbing of my glove."

DiMaggio had received another tremendous ovation when he took the field for the ninth inning in what was as emotional a moment for him as it was for his fans. He later told Reno Barsocchini that it was one of the few times he could remember wanting to cry as a ballplayer. "Joe said he spent the entire top of the ninth inning out there thinking that maybe he could gut out another season," Barsocchini said. "A part of him felt that, despite having thought this would be it, that maybe it had been premature. 'The cheers,' he said. 'You can never know how that pumps you up. It's adrenalin of the heart.' That was a lot coming from Joe."

"I would hope," wrote Ed McAuley of the *Cleveland News*, of DiMaggio's curtain calls, "he calls it a career while the cheers are still fresh on his memory."

In the Yankees victorious clubhouse after the game, DiMaggio was barraged with bats, balls, photographs, and other items that teammates asked him to sign, and Joe did so graciously. When those teammates asked about next year, DiMaggio answered simply: "I've played my last game."

For the record, Joe DiMaggio played his last game on October 10, 1951. After that day, life in baseball and for those with a vested interest in Joe DiMaggio would never be the same. Two days later, William Earl "Bill" Essick, the Yankees' West Coast scout who signed DiMaggio, died in his sleep. It was likely coincidental, but it was indicative of the upheaval in the game Joe's retirement caused.

The pressure, though, was only beginning to mount on DiMaggio returning for yet another season, even though he had announced in spring training that this was his final year. The Yankees didn't want to accept his departure, knowing he was a catalyst in team marketing. Owner Dan Topping insisted on seeing him just days after the end of the World Series, making a plea that DiMaggio use the off-season to consider all options and that he would again be paid $100,000 for the 1952 season, if he were to return. It is not common knowledge now, but DiMaggio still hadn't played his last game. He was about to depart on a Japanese tour on a team that included his brother Dom and Yankee teammates Billy Martin, Eddie Lopat, and others. An estimated crowd of a million cheering Japanese fans lined the streets of Tokyo to give DiMaggio and the Americans a hero's welcome, throwing flowers into Joe's convertible and waving American and Japanese flags.

"He's got a lot of baseball left, in my opinion," said Gene Woodling when he read about DiMaggio's triumphant Japanese tour. "He can play the outfield with any of them in the game today." Gil McDougald, who had just been named Rookie of the Year, said: "DiMaggio is one great guy, and he was swell about helping a new fellow along. But what a student of the game! He asks more questions than the rookies."

In what may actually have been DiMaggio's final at-bat of the 1951 season, he hit a 400-foot home run at Meiji Park in Tokyo in what was his last game on the Japanese tour. When Japanese reporters asked if he was really considering retiring, DiMaggio politely said that the Yankees had asked him not to talk about any decision until he had returned to the United States. DiMaggio, though, left Japan several days ahead of his tour teammates, saying he had urgent business to take care of. He did not say what business it was, but he showed up in Hollywood days later, ostensibly visiting his son Joe III. There, cornered by more reporters asking about his future, he appeared less patient. "It's my decision to make," he said, seeming agitated, "and I'll make it when I'm ready."

DiMaggio likely would not have even been considering retirement had it not been for the paradox of the Yankees' success of winning back-to-back-to-back World Series titles from 1949 through 1951. Those championships had come under the unlikely helm of Casey Stengel, who in that time had also made himself the bane of Joe DiMaggio's existence. DiMaggio had reached a breaking point of feeling he could no longer play for Stengel, according to Barsocchini. On the one hand, DiMaggio never asked for any special star treatment from the Yankees. On the other hand, if anyone had earned such consideration—to rest his aching heels, especially on doubleheader days, and to have it done graciously and without fanfare—it certainly was DiMaggio whose misfortune then was to not have played at a time when superstars could expect and demand such treatment and to possibly give management a Stengel-or-me ultimatum.

For his part, Stengel had taken the high road throughout the season whenever DiMaggio's retirement was brought up by sportswriters. "The day DiMaggio quits," Stengel would tell reporters, "part of the Yankees will be gone, too. In a sense, Joe was the Yankees, just as Babe Ruth was before him." When the Yankees clinched the pennant, Stengel had made a point of walking over to him in the clubhouse and graciously telling him: "Joe, I want to thank you for everything you did." In talking to sportswriters, Stengel also said the Yankees wouldn't have won the pennant had it not been for DiMaggio's leadership and example. "I would say," Stengel added, "that next to his brother Dom, he's still the best fielder in the league."

Meanwhile, those who most closely followed DiMaggio—the New York writers—had little clue of Joe's thinking: Would he definitely retire or wouldn't he? Many of those writers were given to fawning, over-the-top depictions of DiMaggio, like Joe Williams of the *New York World Telegram* who had gushed like a schoolgirl: "He's an artist in the exact sense of the word, a Cezanne with a finger mitt, a Van Gogh with a Louisville slugger." "The New York writers both respected him and feared that he would cut them off," wrote David Halberstam in *Summer of '49*. "They generously described his aloofness, born of uncertainty and suspicion, as elegance."

Nevertheless, neither DiMaggio nor Mantle would realize what kind of bargaining power they might have had in their day until an era later, in the years of multimillion-dollar contracts and superstar demands. "If I were sitting down with [Yankees owner] George Steinbrenner [to discuss a salary] and based on what Dave Winfield got for his statistics, I'd have to say, 'George, you and I are about to become partners,'" DiMaggio said. Mickey felt the same way. "If I were playing today," Mantle told one interviewer, "I'd do what Joe DiMaggio said. I'd go knock on the door at Yankee Stadium and when George Steinbrenner answered I'd say, 'Howdy, pardner.'"

In the fall of 1951, however, DiMaggio's focus had already been diverted from baseball by the obsession that would occupy him for much of the rest of his life. Earlier that year, Joe had come across photographs of the young Marilyn Monroe. She had had brief roles in several films until 1950 when she emerged as a rising new star and captured DiMaggio's attention. According to the long-held story of their romance, Marilyn and Joe did not meet until 1952 in a date arranged through a mutual friend. However, Marilyn's longtime friend Susan Strasberg believed that DiMaggio began trying to meet her in 1951. In a series of interviews in the late 1980s arranged by Hollywood TV host Skip E. Lowe, Strasberg recalled conversations among Marilyn, herself, and Susan's parents—drama coach Lee Strasberg and former actress Paula Strasberg—discussing the turbulent Monroe-DiMaggio relationship that spanned more than a decade. "There were times Marilyn was so upset that she used to say she wished she'd never agreed to meet Joe," said Strasberg, "and she used to say she met him in 1951, just before the holidays, and by the summer of 1952 there were already photographs of them together, so it would have made no sense for her to say she'd met him 'just before the holidays' that year. So the impression we all had was that they met in L.A., not New York, some time in late 1951 but maybe didn't start seeing each other—and being seen together—until 1952."

According to Los Angeles newspaper clippings, DiMaggio was in Los Angeles just before the Thanksgiving holidays of 1951. By then there were also reports of a possible seemingly unimaginable trade in which the Yankees would send DiMaggio to the Red Sox in exchange for Ted Williams. Such talk had occurred before, including the purported deal in 1947 in which, after a night of heavy drinking, Red Sox owner Tom Yawkey and Yankee general manager Lee MacPhail had shaken hands on a trade, only to wake up the next morning and both agreeing it had been drunken wishful thinking. The deal seemed even more unlikely after the 1951 season, though Boston sportswriter Ben Ajemian reported that a trade was being discussed in late November. The only logic seemed to be that the left-handed-hitting Williams, who would still have several tremendous seasons in the 1950s, could challenge Babe Ruth's home-run record with the help of the short right field fence in Yankee Stadium, while the aging DiMaggio might have a rebirth with the even shorter fabled left field wall, the Monster, at Boston's Fenway Park.

DiMaggio's own teammates began lobbying for Joe's return, perhaps realizing that his mere presence now meant almost as much as his dependable hitting had during the peak of his career. Gene Woodling was among the teammates who were shameless in their public pleas. "Please, Joe, come back next year," he told one writer who quoted him. "I need more money to buy shoes for my three kids." General managers of opposing teams estimated that DiMaggio's absence could be catastrophic for the league financially. Each team in the American League stood to lose a quarter-million dollars in ticket sales in the 1952 season without Joe's drawing power, predicted Chicago White Sox general manager Frank Lane.

For DiMaggio, it would not be completely about the money. The day after the Yankees won the World Series, team owner Dan Topping told Joe he would pay him $100,000 for the 1952 season, if not to play, then to move into the broadcast booth as well as to handle the interviews on the postgame television show. That was just talk, though. Topping wanted him on the field. He sensed as much as anyone in the game that the Yankees were in a unique position to win championships for the rest of the decade. They had the best catcher in the league in Yogi Berra, who had an uncanny ability working with the pitching staff. Whitey Ford was coming back from the military. They hoped to get a few more years at shortstop from Phil Rizzuto, and Billy Martin helped complete a strong infield up the middle. Then there was the maturing of the rookies, primarily Mickey Mantle and the Rookie of the Year, Gil McDougald. Topping had seen the inspiration the team got in the World Series from DiMaggio, whose quiet leadership had helped knock off the so-called "team of destiny" Giants.

"He always gave so much of himself on the field that there wasn't much left when the game was over," said pitcher Eddie Lopat. "[But] I think DiMaggio was the loneliest man that I ever knew. He couldn't even eat a meal in a hotel restaurant. The fans wouldn't let him. He led the league in room service."

However, that wasn't the life DiMaggio wanted. It hadn't been the life he wanted when his body and physical prowess were at their height and certainly not what he envisioned for himself as a broken-down athlete unable to do what once came so easily, too quick to show his frustration at his slowness but still holding on to the hope of one last glimmer of youth.

DiMaggio would temporarily find his post-career dream in his love affair with Marilyn, as many of his lifelong friends learned.

"We were playing in a golf tournament at the Merced Country Club, and afterwards all of the guys went to a bar in San Francisco," recalled former high school teammate Dario Lodigiana. "Dominic DiMaggio was partners in this bar, and our buddy Reno Barsocchini was serving drinks—just to help out. 'Hey, Dario!' Barsocchini called out. 'Go down that hall and turn left, the first door you come to. There's a guy down there who wants to see you.'

"So I walked down there and sitting in a chair was Joe DiMaggio. And sitting on his lap was Marilyn Monroe! I was shocked to see her there, I did not expect it. I said, 'Good Night! Oh my God!' Talk about a beautiful girl!"

CHAPTER TWENTY-ONE

Fate and Destiny

If I knew I'd live this long, I would have taken better care of myself.
—MICKEY MANTLE

MICKEY MANTLE USED TO JOKE ABOUT A CURSE ON THE MEN IN HIS family as if it were some kind of defensive mechanism denying his own mortality. At some point in everyone's life, often at an early age, we all come to know that some day we will die. Usually, however, death casts only a faint shadow, like that of a high cloud on an otherwise sunny day. In 1944, at the age of 13, Mickey found that cloud suddenly enveloping him in its shadow. That year Mickey came face-to-face for the first time with what he later would come to call "the Mantle curse."

"Grandpa suddenly became old and feeble, almost overnight," Mickey said, remembering the image of his grandfather withering away. "My father would help him out of bed and support his wobbly legs that used to stride along South Quincy Street with so much vigor . . . Dad was worried sick over Grandpa's condition. He began looking for a place in the country, as far away from the mining areas as Grandpa could get." The mines, though not good for anyone's health, had little to do with Charles Mantle's illness. Mickey's grandfather was suffering from Hodgkin's disease. Shortly after Mickey's first year of baseball, in an attempt to get Charles into a better climate, the Mantles moved to a farm outside Commerce. Mutt swapped the house on Quincy Street for a horse, a tractor, some cows, and 160 acres of land that the family could farm, sharing the crops with the landowner.

At the time, Hodgkin's disease was virtually a terminal illness. It had been named after Thomas Hodgkin of London, who first described it in

1832. It is a cancerous disease that strikes the lymphatic system, which plays a key role in the body's immune defenses. Because the lymphatic system consists of channels that course through the body like blood vessels, the cancer has a ready route to spread to any organ and tissue. The most common symptom of Hodgkin's disease is a painless swelling in the lymph nodes in the neck, underarms, or groin. Other symptoms may include fevers, night sweats, tiredness, weight loss, or itching skin. By Mickey's recollection, his grandfather had all of these symptoms. Modern medicine would eventually develop radiation and chemotherapy treatments to fight the disease, usually with an 80 percent success rate of putting the disease in remission for 10 years and longer.

In the 1990s, Hockey Hall of Famer Mario Lemieux would survive Hodgkin's disease. Major-league reliever Scott Radinsky would miss the 1994 season at the age of 26 with Hodgkin's disease, but returned the following season and continued with his career. But as can be the case with Hodgkin's when untreated or diagnosed too late—especially in 1944—the disease ravaged Charles Mantle's body quickly. He died shortly after the family moved to the farm.

"I never forgot that moment, standing beside the casket with my little twin brothers, Ray and Roy, the three of us looking down on him, and my father whispering, 'Say goodbye to Grandpa,'" said Mickey. "I was just a kid then. I didn't understand death and sickness very well. Even now I don't remember the order of events from that time in my life. It just seemed that all my relatives were dying around me. First, my Uncle Tunney, the tough one, then my Uncle Emmett. Within a few years—before I was thirteen—they had died of the same disease. I knew Uncle Emmett had it because the doctor had to cut the lymph nodes out of his ravaged body for nearly a year. To no avail . . .

"That [molded] my belief that I would die young. I lost my grandfather, my father and two uncles, all to Hodgkin's disease. None of them lived beyond the age of forty-one. I took it for granted that this would be my fate; it took all the Mantle men."

The so-called "Mantle curse" would become part of the lore surrounding Mickey Mantle. By Mantle's own admission, talk of it became trite and melodramatic. "I hope to make it to forty," Mantle said while in his 20s. "Sure, I kid about it, but I think about it, too." Howard Cosell would even go so far as to call Mantle "the doomed Yankees slugger, playing out his career in the valley of death." Understandably, Mantle tired of it. He could not, however, put it out of his mind altogether. Its impact on his psyche was indelible. What man, after all, can be subjectively secure with the concept of his own mortality? At a very early age, Mantle had lost something that cannot be regained. Each succeeding death of a male Mantle relative was one step closer to the abyss. Death seemed to haunt every crucial moment of his childhood and adolescence.

The moment Mantle went down chasing Willie Mays's fly ball in right-center field, he knew his first World Series was over. He was disappointed that it had ended so abruptly, but it would be matched by the suddenness of how quickly his personal life would take another turn. The next morning, on the steps of Lenox Hill Hospital, as Mantle stepped out of a taxi, the life he had known since childhood would begin coming to an end.

"[My father] got out of the cab first, outside the hospital, and then I got out," Mantle remembered years later. "I was on crutches and I couldn't put any weight on the leg that was hurt, so as I got out of the cab I grabbed my father's shoulder to steady myself. He crumpled to the sidewalk. I couldn't understand it. He was a very strong man, and I didn't think anything at all about putting my weight on him that way. He was always so strong."

Both Mickey and Mutt were rushed into the hospital where Mantle underwent more tests confirming two torn ligaments in his right knee. At the same time, doctors at the hospital ran a series of tests on Mutt. Father and son were put in the same room where they watched the remainder of the World Series on television. Years later, Mantle would say that he suspected his father had been ill—that he had noticed some weight loss when Mutt had visited him in Kansas City that summer to confront him about "being a man." If so, Mickey apparently did not act on it, nor did anyone else close to Mutt for that matter. Mantle may have been in denial of anything that threatened the most formidable figure in his life. But if Mantle, in fact, did truly fear that there was something seriously wrong with Mutt's health, his reluctance to urge or insist that he see a doctor only further underscores Mickey's own inability to assert himself with his father. Just three weeks shy of turning 20, a major-league ballplayer on the verge of stardom, and seemingly a world away from Commerce, Oklahoma, Mantle was nevertheless still a child when it came to anything involving his father. His world and his relationship with his father were about to change dramatically. Upon his father's collapse outside the hospital, Mantle said at the time what was probably more accurate than his later recollections: "That was the first time," he said, "that I knew Dad was really sick."

A few days later, the doctor who had examined his father came to see Mickey while he was alone resting in his hospital bed. Mutt had cancer, Mickey was told. It was Hodgkin's disease, the dreaded Mantle curse—the same form of cancer that had killed Mickey's grandfather Charles, and his uncles. The doctor advised taking Mutt home and allowing him to return to work, for as long as he could. The diagnosis offered little of the hope that the suddenly shocked Mantle desperately sought.

"I'm sorry, Mick," the doctor said with finality. "I'm afraid there's not much that can be done. Your father is dying."

The course of self-destruction Mantle would later follow had less to do with celebrity and fame than it did with his impending sense of doom. Having watched so many male members of his family, including his father, succumb to Hodgkin's disease, Mantle was haunted by the fear of an early death. Hank Bauer remembered having once confronted Mickey after seeing him arrive for a game hung over from yet another of his late-night drinking binges. Bauer tried to have a big-brother talk with Mantle, suggesting that he be more serious and stop abusing his body. "My father died young," Mantle said, looking up at Bauer through bloodshot eyes. "I'm not going to be cheated."

For years after, Mantle would remain consumed by thoughts of his father and the feeling that Mutt had been cheated by his early death—cheated of seeing Mickey win the Triple Crown and his every accomplishment, cheated of seeing the grandchildren he had asked for, cheated of the chance to grow old and resolve all the issues shared by fathers and sons. Years later, while researching *Dynasty*, his history on the 1949–1964 Yankees, Peter Golenbock got Mantle to reminisce about his father and their relationship—something Mickey often refused to do with Yankee beat writers.

"Do you still miss him?" Golenbock asked. "Do you still think about him?"

Mantle nodded. "Oh, yes," he said. "I dream about him all the time."

Mantle, in a sense, not wanting to get "cheated," was living out not only the dream his father had for him but the life his father had been denied, too. As psychiatrists and Shakespeare would have it, a son comes into his own when he surpasses his father. In Mantle's case, he continued the race with his father still a prominent figure in his psyche. Mutt would forever be present in Mickey's life, not simply as a memory but as a patriarchal figure from whom Mantle had never broken the ties of a child. Invariably, the tension between fathers and sons requires some form of release, physical and emotional, and with Mickey there had been neither. His nightlife carousing, his sexual infidelity, his showing up hung over for games—it may have been Mantle not wanting "to be cheated," but it also was the rebellion of a son seeking that release.

Author Robert Creamer, who ghostwrote Mantle's book *The Quality of Courage* in 1964, would write years later that the only time he ever saw Mickey drunk was in New York in 1963, after the Yankees had been swept in the World Series by the Dodgers. "It was late at night," said Creamer, "and he was standing in the downstairs lobby of a hotel with a drink in his hand, talking with a small group of baseball people. He wasn't loud or belligerent, just a little sodden and a little wistful about the defeat." Creamer said it did not take long to understand that, more than a dozen years after his death, Mutt Mantle still remained foremost in Mickey's thoughts—and that it was an issue that still affected him deeply. "[Mickey] said, 'What about this book?' It was about courage, I said," Creamer recalled, "and Mantle began talking about his father. He described his strength in holding his family together during the Depression and his courage in the last year of his life, when he knew he was dying of Hodgkin's disease but did not tell Mickey, who was in his precarious rookie season with the Yankees. 'My father was the bravest man I ever knew,' he said. I learned that Mantle was more sensitive than I had imagined from the surly image he had been projecting, and I found he had a subtle sense of humor. After our book was published, I took a copy to Yankee Stadium and asked him to autograph it for my children. When he handed it back, he had a little grin. In his strong, clear hand he had written, 'To Jim, Tom, John, Ellen and Bobby, my best wishes—from the man who taught your father a few lessons in journalism—Your friend, Mickey Mantle.' That was a nice little zinger, and I got a kick out of it."

In 1951, though, Mantle had little of that wit, especially as he faced the uncertainty of his baseball future with the most serious injury of his young career and, at the same time, the certainty of his father's death, which doctors told him likely would come in the following year. The doctors at Lenox Hill Hospital had the same conversation with Mutt, outside of Mickey's presence. Years later, Mickey said he wished he had been in that meeting or that Mutt would have talked to him about it in those days. Instead, they spoke of Merlyn and Holly once again, with Mutt once more insisting that Mickey should "marry one of your kind," and return to Oklahoma with him and the friends who had come to New York with him.

"Mickey would tell me that his father was putting a lot of pressure on him to return to Oklahoma with him, and I guess I thought he would," Holly told me. "Maybe he would have if it hadn't been for his injury, but the doctors wanted him to remain in New York long enough for the swelling to go down on his knee. They were thinking they might have to operate, and they weren't going to be able to operate until the swelling was down. And there was the chance they wouldn't have to, which is what Mickey was hoping for because he didn't want to have any surgery on his legs unless it was absolutely necessary."

By the end of October, Mutt and his friends had returned to Oklahoma, leaving Mickey in New York where the Yankees put him up at the Henry Hudson Hotel near Central Park, convenient for Mantle getting to his doctor's office.

"He was in a cast up to his hip," Holly remembered, "the drawback was that his room at the Henry Hudson Hotel was so small, it was smaller than my walk-in closet. And he asked me if I would stay with him all night. And I said, 'Mick, I'd like to but I can't fit on your bed' because it was like a cot. It wasn't a twin bed. And he said, 'Please,' and his right leg was in a cast up to the hip, and I said, 'Mick, how are you going to get into bed if I'm in there. He said, 'I'll manage,' and he left his leg on the floor and I was pushed up against the wall."

Soon Holly was living with Mickey at the Hudson Hotel where he would watch television all day while she was out hustling acting jobs. Holly's friends were urging her to relocate to Hollywood where they were all getting work on westerns and television, but she wasn't ready to make the move. This was also an exciting time in New York sports, and Mickey was part of it. In the evenings, Mickey and Holly continued to be regulars at Danny's Hideaway, the Stage Deli, and Toots Shor's, where Yankee fans were still all too eager to pick up his tabs. Mickey was also meeting other athletes, among them members of the New York Giants football team that had begun the 1951 season on a roll, unbeaten after the first five games. Like Mickey, many of the Giants players were staying at the Henry Hudson Hotel, sometimes upsetting Mantle.

"When we would get up in the morning to go downstairs to get something to eat, all the football players—you know men make noises if a fellow is with a girl? Well, they were making all those noises, and Mickey was a little upset and he wanted to tell them all," Holly said in an interview, "and I said, 'Mickey, don't worry about it.' So then he moved from there to 53rd near the Stage Delicatessen. I think they were on the fourth floor, and he wanted me there all the time, and I couldn't because I had to work. I would come there after my work, and sometimes I'd work on a movie until 10 or 11 at night, and Mickey would be passed out. He had been drinking all day."

As winter set in, Mantle began planning his return to Oklahoma. The bandages came off his knee, and Holly said that Mickey began insisting he didn't need surgery and could rehabilitate during the off-season. In her 2010 biography *The Last Boy: Mickey Mantle and the End of America's Childhood*, author Jane Leavy concluded that previous reports that Mickey had undergone surgery were wrong. The damage was serious enough to require surgery. Mantle had torn his meniscus, anterior cruciate ligament, and medial collateral ligament, but the injuries were never fully diagnosed at the time. The orthopedic surgeon who analyzed the case history that Leavy compiled said it was likely that in future seasons

Mantle compensated for the torn ACL with what the orthopedist called "neuromuscular genius." Even two years later when Mickey underwent another surgery on the knee, there was no established procedure to repair a torn anterior cruciate ligament.

"Mickey was limping badly when he left New York to go home," said Holly. "He was worried about his father, and he was telling me he wanted us to get married—that he was going to call off the engagement to Merlyn. 'I love you,' he said, 'and I won't give you up.'"

Chapter Twenty-Two

No Longer DiMaggio

I can remember a reporter asking me for a quote, and I didn't know what a quote was. I thought it was some kind of soft drink.

—Joe DiMaggio

In December Joe DiMaggio met with Yankee owners Dan Topping and Del Webb, who prepared themselves for the biggest sales job of their lives: Convincing the greatest, most famous athlete in America that at age 37 he still had another year of baseball left in him—and that he would earn $100,000 for the 1952 season, the same annual salary that Americans were paying President Harry S Truman. Admittedly, DiMaggio's body had begun to break down, and his injuries had taken a physical toll. The pain in his feet was so severe—doctors had removed a three-inch bone spur from his left heel in 1947 and there was now another bone spur in his right heel—that walking alone became agonizing at times. Then there was Joe's right shoulder that would sometimes pop out of its socket on and off the field. DiMaggio, however, had proven in 1951 just how valuable he could be to the Yankees playing in the clutch. There also was no bigger box office draw in the game, and Topping and Webb were willing to allow him to pick his spots on when he would play, just pinch hitting on the road or in the second half of a doubleheader, or perhaps playing mostly in home games at Yankee Stadium.

DiMaggio, though, couldn't see himself as a part-time player, and stubbornly resisted any temptation.

"I'm never putting on that monkey suit again," DiMaggio told the Yankee owners.

"Until yesterday," said Webb, "we had still hoped you would stay. But, since you didn't change your mind, it's a sad day, not only for the Yankees, but for all baseball as well."

DiMaggio memorialized the finality of the moment with the Yankee owners by signing baseballs for both men. His inscription, rendered in black fountain pen, read: "12/11/51 - To Del Webb, my association with you and the Yankees have been happy winning times. Sincerely, Joe DiMaggio."

The formal announcement became one of the biggest press conferences ever held in New York for any sports figure, befitting of a presidential candidate. The Yankees' Fifth Avenue offices in Squibb Tower on the afternoon of December 11 were too small to accommodate the horde of writers, radio reporters with microphones, television cameras, and newsreel crews that packed inside. The team's public relations man, Red Patterson, quickly arranged to spread Joe's final news conference as a player over four rooms. DiMaggio had writer pals prepare a brief statement that he read aloud in one of the rooms.

"I told you fellows last spring I thought this would be my last year. I only wish I could have had a better year, but even if I had hit .350, this would have been the last year for me. I feel I have reached the stage where I can no longer produce for my ball club, my manager, my teammates, and my fans the sort of baseball their loyalty to me deserves. You all know I have had more than my share of physical injuries and setbacks during my career. In recent years these have been much too frequent to laugh off. When baseball is no longer fun, it's no longer a game.

"And so, I've played my last game of ball."

Dan Topping told reporters that accepting DiMaggio's decision had been his biggest disappointment as an owner.

"We tried everything we possibly could to get him to stay," said Topping. "But we couldn't convince him. I don't know why he had to quit. Sick as he was last season he did better than most of the players hanging around."

For DiMaggio, though, "hanging around" was unacceptable. "I once made a solemn promise to myself that I wouldn't try to hang on once the end was in sight," he said. "I've seen too many beat-up players struggle to stay up there, and it's always a sad spectacle."

Never one who wanted to show his emotions in public, DiMaggio was the model of stoicism in announcing his retirement. Some who were at the press conference, however, remembered an air of sadness and resignation among the reporters for whom the dapper DiMaggio in a trendy double-breasted gray suit seemed to offer the image of a powerful but slender man still capable of another season or two.

"The old timing was beginning to leave me, and my reflexes were beginning to slow up," Joe offered to a question of how he could walk away when he still looked like he could play. By the end of the 1951 season, he said, "it had become a chore for me to play. I found it difficult getting out of bed in the morning, especially after a night game. I was full of aches and pains."

DiMaggio turning his back on $100,000, the highest annual salary paid any athlete in the world at the time, was difficult for most people to fathom—and it only seemed to heighten the aura that had long surrounded him.

"Only a man with character and overwhelming pride could take a step like that," wrote *New York Times* columnist Arthur Daley. "The Yankee Clipper has always been a proud man. That's why he was such a great ball player. He was never satisfied with anything less than perfection."

"He had to be perfect every day," said teammate Jerry Coleman. "Joe wasn't happy when he wasn't perfect. He had to be DiMaggio every day."

It was much the same thing that Joe's family had long grown accustomed to and knew. "He quit," said Tom DiMaggio, "because he wasn't Joe DiMaggio any more."

However, there was another problem factoring into DiMaggio's decision that few had bothered considering but that had affected Joe in recent years—night baseball. In 1946 the Yankees played their first game under the lights at Yankee Stadium, and there was no doubt in Joe's mind that night games had changed baseball.

"I honestly believe night ball cut short my days by about two years," DiMaggio said looking back on his decision to retire. "You don't get to bed until two in the morning, or so, and wake up at ten. I found that wasn't enough rest to get the aches and pains out of my system. I'd go to the park for an afternoon game the next day, and sometimes I wouldn't wake up 'til the fifth or sixth inning.

"It should be one way or the other—either all night ball or all days, so that a player can live normally. Maybe it doesn't affect the young fellows that way, but there's no question in my mind that it does at my age."

Reno Barsocchini remembered DiMaggio being unusually gracious that Tuesday afternoon as if soaking up the moments of the last day he would talk to writers as a ballplayer, a ballplayer giving his final interviews as a Yankee.

"There was a snowstorm coming, and Joe wanted to catch a plane out to the coast that night," Barsocchini told me. "He didn't want to be in New York one second longer than he needed to be, not on this trip back there. He knew that any place he went in the city, people would want to commiserate about his career. And, as far as Joe was concerned, he didn't want to look back, not at this time. He wanted to look to the future. He wanted to look ahead to his first Christmas and his first New Year's where he wouldn't have to think about the next season, about spring training, and about all the bullshit of what the Yankees' chances are for winning another championship. He was done with all of that, and that day was the day for putting all that behind him."

DiMaggio answered the same questions from different reporters as long as they wanted to stay—The best hitter he'd ever seen? "That's an easy one," said Joe. "Ted Williams, without question"—and he dutifully posed for every photographer. The television and radio crews as well had a field day with the surprisingly obliging Yankee Clipper until a fuse blew. The Yankee offices went dark, almost as if it was a signal from Joe that it was time for him to go. Minutes later when the lights finally came on again, DiMaggio had disappeared.

CHAPTER TWENTY-THREE

Out at Home

Baseball was my whole life. Nothing's ever been as fun as baseball.
—MICKEY MANTLE

MICKEY MANTLE NEVER BELIEVED FOR ONE MOMENT THAT JOE DIMAG-gio was serious about retiring, not after the way he had delivered in the clutch for the Yankees in the homestretch of the 1951 pennant race and in the World Series. Besides, as Mickey kept hearing teammates asking one another, who in his right mind would walk away from 100 grand when what you were doing in return was playing baseball? Baseball? A game that children played any chance they could?

Mickey didn't believe it until the Wednesday afternoon, the day after Joe's announcement, when his longtime friend Bill Mosely dropped by his family's house in Commerce with the news. Mantle was still limp-ing around the house, wearing a modified brace that allowed his right leg to bend at the knee. This had been an improvement over the full-length brace that locked at the knee that he had worn for six weeks after the injury, until late November. With the modified brace Mickey was supposed to be doing a series of rehabilitation exercises designed to strengthen his knee. The Yankees' team physician, Dr. Sidney Gaynor, had devised a specially weighted boot for Mickey to use in perform-ing the exercises. Mickey, however, lacked the patience and dedication required for the physical rehabilitation it would take to heal the knee to as close to new as possible.

"I lazed around, feeling sorry for myself instead of doing the exercises prescribed by Dr. Gaynor," Mickey was to later say. "I thought the muscles would automatically come back, good as ever. I was twenty years old, and I thought I was a superman."

Learning that DiMaggio had retired, Mickey suddenly felt even more overwhelmed than he had at any time since his demotion to the minor-league Kansas City team that summer. And his bum right leg was the least of it. Since October, Mantle had been trying to come to grips with Mutt's illness and the doctors' diagnosis that gave him only months to live. If he couldn't extend his father's life, Mickey was now determined to make the last months of his existence as comfortable and pleasant as possible. Doing that, however, put Mutt's deathbed wishes at odds with his son's own dreams for his future. Mutt had used the weeks since Mickey's return from New York to intensify his pressure on him to marry Merlyn, and doing it while he was still alive to be at the wedding.

"I think that Mutt knew that if he died before Mickey married Merlyn that Mickey sooner or later would break off the engagement and end up marrying me," Holly Brooke said in an interview half a century later. "When he left New York to go home that winter, he was intent on telling his father that he couldn't marry Merlyn because he had asked me to marry him—and that we were going to get married. I have no doubt those were his intentions, but I don't think he was prepared to see his father in the condition he found him, dying and with little time to live. Mickey wrote me that his father's condition had deteriorated and might not have long to live. I had a sense then that things had gotten out of Mickey's control. Mutt had a way of knowing how to pull Mickey's strings, and Mickey still hadn't found a way of standing on his own against his father. And it would be many years before he would be able to get out from under Mutt's thumb."

Not surprisingly, when Mickey returned to Commerce after the World Series, a sense of portending doom clouded any celebration. Mantle had completed his first major-league season. The Yankees had won the World Series, giving Mickey's income for his rookie year an additional boost. With his World Series share, Mantle even put a down payment on a new home for his mother and father. The new house at 317 South River Street had seven rooms and even the Mantles' own party line telephone. "Two rings meant us," said Mickey.

Mutt had first broached the idea of Mickey marrying Merlyn the previous winter when, sensing that his son would soon wind up with the Yankees' big-league team, he had begun worrying that Mickey's career would end up sidetracked if he were to play in New York while remaining single. "After you make the majors," Mutt told his son just before Christmas in 1950, "I'd like to see you marry Merlyn, and I'd like to have a little freckle-faced, redheaded grandson." Mutt repeated this wish again in New York after meeting Mickey's Holly Brooke, and he wasted no time in bringing it up again when Mickey was back in Commerce.

Mickey and Merlyn were married on December 23, 1951, in a small ceremony at the home of Merlyn's parents in Picher. Mickey had just turned 20 that October. Merlyn was 19. Mutt's hand in the wedding was obvious. Mickey's best man was Turk Miller, his father's closest friend. Only the immediate families attended, and Merlyn's mother's cousin played the wedding march on the Johnson family piano. "The wedding was happy and tearful at the same time," Merlyn wrote in *A Hero All His Life*. "His father looked on, and we both knew this ceremony was partly for him. Next to me, the groom's father was the happiest person in the room. Mick was somewhere in the top five. He would have done anything for his parents, and his lingering sadness was the fact that he was not able to do it sooner."

The honeymoon, however, turned out to be a small disaster. First, the new Mantles took along Mickey's friend Bill Mosely and his girlfriend on what they thought was going to be a fabulous, all-expenses-paid weekend in the bridal suite of a luxurious hotel in Hot Springs, Arkansas. In his typically unsuspecting manner, Mickey had believed a guy who claimed to be from the Hot Springs Chamber of Commerce. Of course, there was no free honeymoon, and Mickey and Bill barely had enough to pay for one night at a motel. Back home, the newlyweds moved into a small motel on Main Street in Commerce. Mutt would stop by to check on them each night because he was afraid that the motel's open draft heaters might malfunction and harm them with a deadly gas leak.

Merlyn, however, quickly realized that her new husband was an extremely distracted newlywed as she found herself competing with the two most important things of Mantle's life: his love for his father and his career. Mutt had been forced to retire from his job at the mine. Shortly after the new year in 1952, Merlyn and Mickey drove Mutt through snow-covered and ice-slicked roads to the Mayo Clinic in Rochester, Minnesota. There, Mutt underwent exploratory surgery, from which the doctors learned that the disease was so advanced that he only had months to live. "They gave him treatments that eased his pain, but there was nothing anybody could do to cure him," Mantle said years later. "When I saw the despair settle deeply in his eyes, I began to doubt God . . . All I knew was a bottomless sorrow, and I couldn't express it to anyone."

Least of all, it seemed, to Merlyn. She was to bitterly complain years later about feeling locked out by Mickey in his suffering and pain over his father's illness. Mantle would never adequately explain the reason for shutting his wife out of the emotional despair he felt over seeing his father wither away. He was equally reclusive over their years together in talking to her about his injuries and the prescribed rehabilitation programs that he invariably failed to follow. That winter, the days leading to spring training passed without Mantle investing any time or effort in rehabilitating his knee, even after DiMaggio formally announced his retirement and learning that Stengel planned to move him over to center field. Unfortunately for Mickey, this would become a bad ritual for much of his career. An untimely injury—and they would be numerous—would curtail a promising season, sending Mantle into an abyss of self-pity and a period of halfhearted rehabilitation. "I hated getting hurt," Mickey would say in one conversation. "That's why I hated going to doctors. I didn't want to see them because I didn't want to know what they would tell me."

Dr. Gaynor years later explained that Mickey's tendencies to injure himself were the result of his muscles being too strong for his bones, a condition that led to an unusual number of torn ligaments and cartilage during his career. Mickey would subsequently downplay his injuries. "They keep talking about me getting hurt," he said. "I still played eighteen years. I played in more games than anyone else in Yankee history."

As 1951 ended, though, Mickey's mind wasn't on the first of those injuries that would haunt his career. His mind was on the personal decision that would haunt him the rest of his life. Once again, as he had all his life, Mantle's father had decided his future, and Mickey had neither the courage nor the ability to protest.

"Mickey called to tell me that he had married Merlyn—that he hadn't had any choice," said Holly. "He was in tears, and he asked me to forgive him. He sounded like such a wreck, you couldn't help but feel sorry for him. And I knew Mickey and how he always seemed to bend to suit to whatever his father wanted.

"'Mickey,' I said. 'Call me when you're back in New York. We'll talk then.' He said, 'Okay, Holly. I love you.' He didn't have to tell me. I knew he did. 'I love you, too, Mickey,' I said. 'Take care of your father.'"

DiMaggio was in California just after Christmas when he heard the news that Mantle had gotten married.

"Joe was in L.A. seeing someone—it turned out to be Marilyn, though I didn't know it at the time," said Reno Barsocchini. "And I was talking to him on the phone and joked with him that the kid Mantle had tied the knot. All Joe said was, 'Good for him. Good for him.'

"I think Joe was happy for Mickey, and maybe envious. Mickey was young, playing for the New York Yankees, and prince of the city. He was everything Joe had once been."

Epilogue

Baseball isn't statistics. It's Joe DiMaggio rounding second base.
—Jimmy Breslin

Joe DiMaggio once advised Mickey Mantle to keep his feelings hidden from the public. It was in June 1951, and Mantle had just struck out several times in a game, taking out his frustration on a water cooler just as he would for years. Mickey nodded as Joe spoke to him as if he would heed the advice, DiMaggio later remembered, and a couple of days later the Yankee rookie threw yet another temper tantrum.

"We were teammates, and we each were outstanding ballplayers in our own way," DiMaggio would tell a couple of drinking pals in San Francisco. "But I don't think we had anything else in common."

Perhaps not, at least not until toward the end of Mantle's own career, a downslide that began in the mid-1960s. In 1961 Mickey and Roger Maris chased Babe Ruth's single-season home-run record, with Maris breaking it with his 61st home run. Mantle finished with 54 home runs, his season ending early in September when an abscessed hip from a vitamin shot infection forced him to be unexpectedly hospitalized. The Yankees won back-to-back World Series championships in 1961 and 1962, the last of Mickey's seven series titles. Mantle batted .317 and .321 in those two seasons and then hit .303 with 35 home runs and 111 RBIs in 1964, which would be his last good year. In 1964 against the St. Louis Cardinals, Mickey broke Ruth's World Series record and set the existing World Series mark of 18 home runs. The Cardinals, however, ultimately won the World Series in seven games, in what effectively became the end of Mickey Mantle's career as baseball's most feared switch hitter. Unfortunately, unlike DiMaggio, Mantle did not leave near the top of his game. His dramatic decline in the coming seasons would mirror the Yankees' own slide. In 1965, the Yankees slipped into the second division for the first time in 40 years. In 1966, they finished last in the American League for the first time since 1912, and they were next-to-last in 1967.

The Yankees compensated by celebrating Mickey Mantle Day at Yankee Stadium. In fact, Mickey became the only player to have four days in his honor at Yankee Stadium: Mickey Mantle Day in 1965, Mickey Mantle Fan Appreciation Day in 1966, Mickey Mantle Day after his retirement in 1969, and Mickey Mantle Day in 1997, two years after his death. On that first Mickey Mantle Day, a sellout crowd packed the Stadium where Mickey was presented with a new car; two quarter horses; vacation trips to Rome, Nassau, and Puerto Rico; a mink coat for Merlyn; a six-foot, hundred-pound Hebrew National salami; a Winchester rifle; and more, as well as the adoration of the city, the fans, and the Yankee organization. Large banners read "Don't Quit, Mick" and "We Love the Mick." Author Gay Talese, in his *Esquire* profile of DiMaggio, would call the celebration, which even the archbishop of New York, Francis Cardinal Spellman, had helped promote, "an almost holy day for the believers who had crammed the grandstands early to witness the canonization of a new stadium saint."

DiMaggio flew to New York to make the introduction of Mantle. Over the years, Joe and Mickey would see each other not only at the annual Yankee Old Timers' Day games but also almost every spring because DiMaggio attended the Yankees' spring training camps as a special instructor. Invariably, photographers would flock to them, and they were regularly photographed together. In 1961, photographer Ozzie Sweet, whose portraits often graced the cover of *Sport* magazine, arranged to photograph the two legendary Yankee center fielders together. His account of the photo session contradicts any notion that Mantle felt uncomfortable in DiMaggio's presence. On the contrary, according to Sweet, it was Mantle who looked "relaxed and confident" and DiMaggio who appeared "antsy and uncomfortable." DiMaggio was his typical distant self, causing Sweet to tread lightly. "With anyone else, I might say, 'Adjust your cap . . . '" said Sweet. "But with Joe, I didn't dare. I just wanted to quickly get some images of the two of them together." In one photograph from that session, DiMaggio can be seen straining his neck as he tried to move his head closer to Mantle's [face]. "I didn't know what the heck he was doing there," said Sweet. "But with Joe, I didn't want to fool around for long. I didn't want to say, 'Mr. DiMaggio, could you please change the angle of your neck so you don't look like a turtle?' I think he might have walked away!"

DiMaggio was also one to brood on small slights, or even perceived slights. In one Old-Timers' Game at Yankee Stadium, the public address announcer made an unintentional slip of protocol and introduced the great Yankee Clipper ahead of Mantle, instead of last as was customary with DiMaggio. With Mickey introduced at the end, with the fans' energy and enthusiasm at a fever's pitch, it appeared that Mantle had received the biggest and loudest ovation. Mickey himself was aware of it and even remarked with great satisfaction, "I heard Joe was pissed off about it." The rivalry, of course, worked both ways. Songwriter Paul Simon told author David Halberstam how amid the social and political upheaval of the 1960s he came to write the lyric about DiMaggio in his song "Mrs. Robinson." Simon said Mickey Mantle asked why he'd used DiMaggio and not him. Rather than get into the complex idea of the simpler times of DiMaggio, Simon said, "It was syllables, Mickey. The syllables were all wrong."

Since his retirement, DiMaggio had carefully guarded his image. With the exception of Joe's courtship of Marilyn Monroe and their marriage and divorce, all that the public had seen of DiMaggio in recent years was the packaged grace and magnanimity, the exquisitely tailored pin-striped suits, the regal image of suave detachment, an American hero transformed into a national aristocrat. That is how DiMaggio came off at that first Mickey Mantle Day, with the Yankee franchise in decline and Mickey already talking about retirement.

When DiMaggio was introduced to the packed Yankee Stadium that afternoon, he walked with his customary grace from the dugout onto the field. Then, as he waved to the cheering crowd, DiMaggio noticed Mickey's mother Lovell standing off, almost ignored, to one side. DiMaggio unexpectedly cupped her elbow in his hand and escorted her to where all the players and dignitaries were lined up along the infield grass. As he stood near home plate acknowledging the fans and the dignitaries on the field, DiMaggio happened to glance back at Mantle, who was still in the Yankee dugout with Merlyn and the boys. But what caught his eye was the figure of Senator Robert F. Kennedy, who was walking back and forth in the dugout, anticipating his own introduction. DiMaggio despised both Bobby Kennedy and his brother, the late president, for their romantic involvement with Marilyn Monroe. He blamed them, among others, for her personal demise. Marilyn had been the love of Joe's life, and his devotion to her continued long past their nine-month marriage in 1954. DiMaggio had reportedly told close friends that he had believed a reconciliation might be possible and was shocked when she was found dead of an overdose in 1962. DiMaggio had vowed never to have anything to do with the Kennedys, but now he was faced with the prospect of exchanging at least cordial greetings with one of them. This was, however, a Stadium filled with people still enamored with him, and he would not disappoint. DiMaggio turned his attention to Mickey and the fans there to honor him. "I'm proud," he announced, "to introduce the man who succeeded me in center field in 1951."

The applause in the Stadium was thunderous and sustained for Mickey as he and his family walked on to the field. Mantle waved to the crowd, which was on its feet, then posed with his wife and sons for the photographers kneeling in front of them. Mantle then gave a typically short speech. "A lot has been written about the pain that I've played with," he said. "When one of the fans says, 'Hi, Mick, how ya doin'? How's the leg?' It makes it all worth it. I just wish I had fifteen more years to play here."

Moved almost to tears, Mantle turned and began shaking hands with the all the dignitaries standing nearby. "Among them now," wrote Talese, "was Senator Kennedy, who had been spotted in the dugout five minutes before by Red Barber, and had been called out and introduced. Kennedy posed with Mantle for a photographer, then shook hands with the Mantle children, and with Toots Shor and [New York political leader] James Farley and others. DiMaggio saw him coming down the line and at the last second he backed away, casually, hardly anybody noticing it, and Kennedy seemed not to notice it either, just swept past shaking more hands. . . ."

Mantle later told me he had been drunk on Mickey Mantle Day.

"Which one?" I asked.

"I dunno," he said. "Maybe all of them."

Amazingly, until years later, no one in the inner circle of Mickey's friends stepped forward to help him confront the drinking that had put his personal life in a downward spiral. Perhaps they expected the family members to initiate the process. Maybe, too, the idea of admitting that one of America's heroes was drinking himself to death was too much to acknowledge. Certainly the public incidents of Mantle crying out for help were clear and numerous. Once Mickey flew from Florida into Love Field in Dallas, drinking hard most of the way. Fortunately for Mantle, pro golfers Tony Lema and Jackie Cupit were on the same flight and saw that he needed help. It was a wet winter night in Dallas with the roads all dangerously slick with sleet. When Mickey refused their offers to drive him home, the golfers followed him in their car. They saw Mickey's car go out of control, go over a curb, and blow a tire. Lema and Cupit then drove him home and left the Mantle house only after Mickey promised not to go out in his condition to retrieve his car. The moment they left, Mickey hopped on the motorcycle the Yankees had given him on one of the Mickey Mantle Days at the Stadium, taking Mickey Jr. along. After Mickey Jr. put the spare tire on the car, Mantle got behind the wheel and drove home with his nervous son following on the motorcycle.

Another time, Mickey suffered an anxiety attack in an incident that made the national news. On a flight home to Dallas, Mickey began to hyperventilate on the plane. Believing he was having a heart attack, Mantle asked a flight attendant to check if there was a doctor on the plane. The flight attendant immediately snapped an oxygen mask over Mickey's face, and the pilot radioed ahead to have paramedics meet the plane upon its arrival at Love Field. Mantle was taken away from the terminal in a stretcher, and he later tried to make light of the incident by saying a fan had stuck a ball in his face and asked for his autograph despite his condition. Fortunately, Mickey had not had a heart attack, nor was there anything wrong with his heart. The problem, instead, was related to Mickey's excessive drinking.

In New York, some 30 years after tearing up a knee avoiding DiMaggio and slipping on a Yankee Stadium drainage gutter, a drunken Mickey Mantle stepped out of a limousine and tripped and fell into a gutter outside the St. Moritz Hotel. A friend kneeled down to help, and Mickey looked up with a crooked grin and cracked, "A helluva place for America's hero, ain't it?"

The signs of Mickey's drinking problems were all there dating back to his rookie season. The Yankee management didn't see it until a few years later when George Weiss started keeping tabs on Mantle and Billy Martin. The Yankee general manager hired private investigators and began compiling a dossier—not so much on Mickey but on Billy—and building a case strong enough to override any protests from Casey Stengel, Martin's longtime protector. Weiss also had to convince Yankee owners Topping and Webb that Martin had become a cancer threatening the future of the ballclub.

Along the way, Weiss was aided in his project by what would be, for him, a fortuitous turn of events. In June 1956, arguably Mickey's career year, the FBI contacted the Yankees with a request to interview Mantle. According to FBI files obtained through the Freedom of Information Act, federal officials had received information from unnamed sources that Mantle was being "blackmailed for $15,000 after being found in a compromising position with a married woman."

The incident only further convinced Weiss and the Yankee owners that Mantle's personal life was out of control, even though there was no violation of federal law on Mickey's part. "Mr. Mantle subsequently denied ever having been caught in a compromising situation," a memo in Mantle's FBI file states. "Mr. Mantle readily admitted that he had 'shacked up' with many girls in New York City, but stated that he had never been caught."

"That sounds like him," said Phil Pepe, a former sportswriter for the *New York Daily News* who covered many of Mantle's escapades with the Yankees and later cowrote a book with him. "Not that I have firsthand knowledge of it, but I had my suspicions when I traveled with him. He had friends, he had ladies who he was friendly with, and he would be the first to admit that his marriage was always rocky and shaky."

Through the early and mid-1950s, Mantle tried his best to keep his womanizing a secret from Merlyn. Sometimes Mickey went to Olympian, if not absurd, lengths to hide those affairs from his wife, as when he and

Merlyn flew to Cuba with friend and wealthy contractor Harold Young-man and his wife Stella of Baxter Springs, Kansas, in their twin-engine Beechcraft in the spring of 1957. At an airport in Montgomery, Alabama, where they had stopped to refuel, Harold tugged at Mantle and pointed to a newsstand in the terminal. "Hey, Mickey," said his friend, "is that your picture?"

Mantle's photograph was on the cover of *Confidential* magazine, a celebrity gossip rag bought by 4.5 million readers each week, with a picture and accompanying story about Holly Brooke, whom he had continued to see even after his marriage. Mantle immediately bought all the copies of *Confidential* that were on display at the newsstand and threw them in the trash. Trying to keep Merlyn from seeing the magazine, Mickey and Youngman then proceeded to sprint out of the plane at every airport on that trip to buy up all the copies and dump them all out of sight.

Mantle's efforts, however, were to no avail. When they returned home from the trip, Mickey and Merlyn found a stack of the magazines sitting in their front yard. The *Confidential* story, apparently written by Brooke, was an exposé of their affair and how they had met in his rookie season through shyster Alan Savitt's fraudulent endorsement scam. "I OWN 25% OF MICKEY MANTLE," the magazine teased, "and there were times when he was mine—100%." Holly had been paid $1,250 for the story, according to the magazine's records, almost the same amount she had paid Savitt to invest in the scam in 1951.

The *Confidential* article became an embarrassing nightmare for Mickey, with the story laying out his relationship with Holly, including how she called him "Mickey Mouse" in their intimate moments. "Plenty of times we'd sit in my car in the wee small hours of the morning and watch the sun rise over Manhattan," Holly's story reported. "Those all-night rendezvous might come after an afternoon of baseball or golf, but the Mick was never too tired for a night game . . . More than once, Mickey would ask me how I felt about marrying him, owning 100 percent . . . permanently. But he always answered his own question. 'No, I guess not,' he'd say. 'You'd never be happy in a little town like Commerce.'"

No one came out a winner in the *Confidential* article, which made Holly appear to be a conniving gold digger trying to shake Mickey down now that he was the Yankees' big star—something that she repeatedly denied in my interviews with her five decades later. Holly maintained she had been naïvely lured to some unmarked editorial offices in Manhattan unaware she was meeting writers for *Confidential*, and that she had been deceived and taken advantage of as much as Mickey by the sleazy tabloid.

"I would never have done that to Mickey," she said. "If I had known who these people were, I would never have gone there and talked to them. They interviewed me and then twisted around what I said and tried to make it seem like I wrote the article."

However, at the time there did appear to be some difference over money between Mickey and Holly, dating back to her 1951 investment of $1,500 with Alan Savitt who apparently never repaid her nor produced any of the earnings he had promised. In the homestretch of Mantle's 1956 Triple Crown season, Holly wrote in *Confidential*, Mickey and she were still carrying on their love affair—and he had asked her to come stay with him while the Yankees were playing the Red Sox in Boston. When she arrived, she asked him again about getting back the money she had lost to Savitt. "Don't worry," she said Mickey told her, "the Yankees will take care of it." She remembered that their song was playing in the background. "It's time," she wrote, "he went to bat—for me." In her January 31, 1958, nationally syndicated column, Dorothy Kilgallen reported that, "Actress Holly Brooke settled her lawsuit with Mickey Mantle out of court and quietly—for a sum reported to be in five figures. The Yankees' legal battery handled the case, keeping Mickey out of the headlines."

Merlyn eventually learned about all of Mickey's infidelities, writing in *A Hero All His Life* that "he was married in a very small geographic area of his mind." Unfortunately for Merlyn, Holly Brooke put not only a name but also a beautiful face on what had filled the bigger share of Mickey's life.

"There was a side of him," said Merlyn, with apparent regret, "that would always be drawn to that kind of woman."

What Merlyn, like Mickey's father, may have never understood, though, is that Holly Brooke had symbolized more than just another woman in his life. Over the years, as in 1951, she came to represent a life that, for Mantle, matched the ambitions that he had come to fulfill as the biggest thing to hit New York since, well, Joe DiMaggio.

"American sports heroes like Joe DiMaggio and Mickey Mantle are different than you and me and everyone who worships them," the Hollywood author and journalist James Bacon said in an interview discussing fame. "Joe and Mickey had more in common with Frank Sinatra, John Wayne and the idols of celebrity than they did with the life into which they were born. It wasn't anyone's fault and certainly not theirs. It's what came with what they did so wonderfully well and with the inevitability of their success.

"And love stories like that of Joe and Marilyn. It's gods and goddesses. And who are we to judge?"

Author's Note

Booze, Baseball, and Sex. A musician friend with the American rock band Styx thought that should have been the subtitle of my 2002 biography, *Mickey Mantle: America's Prodigal Son.* Perhaps he was right. Since the days of Babe Ruth, booze and sex had been synonymous with some of the legends of the game. And, in that, Mantle may have been Ruth's successor. My friend's subtitle suggestion may have been my favorite response from any reader in the countless letters, e-mails, and communications that I received over the years. Then in 2006, I opened an e-mail from someone whose correspondence would eventually lead to the writing of *DiMag & Mick.*

> *Mr. Castro:*
>
> *I was recently "googling" for information on my Aunt Holly (Brooke) and came across the following: "Castro maintains, Mutt Mantle controlled his son's personal life, disapproving of Mantle's relationship with showgirl Holly Brooke and insisting that he . . ."*
>
> *I'm looking forward to reading your book and getting a different perspective from the stories I grew up with from Aunt Holly. I cringe when I see articles portraying her as a "showgirl"; Holly was much more than showgirl . . . she was an artist (with paintings hanging in Gracie Mansion), a columnist (the one I recall is "The Babbling Brooke"), she performed on Broadway in plays such as "Portrait of a Queen," she is also the Aunt/Great Aunt of Robert Sean Leonard and Brett Harrison, close friends to stars such as Jimmy Durante and Roy Rodgers [sic], she worked as a lab technician on the Manhattan Project (where she lost her sense of smell in an accident), I could go on and on . . . she has led quite a life. The one thing she has always wanted to do but never gotten around to finishing is an autobiography.*
>
> *The great news is that she is alive and well (she visited for Christmas). She just recently gave me an autographed photo Mickey gave her*

back in the days when they were engaged (I'm not sure if it is a copy or original . . . Holly insists she gave me the original, but it looks like it may be a copy). I know a slightly different version of how Mickey Mantle married his hometown sweetheart, but there's no reason to go into any of that; might just cause folks pain that will do no one any good. Suffice to say, Holly and Mickey remained close friends until he passed away.

Keith Huylebroeck (pronounced holly-brooke . . . hence her stage name)

Bethlehem, PA

Keith Huylebroeck eventually put me in contact with Holly Brooke, and it began a decadelong friendship in which we spoke often, and in those interviews she helped me in reconstructing the year 1951 for this book. Holly especially remembered the times when DiMaggio would visit with Mantle at Danny's Hideaway, and of being with Mickey on several occasions when Mantle dined with Joe and other guests both during and after 1951, including Marilyn Monroe. She recalled numerous other times when DiMaggio had called on Mantle or when Mickey mentioned to her of having spoken to or having heard from Joe. Most memorable of all was her recollection of at least one telephone call of encouragement she says Mantle received from DiMaggio that summer of 1951 when the Yankees had demoted the slumping Mickey to Kansas City, then one of the team's minor-league affiliates. According to Brooke, she was staying with Mantle in Kansas City while he was in the minors and witnessed Mickey receiving that call. She also strongly denied that Mantle, either as a rookie or later when they were involved in an extramarital affair, would become physically ill whenever DiMaggio visited the Yankee clubhouse as portrayed in Billy Crystal's endearing but flawed HBO film, *61*, about Mantle and Roger Maris's chase of Babe Ruth's single season home-run record.

Holly Brooke's corroboration of my earlier interviews with the other two most significant women in Mantle's life—wife Merlyn, and Greer Johnson, his companion the last 10 years of his life—and longtime DiMaggio pal Reno Barsocchini provided virtually unassailable confirmation that

Joe and Mickey's true relationship was hardly what the world had been led to believe it had been. Their accounts reveal for the first time that, much to the contrary of the long-held myth of DiMaggio and Mantle as unfriendly antagonists, the relationship between the two men was actually that of symbiotic teammates and heroes cast into the national spotlight in 1951—DiMaggio's final season and Mantle's rookie year—and lasting until Mickey's death in 1995. It debunks all those DiMaggio-can't-stand-Mantle-and-vice-versa stories as being untrue and at best as the well-intentioned made-up stories of Mickey's teammates attempting to protect him from the boogeyman they created of DiMaggio—though Mickey Mantle really needed no protection. Mickey more than held his own with the fabled Yankee Clipper on the field, and today he is perhaps remembered more fondly than DiMaggio by their fans.

What hopefully emerges in *DiMag & Mick* is a portrait of DiMaggio and Mantle as the old and young exemplars of what was a more confident, masterful age not only in baseball but in the country where they were held up as cultural heroes over two generations, symbolic of an America celebrating its recent triumph over Nazism and ever-curious about the new age of color television, rocket ships, and technology it had entered.

Additionally, the book is about fathers and sons, rebels and heroes, and the rite of passage of two men who would go down in baseball immortality—DiMaggio as he reluctantly prepares to leave the spotlight of adoration and hero-worship for the glitzy world of Marilyn's exploding Hollywood celebrity, and Mantle in his awkward attempt to leave his country roots of Dust Bowl Oklahoma for the big-city exposure and expectations of greatness being placed on him.

Yankee legend and glory holds a special magic all its own, and this book examines the heart and soul of that mystique, especially the bond of the players themselves and how that came to breed and spread the perception that there was any enmity and animosity between DiMaggio and Mantle—two polarizing personalities who drove many teammates away from one and galvanized their friendship with the other.

I grew up with DiMaggio as my father's hero and Mantle as mine. Among my oldest memories was the day my father brought home a newspaper sports page that had a picture of Joe DiMaggio with his arm around a hotshot rookie that my dad informed me "will be even better than DiMaggio." I could only imagine. After all, a near life-size poster of Joe DiMaggio even dwarfed a crucifix over my bed, much to my mother's chagrin. But then that was my father's doing. Three things have always been important to him: God, family, and baseball, though not necessarily in that order. My father, of course, was right about Mickey Mantle. In my mind, he would wind up being greater than DiMaggio, although not for the reasons some baseball purists would argue.

Much like my Mantle biography, this book obviously had some of its genesis in a childhood in the so-called golden age of baseball years ago but didn't begin taking shape until Mantle and DiMaggio were both in their own golden years. When I was a columnist at the *Los Angeles Herald Examiner*, I had set out to write a biography of Joe DiMaggio. Although Mantle had been my hero, DiMaggio had been my father's baseball idol—and I think I'd wanted to write that book for my father. So for a number of years, my idea had been to research and write the DiMaggio book.

DiMaggio, of course, wasn't an easy interview to land. When I finally was able to meet DiMaggio, it was through a strange set of circumstances that produced informal interviews from the late 1970s to the 1980s and a few times in the early 1990s. I had been in Reno Barsocchini's bar several times during visits to San Francisco and had struck up a friendship of sorts with Reno. I'm not altogether sure why. A lot of reasons, I suppose. He got to know of my interest in baseball and DiMaggio. I'd told him the story of the poster-size photo of DiMaggio hung over my bed when I was young and how my mother would take it down anytime our parish priest would visit and replace it with a crucifix. Anyway, back in L.A., I would occasionally get a call from Reno telling me, "The Clipper's in town. Wanna talk to him?" I would catch a Pacific Southwest Airlines flight out of LAX after work and sometimes catch him at Reno's that night or the next. I wouldn't say I struck up a friendship with DiMaggio, but I found myself in a kind of friendly gathering of drinking pals to which he could talk about whatever was on his mind. I got the sense that Reno would call out to people such as myself to have this court there for his friend. Years later I would learn from golf writer Art Spander that he had gotten to know DiMaggio much the same way, through Reno who would also alert him to whenever Joe was in town.

However, I found that while DiMaggio could be generous with his time and observations in talking about other subjects—as diverse as immigrants and immigration to baseball and Mantle, he could be guarded to the point of being abrupt and rude when the subject of conversation turned toward him. I had been told—and I knew from everything I'd read and knew about him, too—that DiMaggio wouldn't talk about himself, but I was able to get him to open up and talk about Mickey. Eventually I became convinced that I could write a better, more definitive biography about Mantle than I could about DiMaggio.

I first met Mickey Mantle in 1970, the year after his retirement and shortly after he had returned to Dallas from a frustrating season as a coach of the New York Yankees. Mickey had lived in Dallas since the late 1950s, and only earlier that year I had joined the reporting staff of the *Dallas Times Herald* right out of college. One of the first things I did upon going to work at the *Times Herald* was to check the Mickey Mantle files at the newspaper's morgue. I was stunned to see the scarcity of any Mantle clips since his retirement. No lifestyle pieces, no Mick-in-retirement articles. You would have thought Mantle didn't reside in Dallas. A couple of national pieces had been written about Mickey in retirement, but nothing locally. I lobbied for an assignment to interview Mantle, which came my way because no one else was interested. Heck, my editors themselves weren't interested.

When I first contacted Mantle, I started getting a sense of why no one was writing about him. Even after I explained that his home telephone number had been in our City Desk files, Mickey seemed miffed. I remember his words as something that might have come from Yogi Berra. "Well," Mickey said over the phone, "I only gave out that number so that I could be reached whenever someone needed to talk to me."

Mickey was close to an hour late to our lunch interview. As I write in the book, he had wanted to meet at a trendy burger shop in the Turtle Creek section of North Dallas. When he finally arrived, Mickey apologized in a matter-of-fact manner. He said, "There was a screw-up on our tee time this morning."

I was immediately blown away. Not because I was finally meeting my boyhood hero, face-to-face, but because as I saw him—slightly red-eyed, smiling crookedly, slurring some of his words—I thought to myself, *My God, it's like meeting my father.* They both were heroes, and they both were drinkers. And not happy drunks either. Of course, I didn't tell Mickey he reminded me of my father. Nor did I tell my father that he reminded me of Mickey. But from experience, I had an understanding of how to deal with Mantle. An interview, a formal question and answer interview, was out of the question. Instead, over charbroiled cheeseburgers and beers, Mickey rambled in a disjointed exercise of free association for which I wasn't prepared.

We talked for close to two hours that afternoon, and I remember being panic-stricken the longer the interview went on because I feared that I actually had little to use in a traditional story about Mickey in retirement. He would clam up when the conversation turned to things he was doing now. A bowling alley bearing Mickey's name in Dallas had closed down, and then reopened, and Mickey was unclear as to what the status of it was. He didn't want to talk about his investments, and he was equally evasive on questions about his life with his sons. There was one comment I wrote several times in my notebook: "We're doing a lot more things together now, that's for sure." My time with Mickey might have ended that afternoon had we not started talking about golf, one of the few things over which he showed any passion. I happened to live in a town house complex that was adjacent to the Preston Trail Golf Club in far North Dallas. Mickey was a member of Preston Trail. I wasn't—this was one of the most exclusive golf courses in Dallas—but I'd sneaked onto the course a few times and attended the Byron Nelson Classic at Preston Trail earlier that year. So when Mickey told me of a particularly tricky par 5 that he said he had driven the length of with a slight breeze, I knew exactly which one he was talking about. I was a duffer, but golf is the consummate game for eternal optimists. The next thing I knew, I had a golf date with Mickey a few days later. We played with two other members from whom Mickey cajoled a stroke per hole handicap for me, even though I kept assuring him I wasn't that bad. "Believe me," he said to me, "you are." We won all 18 holes at $10 a hole, and Mickey won a

side bet with each of the two fellow members. He insisted I keep the win-
nings from the main bet, and I sensed that, in a way, Mickey got as big a
kick out of winning $100 bets from each of the two men as he did from a
World Series share when he was playing baseball.

As for the interview itself, I think it was Gore Vidal who described
interviews like these as "encounters"—and I had several of these types
of encounters with Mickey in the 1970s and in the 1980s. In 1973, I
was working for the PBS *Newsroom* show that Jim Lehrer had created in
Dallas, and we wanted Mantle to appear on our live show to discuss the
young Texas Rangers baseball team. Since I knew Mickey, I contacted
him and we immediately faced two insurmountable problems. First,
Mickey wanted to be paid. He had no idea what PBS was but thought
if it was live he should be paid. Secondly, Mickey really didn't want to
appear live but wanted the interview to be taped, which went against the
format of the show. The whole thing was a wash. In 1985, while at *Sports
Illustrated*, I proposed and had approval for a Mickey Mantle profile that
resulted in several phone conversations with Mickey, and equally as many
broken dates for face-to-face meetings. As we were to learn later, Mickey
was drinking himself to death during these years. His family life was also
not good. There were ongoing problems with his son Billy, and he and
Merlyn were breaking up. They didn't divorce, but they lived apart for the
last seven years of his life. I spoke with him twice in late 1994, planning
to meet with him during an upcoming card show appearance on the West
Coast. But then he had to cancel the show because of stomach problems
that worsened until his death.

Although I spoke to Merlyn Mantle numerous times in the 1970s, as
I acknowledged in my Mantle biography, she did not cooperate with me
as I was later researching that book, having learned that I was relying on
interviews with Greer Johnson. Merlyn had long bitterly resented Mickey's relationship with Miss Johnson and denied access to anyone whom
she knew to be working with her. When Mantle was hospitalized and
dying in 1995, the Mantle family had gone so far as to forbid her from
visiting Mickey on his deathbed, refusing to allow her to bid him a final
good-bye. The Mantles had also tried to keep her from attending Mickey's memorial service. And although I had notes from my conversations in

the early 1970s with Merlyn, I honored her request that I not write about his time with her and Mickey until after her death. She died in 2009.

Through all those years, Mickey continued a close friendship with Holly Brooke, according to her account. They remained lovers even after Mantle's marriage, and her recollections reveal that Mickey regularly unloaded his heart to her about what was sometimes a turbulent married life. Holly continued working as an actress as well as a painter and writer, raising her son as a single mom, and later marrying Broadway producer Henry Clay Blaney.

"Mickey Mantle was just a wonderful man," Holly said, summing him up. "He's also the most honest man I've ever met in my whole life. Mickey just wouldn't tell a lie. He would try not to hurt anybody. I don't know how many people you can say that about. He was remarkable."

Acknowledgments

DiMag & Mick: Sibling Rivals, Yankee Blood Brothers would not have been possible without the assistance of many individuals.

First, acknowledgment must go to my literary agent and friend, Leticia Gomez, without whose professional skills, constant encouragement, and unstinting moral support, this book would never have been completed.

Holly Brooke has been a good friend and source whose recollections of her life with Mickey Mantle in New York in 1951 and later were critical to the development and writing of the book. The same is true for Reno Barsocchini, whose friendship was invaluable in understanding Joe DiMaggio and his relationship with Mantle. And, of course, the time and assistance of Joe DiMaggio and Mickey Mantle provided firsthand insight into their lives.

James Bacon, my former desk mate at the *Los Angeles Herald Examiner*, was an inspiring mentor with his friendship and countless stories about Hollywood stars from Sinatra to Marilyn, not to mention his whiskey and his introduction to numerous contacts, among them Reno Barsocchini.

Pete Rose was magnanimous in sharing his memories and recollections of the time he spent with Mantle and DiMaggio and in helping me understand the unique culture and dynamics of the major-league clubhouse.

Tom Catal and Andrew Vilacky of the Mickey Mantle Museum in Cooperstown have always been both gracious and generous in their hospitality to me and my family, as well as sharing their library.

Greer Johnson, Mantle's "soul mate" the last 10 years of his life, was extremely kind in reminiscing about Mickey and graciously trusting me with her memories and remembering Mickey's conversations with her about his father, DiMaggio, Roger Maris, and many of the other important people in her life. This book, like *Mickey Mantle: America's Prodigal*

Son, would not be as complete in its assessment of Mantle without her assistance.

The late Ray Mantle, one of Mickey's brothers, shared his memories of growing up with Mickey, especially in clearing up discrepancies in previous accounts of Mantle's early life, as well as Mickey's relationship with DiMaggio. Ray also offered tremendous insight into Mickey's relationship with their father and Mickey's friendship with Billy Martin.

A number of people were helpful in providing information or putting me in touch with prospective interviewees but especially: DiMaggio biographer Richard Ben Cramer, who shared his thoughts on why he believed Joe and Mickey intensely disliked each other; author Phil Berger, who graciously shared his insights and contacts on Mantle, the subject of one of his numerous books; and Michael A. Stoner, attorney for Greer Johnson.

I am deeply appreciative of the acceptance and assistance from my publisher, The Rowman & Littlefield Publishing Group, and especially the support and editorial assistance of Meredith Dias, Josh Rosenberg, Stephanie Scott, and Ashley Benning.

Special thanks also to these individuals for their support or assistance in tangible and intangible ways: Hank Aaron, Art Aguilar, Marty Appel, Bobby Asnas, Ed Attanasio, Jim Bacon, Sallie Baker, Pat Barsocchini, Cameron Bebehani, Jim Bellows, Keven Bellows, Yogi Berra, Hollis Biddle, Alan and Jan Block, Roy Bode, Barry Bonds, John Borunda, Jim Bouton, Brian Brassfield, Marty Brennaman, Jimmy Breslin, Tony Brooklier, Jerry Brown, Jim Brown, Jeff and Cindy Brynan, Jim Bunning, Ken Burns, George W. Bush, Roger Butler, Al Campanis, Dave Campbell, Frank and Lucy Casado, Patricia Casado, Rick Cerrone, Laura Chester, Barbara Cigarroa, Paul Cohen, John B. Connally, Alfredo Corchado, Bob Costas, Kevin Costner, Warren Cowan, Billy Crystal, Francis Dale, Tina Daunt, Teo Davis, Gavin deBecker, Cody Decker, Mary Anne Dolan, Joe DiMaggio, James Duarte, Mel Durslag, Charlie Ericksen, Carl Erskine, Roy Firestone, Bob Fishel, Robert Fitzgerald, Whitey Ford, Don Forst, Dudley Freeman, Glenn Frey, Carlos Fuentes, Randy Galloway, Peter Gammons, Art Garfunkel, Brian Gauthier, Paul Gelb, Mikal Gilmore, Rudolph Giuliani, Carole Player Golden, Peter Golenbock, Johnny Grant, Kathy Griffin, Carlos

Guerra, Mary Frances Gurton, Chris Gwynn, Jacleen Haber, David Halberstam, Mike Hamilburg, Arnold Hano, Thomas Harris, Ray Harper, Lew Harris, Jickey Harwell, Don Henley, Mickey Herskowitz, Tom Hoffarth, Gerald Holland, Joe Holley, Ken Holley, Emory Holmes, Bill Hudson, Ed Hunter, Matty Ianniello, Alex Jacinto, Derek Jeter, Chipper Jones, David Justice, Ron Kaye, Ray Kelly, Kitty Kelley, Preston Kirk, Steve Kraly, Doug Krikorian, Sandy Koufax, Tony Kubek, Deborah Larcom, Ring Lardner Jr., Don Larsen, Tommy Lasorda, Daniel Lastra, Tim Layana, Timothy Leary, Mike Leggett, Jill Lieber, Carole Lieberman, Skip E. Lowe, Mike Lupica, Larry Lynch, Professor Ralph Lynn, Bob Mallon, John Mankiewicz, Mickey Mantle, Willie Mays, Bill McAda, Barbara McBride-Smith, Julie McCullough, Mark McGwire, David McHam, Frank Messer, Lidia Montemayor, Jim Montgomery, Louis F. Moret, Mark Mulvoy, Marcus Musante, Stan Musial, Joe Namath, Yolanda Nava, Jack Nelson, Don Newcombe, Jose Oliveros, Peter O'Malley, Edward James Olmos, Bill Orozco, Robert Patrick, Octavio Paz, Professor Thomas Pettigrew, Vic Prado, Tony Pederson, John Robert Pharr, George Pla, Charles Rappleye, Robert Redford, Jimmy Reese, Pee Wee Reese, Rick Reilly, Bobby Richardson, Wanda Rickerby, Phil Rizzuto, Tim Robbins, Phil Alden Robinson, Gregory Rodriguez, Jim Rome, Carol Rose, Emilio Sanchez, Richard Sandomir, Susan Sarandon, Dick Schaap, Dutch Schroeder, Vin Scully, Modesta Garcia Segovia, Diane K. Shah, Gail Sheehy, Charlie Sheen, Ron Shelton, Bob Sheppard, Blackie Sherrod, Ivan Shouse, Buck Showalter, T.J. Simers, Paul Simon, Marty Singer, Bill Skowron, April Smith, George Solotaire, Stephanie Sowa, Lee Strasberg, Susan Strasberg, Ben Stein, George Steinbrenner, Randy Swearingen, Sallie Taggart, Gay Talese, Don Tanner, J. Randy Taraborrelli, Joe Torre, John Tuthill, Peter Ueberroth, George Vecsey, Antonio Villaraigosa, Judy Wammack Rice, Sander Vanocur, Robert Vickrey, Don Wanlass, Tommy West, Ted Williams, Tom Wolfe, Gene Woodling, Steve Wulf, and Don Zimmer.

My appreciation to the entire staff of the Baseball Hall of Fame Museum Library in Cooperstown, New York, for their cooperation on so many levels. Thanks also to the library staffs of *Time* and *Sports Illustrated*, the *Sporting News*, the Associated Press, the *Los Angeles Times*, the *New York Times*, the *New York Post*, the *New York Daily News*, *Newsday*, the

Washington Post, the *Boston Globe*, the *Dallas Morning News*, the *Houston Chronicle*, the *Detroit Free Press*, the *Kansas City Star*, the *Oklahoman*, and the *Tulsa World*; ESPN Archives, MLB.com, the New York Yankees, Susan Naulty of the Richard Nixon Presidential Library in Yorba Linda, California, the National Archives and Records Administration, the reference departments at the New York Public Library, the Beverly Hills Public Library, the Santa Monica Public Library, the Dallas Public Library, and the Library of Congress; and the administration of the Commerce [Oklahoma] Unified School District.

I want to thank, too, Christina Kahrl, my editor on my Mickey Mantle biography at Brassey's Inc., for her sensitive editing and commentary on drafts of the manuscript. Christina isn't just a great editor but one of the most knowledgeable baseball writers in America. Although she wasn't involved in editing *DiMag & Mick*, her contributions on *Mickey Mantle: America's Prodigal Son* were invaluable in developing the DiMaggio-Mantle dual biography.

As always, I am especially indebted to my late parents: my mother, Maria Emma, for always encouraging my interest in heroes in general and Mickey Mantle in particular; my father, Antonio Sr., for sparking my love of baseball as a youth and spending countless hours over the years talking baseball and forever debating the merits of DiMaggio and Mantle.

Special gratitude goes out to my muse, Jeter, the prince of all Labrador retrievers.

This book might never have been written without the inspiration and sacrifice of my wife and our sons. Both Trey and Ryan have helped at various times in the research, writing, and editing of the book, relentless in inspiring the pursuit of the smallest details and the most obscure of anecdotes while holding back a Yankee fan's overzealous romanticism of both DiMaggio and Mantle. My wife Renee, the fairest of them all, has been the guiding light of the book from the very beginning—willing to sacrifice vacations, movie nights, and more for whatever research and work the project required. Her devotion and love—and the love of my sons—are my proof once again that there is a God.

Tony Castro
Coronado Island, California

APPENDIX A

MICKEY MANTLE'S HALL OF FAME SPEECH
AUGUST 12, 1974, COOPERSTOWN, NEW YORK

Thank you very much, Commissioner. I would really like to thank you for leaving out those strikeouts. He gave all those records, but he didn't say anything about all those strikeouts. I was the world champion in striking out and everything, I'm sure. I don't know for sure, but I'm almost positive I must have had that record in the World Series, too. I broke Babe Ruth's record for all-time strikeouts. He only had, like, 1,500 I think. I ended up with 1,710. So that's one that no one will ever break probably, because, if you strike out that much, you don't get to play very long. I just lucked out.

One of the reasons I'm in the Hall of Fame right now is not because of my speaking, so everybody be patient here. I know it's hot and I'll try to get through with what I gotta say real fast here. I was named after a Hall of Famer. I think this is the first time it's ever happened that a guy's ever come into the Hall of Fame that was named after one. Before I was born, my father lived and died for baseball and he named me after a Hall of Famer: Mickey Cochrane. I'm not sure if my dad knew it or not, but his real name was Gordon. I hope there's no Gordons here today, but I'm glad that he didn't name me Gordon.

He had the foresight to realize that someday in baseball that left-handed hitters were going to hit against right-handed pitchers and right-handed hitters were going to hit against left-handed pitchers; and he taught me, he and his father, to switch-hit at a real young age, when I first started to learn how to play ball. And my dad always told me if I could hit both ways when I got ready to go to the major leagues, that I would have a better chance of playing. And believe it or not, the year that I came to the Yankees is when Casey started platooning everybody. So he did realize that that was going to happen someday, and it did. So I was lucky that they taught me how to switch-hit when I was young.

We lived in a little town called Commerce, Oklahoma, and my mother, who is here today—I'd like to introduce her right now . . . Mom. We didn't have a lot of money or anything. She used to make my uniforms and we would buy the cleats or get 'em off of somebody else's shoes or somethin' and then we would take 'em and have 'em put onto a pair of my street shoes that were getting old. So that's how we started out. We lived in Commerce till I can remember I was about in high school, then we moved out to a farm. We had a 160-acre farm out in Whitebird, Oklahoma, I remember. I had three brothers, but one of them was too little. My mom used to have to make the twins come out and play ball with me. We dozed a little ballpark out in the pasture and I think that I probably burnt my twins out on baseball. I think by the time the twins got old enough to play ball they were tired of it, because I used to make 'em shag flies for me and play all day, which I'm sorry of because they could have been great ballplayers.

My dad really is probably the most influential thing that ever happened to me in my life. He loved baseball, I loved it and, like I say, he named me after a baseball player. He worked in the mines, and when he came home at night, why, he would come out and, after we milked the cows, we would go ahead and play ball till dark. I don't know how he kept doing it.

I think the first real baseball uniform—and I'm sure it is—the most proud I ever was was when I went to Baxter Springs in Kansas and I played on the Baxter Springs Whiz Kids. We had—that was the first time—I'll never forget the guy, his name was Barney Burnett, gave me a uniform and it had a BW on the cap there and it said Whiz Kids on the back. I really thought I was somethin' when I got that uniform. It was the first one my mom hadn't made for me. It was really somethin'.

There is a man and a woman here that were really nice to me all through the years, Mr. and Mrs. Harold Youngman. I don't know if all of you have ever heard about any of my business endeavors or not, but some of 'em weren't too good. Probably the worst thing I ever did was movin' away from Mr. Youngman. We went and moved to Dallas, Texas, in 1957, but Mr. Youngman built a Holiday Inn in Joplin, Missouri, and called it Mickey Mantle's Holiday Inn. And we were doin' pretty good there, and Mr. Youngman said, 'You know, you're half of this thing, so why don't you do something for it.' So we had real good chicken there and I made up a slogan. Merlyn doesn't want me to tell this, but I'm going to tell it anyway. I made up the slogan for our chicken and I said, "To get a better piece of chicken, you'd have to be a rooster." And I don't know if that's what closed up our Holiday Inn or not, but we didn't do too good after that. No, actually, it was really a good deal.

Also, in Baxter Springs, the ballpark is right by the highway, and Tom Greenwade, the Yankee scout, was coming by there one day. He saw this ball game goin' on and I was playing in it and he stopped to watch the game. I'm making this kind of fast; it's getting a little hot. And I hit three home runs that day and Greenwade, the Yankee scout, stopped and talked to me. He was actually on his way to Broken Arrow, Oklahoma, to sign another shortstop. I was playing shortstop at that time, and I hit three home runs that day. A couple of them went in the river—one right-handed and one left-handed—and he stopped and he said, "You're not out of high school yet, so I really can't talk to you yet, but I'll be back when you get out of high school."

In 1949, Tom Greenwade came back to Commerce the night that I was supposed to go to my commencement exercises. He asked the principal of the school if I could go play ball. The Whiz Kids had a game that night. He took me. I hit another home run or two that night, so he signed me and I went to Independence, Kansas, Class D League, and started playing for the Yankees. I was very fortunate to play for Harry Craft. He had a great ballclub there. We have one man here in the audience today who I played with in the minors, Carl Lombardi. He was on those teams, so he knows we had two of the greatest teams in minor-league baseball at that time, or any time probably, and I was very fortunate to have played with those two teams.

I was lucky when I got out. I played at Joplin. The next year, I came to the Yankees. And I was lucky to play with Whitey Ford, Yogi Berra, Joe DiMaggio, Phil Rizzuto—who came up with me—and I appreciate it. He's been a great friend all the way through for me. Lots of times I've teased Whitey about how I could have played five more years if it hadn't been for him, but, believe me, when Ralph Houk used to say that I was the leader of the Yankees, he was just kiddin' everybody. Our real leader was Whitey Ford all the time. I'm sure that everybody will tell you that.

Casey Stengel's here in the Hall of Fame already and, outside of my dad, I would say that probably Casey is the man who is most responsible for me standing right here today. The first thing he did was to take me off of shortstop and get me out in the outfield where I wouldn't have to handle so many balls.

At this time I'd like to introduce my family. I introduced my mother. Merlyn, my wife, we've been married 22 years. That's a record where I come from. Mickey, my oldest boy, David, Billy, and Danny. That's my family that I've been with for so long.

I listened to Mr. Terry make a talk last night just for the Hall of Famers, and he said that he hoped we would come back, and I just hope that Whitey and I can live up to the expectation and what these here guys stand for. I'm sure we're going to try to. I just would—before I leave—would like to thank everybody for coming up here. It's been a great day for all of us and I appreciate it very much.

Appendix B

Bob Costas's Eulogy

It occurs to me as we're all sitting here thinking of Mickey, he's probably somewhere getting an earful from Casey Stengel, and no doubt quite confused by now.

One of Mickey's fondest wishes was that he be remembered as a great teammate, to know that the men he played with thought well of him.

But it was more than that. Moose and Whitey and Tony and Yogi and Bobby and Hank, what a remarkable team you were. And the stories of the visits you guys made to Mickey's bedside the last few days were heartbreakingly tender. It meant everything to Mickey, as would the presence of so many baseball figures past and present here today.

I was honored to be asked to speak by the Mantle family today. I am not standing here as a broadcaster. Mel Allen is the eternal voice of the Yankees and that would be his place. And there are others here with a longer and deeper association with Mickey than mine.

But I guess I'm here, not so much to speak for myself as to simply represent the millions of baseball-loving kids who grew up in the 50s and 60s and for whom Mickey Mantle was baseball.

And more than that, he was a presence in our lives—a fragile hero to whom we had an emotional attachment so strong and lasting that it defied logic. Mickey often said he didn't understand it, this enduring connection and affection—for men now in their 40s and 50s, otherwise perfectly sensible, who went dry in the mouth and stammered like schoolboys in the presence of Mickey Mantle.

Maybe Mick was uncomfortable with it, not just because of his basic shyness, but because he was always too honest to regard himself as some kind of deity.

But that was never really the point. In a very different time than today, the first baseball commissioner, Kenesaw Mountain Landis, said every boy builds a shrine to some baseball hero, and before that shrine, a candle always burns.

For a huge portion of my generation, Mickey Mantle was that baseball hero. And for reasons that no statistics, no dry recitation of facts can possibly capture, he was the most compelling baseball hero of our lifetime. And he was our symbol of baseball at a time when the game meant something to us that perhaps it no longer does.

Mickey Mantle had those dual qualities so seldom seen, exuding dynamism and excitement but at the same time touching your heart— flawed, wounded. We knew there was something poignant about Mickey Mantle before we knew what poignant meant.

We didn't just root for him, we felt for him.

Long before many of us ever cracked a serious book, we knew something about mythology as we watched Mickey Mantle run out a home run through the lengthening shadows of a late Sunday afternoon at Yankee Stadium.

There was greatness in him, but vulnerability too.

He was our guy. When he was hot, we felt great. When he slumped or got hurt, we sagged a bit too. We tried to crease our caps like him; kneel in an imaginary on-deck circle like him; run like him heads down, elbows up.

Billy Crystal is here today. Billy says that at his bar mitzvah he spoke in an Oklahoma drawl. Billy's here today because he loved Mickey Mantle, and millions more who felt like him are here today in spirit as well.

It's been said that the truth is never pure and rarely simple.

Mickey Mantle was too humble and honest to believe that the whole truth about him could be found on a Wheaties box or a baseball card. But the emotional truths of childhood have a power to transcend objective fact. They stay with us through all the years, withstanding the ambivalence that so often accompanies the experiences of adults.

That's why we can still recall the immediate tingle in that instant of recognition when a Mickey Mantle popped up in a pack of Topps bubble gum cards—a treasure lodged between an Eli Grba and a Pumpsie Green.

That's why we smile today, recalling those October afternoons when we'd sneak a transistor radio into school to follow Mickey and the Yankees in the World Series.

Or when I think of Mr. Tomasee, a very wise sixth-grade teacher who understood that the World Series was more important, at least for one day, than any school lesson could be. So he brought his black-and-white TV from home, plugged it in and let us watch it right there in school through the flicker and the static. It was richer and more compelling than anything I've seen on a high-resolution, big-screen TV.

Of course, the bad part, Bobby, was that Koufax struck 15 of you guys out that day.

My phone's been ringing the past few weeks as Mickey fought for his life. I've heard from people I hadn't seen or talked to in years—guys I played stickball with, even some guys who took Willie's side in those endless Mantle-Mays arguments. They're grown up now. They have their families. They're not even necessarily big baseball fans anymore. But they felt something hearing about Mickey, and they figured I did too.

In the last year, Mickey Mantle, always so hard on himself, finally came to accept and appreciate that distinction between a role model and a hero. The first he often was not, the second he always will be.

In the end, people got it. And Mickey Mantle got from America something other than misplaced and mindless celebrity worship. He got something far more meaningful. He got love—love for what he had been; love for what he made us feel; love for the humanity and sweetness that was always there mixed in with the flaws and all the pain that wracked his body and his soul.

We wanted to tell him that it was OK, that what he had been was enough. We hoped he felt that Mutt Mantle would have understood and that Merlyn and the boys loved him.

And then in the end, something remarkable happened—the way it does for champions. Mickey Mantle rallied. His heart took over, and he had some innings as fine as any in 1956 or with his buddy, Roger, in 1961.

But this time, he did it in the harsh and trying summer of '95. And what he did was stunning. The sheer grace of that ninth inning—the humility, the sense of humor, the total absence of self-pity, the simple eloquence and honesty of his pleas to others to take heed of his mistakes.

All of America watched in admiration. His doctors said he was, in many ways, the most remarkable patient they'd ever seen. His bravery, so stark and real, that even those used to seeing people in dire circumstances were moved by his example.

Because of that example, organ donations are up dramatically all across America. A cautionary tale has been honestly told and perhaps will affect some lives for the better.

And our last memories of Mickey Mantle are as heroic as the first.

None of us, Mickey included, would want to be held to account for every moment of our lives. But how many of us could say that our best moments were as magnificent as his?

This is the cartoon from this morning's *Dallas Morning News*. Maybe some of you saw it. It got torn a little bit on the way from the hotel to here. There's a figure here, St. Peter I take it to be, with his arm around Mickey, that broad back and the number 7. He's holding his book of admissions. He says, "Kid, that was the most courageous ninth inning I've ever seen."

It brings to mind a story Mickey liked to tell on himself and maybe some of you have heard it. He pictured himself at the pearly gates, met by St. Peter who shook his head and said "Mick, we checked the record. We know some of what went on. Sorry, we can't let you in. But before you go, God wants to know if you'd sign these six dozen baseballs."

Well, there were days when Mickey Mantle was so darn good that we kids would bet that even God would want his autograph. But like the cartoon says, I don't think Mick needed to worry much about the other part.

I just hope God has a place for him where he can run again. Where he can play practical jokes on his teammates and smile that boyish smile, 'cause God knows, no one's perfect. And God knows there's something special about heroes.

So long, Mick. Thanks.

APPENDIX C

Joe DiMaggio's 56-Game Hitting Streak, 1941

GAME	DATE	PITCHER(S)	TEAM	AB	R	H	2B	3B	HR	RBI
1	5-15	Eddie Smith	Chicago	4	0	1	0	0	0	1
2	5-16	Thornton Lee	Chicago	4	2	2	0	1	1	1
3	5-17	Johnny Rigney	Chicago	3	1	1	0	0	0	0
4	5-18	Bob Harris Johnny Niggeling	St. Louis	3	3	2 1	1	0	0	1
5	5-19	Denny Galehouse	St. Louis	3	0	1	1	0	0	0
6	5-20	Elden Auker	St. Louis	5	1	1	0	0	0	1
7	5-21	Schoolboy Rowe Al Benton	Detroit	5	0	1 1	0	0	0	1
8	5-22	Archie McKain	Detroit	4	0	1	0	0	0	1
9	5-23	Dick Newsome	Boston	5	0	1	0	0	0	2
10	5-24	Earl Johnson	Boston	4	2	1	0	0	0	2
11	5-25	Lefty Grove (HOF)	Boston	4	0	1	0	0	0	0
12	5-27	Ken Chase Red Anderson Alex Carrasquel	Washington	5	3	1 2 1	0	0	1	3
13	5-28	Sid Hudson	Washington	4	1	1	0	1	0	0
14	5-29	Steve Sundra	Washington	3	1	1	0	0	0	0

GAME	DATE	PITCHER(S)	TEAM	AB	R	H	2B	3B	HR	RBI
15	5-30	Earl Johnson	Boston	2	1	1	0	0	0	0
16	5-30	Mickey Harris	Boston	3	0	1	1	0	0	0
17	6-01	Al Milnar	Cleveland	4	1	1	0	0	0	0
18	6-01	Mel Harder	Cleveland	4	0	1	0	0	0	0
19	6-02	Bob Feller (HOF)	Cleveland	4	2	2	1	0	0	0
20	6-03	Dizzy Trout	Detroit	4	1	1	0	0	1	1
21	6-05	Hal Newhouser (HOF)	Detroit	5	1	1	0	1	0	1
22	6-07	Bob Muncrief Johnny Allen George Caster	St. Louis	5	2	1 1 1	0	0	0	1
23	6-08	Elden Auker	St. Louis	4	3	2	0	0	2	4
24	6-08	George Caster Jack Kramer	St. Louis	4	1	1 1	1	0	1	3
25	6-10	Johnny Rigney	Chicago	5	1	1	0	0	0	0
26	6-12	Thornton Lee	Chicago	4	1	2	0	0	1	1
27	6-14	Bob Feller (HOF)	Cleveland	2	0	1	1	0	0	1
28	6-15	Jim Bagby	Cleveland	3	1	1	0	0	1	1
29	6-16	Al Milnar	Cleveland	5	0	1	1	0	0	0
30	6-17	Johnny Rigney	Chicago	4	1	1	0	0	0	0
31	6-18	Thornton Lee	Chicago	3	0	1	0	0	0	0

GAME	DATE	PITCHER(S)	TEAM	AB	R	H	2B	3B	HR	RBI
32	6-19	Eddie Smith / Buck Ross	Chicago	3	2	1 / 2	0	0	1	2
33	6-20	Bobo Newsom / Archie McKain	Detroit	5	3	2 / 2	1	0	0	1
34	6-21	Dizzy Trout	Detroit	4	0	1	0	0	0	1
35	6-22	Hal Newhouser (HOF) / Bobo Newsom	Detroit	5	1	1 / 1	1	0	1	2
36	6-24	Bob Muncrief	St. Louis	4	1	1	0	0	0	0
37	6-25	Denny Galehouse	St. Louis	4	1	1	0	0	1	3
38	6-26	Elden Auker	St. Louis	4	0	1	1	0	0	1
39	6-27	Chubby Dean	Philadelphia	3	1	2	0	0	1	2
40	6-28	Johnny Babich / Lum Harris	Philadelphia	5	1	1 / 1	1	0	0	0
41	6-29	Dutch Leonard	Washington	4	1	1	1	0	0	0
42	6-29	Red Anderson	Washington	5	1	1	0	0	0	1
43	7-01	Mickey Harris / Mike Ryba	Boston	4	0	1 / 1	0	0	0	1
44	7-01	Jack Wilson	Boston	3	1	1	0	0	0	1
45	7-02	Dick Newsome	Boston	5	1	1	0	0	1	3
46	7-05	Phil Marchildon	Philadelphia	4	2	1	0	0	1	2

GAME	DATE	PITCHER(S)	TEAM	AB	R	H	2B	3B	HR	RBI
47	7-06	Johnny Babich Bump Hadley	Philadelphia	5	2	2 2	1	0	0	2
48	7-06	Jack Knott	Philadelphia	4	0	2	0	1	0	2
49	7-10	Johnny Niggeling	St. Louis	2	0	1	0	0	0	0
50	7-11	Bob Harris Jack Kramer	St. Louis	5	1	3 1	0	0	1	2
51	7-12	Elden Auker Bob Muncrief	St. Louis	5	1	1 1	1	0	0	1
52	7-13	Ted Lyons (HOF) Jack Hallett	Chicago	4	2	2 1	0	0	0	0
53	7-13	Thornton Lee	Chicago	4	0	1	0	0	0	0
54	7-14	Johnny Rigney	Chicago	3	0	1	0	0	0	0
55	7-15	Eddie Smith	Chicago	4	1	2	1	0	0	2
56	7-16	Al Milnar	Cleveland	4	3	2	1	0	0	0

Appendix D

Mickey Mantle's Batting Statistics

Minor League Career

Year	Team	G	AB	R	H	2B	3B	HR	RBI	Avg.	SLG.
1949	Independence K-O-M	89	323	54	101	15	7	7	63	.313	.467
1950	Joplin W.A.	137	519	141	199	30	12	26	136	.383	.638
1951	Kansas City A.A.	40	166	32	60	9	3	11	50	.361	.651

Major League Regular Season

Year	G	AB	R	H	2B	3B	HR	RBI	AVG.	BB	K	OBP	SLG.
1951	96	341	61	91	11	5	13	65	.267	43	74	.349	.443
1952	142	549	94	171	37	7	23	87	.311	75	111	.394	.530
1953	127	461	105	136	24	3	21	92	.295	79	90	.398	.497
1954	146	543	129	163	17	12	27	102	.300	102	107	.408	.525
1955	147	517	121	158	25	11	37	99	.306	113	97	.431	.611
1956	150	533	132	188	22	5	52	130	.353	112	99	.464	.705
1957	144	474	121	173	28	6	23	94	.365	146	75	.512	.665
1958	150	519	127	158	21	1	42	97	.304	129	120	.443	.592
1959	144	541	104	154	23	4	31	75	.285	94	126	.390	.514
1960	153	527	119	145	17	6	40	94	.275	111	125	.399	.558
1961	153	514	132	163	16	6	54	128	.317	126	112	.448	.687
1962	123	377	96	121	15	1	30	89	.321	122	78	.486	.605
1963	65	172	40	54	8	0	15	35	.314	40	32	.441	.622
1964	143	465	92	141	25	2	35	111	.303	99	102	.423	.591
1965	122	361	44	92	12	1	19	46	.255	73	76	.379	.452
1966	108	333	40	96	12	1	23	56	.288	57	76	.389	.538
1967	144	440	63	108	17	0	22	55	.245	107	113	.391	.434
1968	144	435	57	103	14	1	18	54	.237	106	97	.385	.398
Totals	2401	8102	1677	2415	344	72	536	1509	.298	1734	1710	.421	.557

World Series

Year	Opponent	G	AB	R	H	2B	3B	HR	RBI	AVG.	BB	K	OBP	SLG.	SB
1951	New York (N)	2	5	1	1	0	0	0	0	.200	0	1	.429	.200	0
1952	Brooklyn	7	29	5	10	1	1	2	3	.345	3	4	.406	.655	0
1953	Brooklyn	6	24	3	5	0	0	2	7	.208	3	8	.296	.458	0
1955	Brooklyn	3	10	1	2	0	0	1	1	.200	0	2	.200	.500	0
1956	Brooklyn	7	24	6	6	1	0	3	4	.250	6	5	.400	.667	1
1957	Milwaukee	6	19	3	5	0	0	1	2	.263	3	1	.364	.421	0
1958	Milwaukee	7	24	4	6	0	1	2	3	.250	7	4	.419	.583	0
1960	Pittsburgh	7	25	8	10	1	0	3	11	.400	8	9	.545	.800	0
1961	Cincinnati	2	6	0	1	0	0	0	0	.167	0	2	.167	.167	0
1962	San Francisco	7	25	2	3	1	0	0	0	.120	4	5	.241	.160	2
1963	Los Angeles	4	15	1	2	0	0	1	1	.133	1	5	.187	.333	0
1964	St. Louis	7	24	8	8	2	0	3	8	.333	6	8	.467	.792	0
Totals		65	230	42	59	6	2	18	40	.257	43	54	.374	.535	3

Mickey Mantle's Career Home Runs

THE COMPLETE YEAR BY YEAR LIST
PLUS WORLD SERIES AND ALL-STAR GAMES

Includes Date, Lefty or Righty, Location, Team, and Pitcher
(First number is career HR total; number in parentheses is HR number
for season).

1951: 13 Home Runs

1 (1). May 1, 1951, LH, Comiskey Park vs. Chicago White Sox, Pitcher:
Randy Gumpert (RH)

2 (2). May 4, 1951, LH, Sportsman's Park vs. St. Louis Browns, Pitcher:
Duane Pillette (RH)

3 (3). May 13, 1951, RH, Shibe Park vs. Philadelphia A's, Pitcher: Alex
Kellner (LH)

4 (4). May 16, 1951, RH, Yankee Stadium vs. Cleveland Indians, Pitcher: Dick Rozek (LH)

5 (5). June 19, 1951, LH, Yankee Stadium vs. Chicago White Sox,
Pitcher: Lou Kretlow (RH)

6 (6). June 19, 1951, LH, Yankee Stadium vs. Chicago White Sox,
Pitcher: Joe Dobson (RH)

7 (7). July 7, 1951, LH, Fenway Park vs. Boston Red Sox, Pitcher: Ellis
Kinder (RH)

8 (8). August 25, 1951, LH, Municipal Stadium vs. Cleveland Indians,
Pitcher: Mike Garcia (RH)

9 (9). August 29, 1951, LH, Sportsman's Park vs. St. Louis Browns,
Pitcher: Satchel Paige (RH)

10 (10). September 8, 1951, LH, Yankee Stadium vs. Washington Senators, Pitcher: Sid Hudson (RH)

11 (11). September 9, 1951, LH, Yankee Stadium vs. Washington Senators, Pitcher: Dick Starr (RH)

12 (12). September 12, 1951, LH, Yankee Stadium vs. Detroit Tigers, Pitcher: Virgil Trucks (RH)

13 (13). September 19, 1951, LH, Yankee Stadium vs. Chicago White Sox, Pitcher: Lou Kretlow (RH)

Number of games in which Mickey homered in 1951: 13
Yankees record in 1951 in games in which Mickey homered: 11-2 (.846)

1952: 23 Home Runs
14 (1). April 21, 1952, RH, Yankee Stadium vs. Philadelphia A's, Pitcher: Bobby Shantz (LH)

15 (2). April 30, 1952, RH, Yankee Stadium vs. St. Louis Browns, Pitcher: Bob Cain (LH)

16 (3). May 30, 1952, RH, Yankee Stadium vs. Philadelphia A's, Pitcher: Bobby Shantz (LH)

17 (4). June 15, 1952, LH, Municipal Stadium vs. Cleveland Indians, Pitcher: Bob Lemon (RH)

18 (5). June 17, 1952, RH, Briggs Stadium vs. Detroit Tigers, Pitcher: Billy Hoeft (LH)

19 (6). June 22, 1952, LH, Comiskey Park vs. Chicago White Sox, Pitcher: Marv Grissom (RH)

20 (7). June 27, 1952, LH, Yankee Stadium vs. Philadelphia A's, Pitcher: Bob Hooper (RH)

21 (8). July 5, 1952, RH, Shibe Park vs. Philadelphia A's, Pitcher: Alex Kellner (LH)

22 (9). July 6, 1952, RH, Shibe Park vs. Philadelphia A's, Pitcher: Bobby Shantz (LH)

23 (10). July 13, 1952, LH, Yankee Stadium vs. Detroit Tigers, Pitcher: Marlin Stuart (RH)

24 (11). July 13, 1952, RH, Yankee Stadium vs. Detroit Tigers, Pitcher: Hal Newhouser (LH)

25 (12). July 15, 1952, LH, Yankee Stadium vs. Cleveland Indians, Pitcher: Early Wynn (RH)

26 (13). July 17, 1952, LH, Yankee Stadium vs. Cleveland Indians, Pitcher: Steve Gromek (RH)

27 (14). July 25, 1952, LH, Briggs Stadium vs. Detroit Tigers, Pitcher: Art Houtteman (RH)

28 (15). July 26, 1952, RH, Briggs Stadium vs. Detroit Tigers, Pitcher: Ted Gray (LH)

29 (16). July 29, 1952, RH, Comiskey Park vs. Chicago White Sox, Pitcher: Chuck Stobbs (LH)

30 (17). August 11, 1952, LH, Yankee Stadium vs. Boston Red Sox, Pitcher: Sid Hudson (RH)

31 (18). August 11, 1952, LH, Yankee Stadium vs. Boston Red Sox, Pitcher: Ralph Brickner (RH)

32 (19). August 30, 1952, LH, Yankee Stadium vs. Washington Senators, Pitcher: Randy Gumpert (RH)

33 (20). September 14, 1952, RH, Municipal Stadium vs. Cleveland Indians, Pitcher: Lou Brissie (LH)

34 (21). September 17, 1952, RH, Briggs Stadium vs. Detroit Tigers, Pitcher: Bill Wight (LH)

35 (22). September 24, 1952, RH, Fenway Park vs. Boston Red Sox, Pitcher: Mel Parnell (LH)

36 (23). September 26, 1952, LH, Shibe Park vs. Philadelphia A's, Pitcher: Harry Byrd (RH)

Number of games in which Mickey homered in 1952: 22
Yankees record in 1952 in games in which Mickey homered: 14-8 (.636)

1953: 21 Home Runs

37 (1). April 17, 1953, RH, Griffith Stadium vs. Washington Senators, Pitcher: Chuck Stobbs (LH)

38 (2). April 23, 1953, LH, Yankee Stadium vs. Boston Red Sox, Pitcher: Ellis Kinder (RH)

39 (3). April 28, 1953, RH, Busch Stadium vs. St. Louis Browns, Pitcher: Bob Cain (LH)

40 (4). April 30, 1953, RH, Comiskey Park vs. Chicago White Sox, Pitcher: Gene Bearden (LH)

41 (5). May 9, 1953, RH, Fenway Park vs. Boston Red Sox, Pitcher: Willie Werle (LH)

42 (6). May 25, 1953, RH, Yankee Stadium vs. Boston Red Sox, Pitcher: Mickey McDermott (LH)

43 (7). June 4, 1953, RH, Comiskey Park vs. Chicago White Sox, Pitcher: Billy Pierce (LH)

44 (8). June 5, 1953, LH, Busch Stadium vs. St. Louis Browns, Pitcher: Bobo Holloman (RH)

45 (9). June 11, 1953, LH, Briggs Stadium vs. Detroit Tigers, Pitcher: Art Houtteman (RH)

46 (10). June 18, 1953, RH, Yankee Stadium vs. St. Louis Browns, Pitcher: Bob Cain (LH)

47 (11). June 21, 1953, RH, Yankee Stadium vs. Detroit Tigers, Pitcher: Hal Newhouser (LH)

48 (12). June 23, 1953, LH, Yankee Stadium vs. Chicago White Sox, Pitcher: Virgil Trucks (RH)

49 (13). July 16, 1953, RH, Connie Mack Stadium vs. Philadelphia A's, Pitcher: Frank Fanovich (LH)

50 (14). July 26, 1953, RH, Briggs Stadium vs. Detroit Tigers, Pitcher: Al Albert (LH)

51 (15). July 26, 1953, LH, Briggs Stadium vs. Detroit Tigers, Pitcher: Steve Gromek (RH)

52 (16). August 7, 1953, LH, Yankee Stadium vs. Chicago White Sox, Pitcher: Connie Johnson (RH)

53 (17). September 1, 1953, LH, Comiskey Park vs. Chicago White Sox, Pitcher: Virgil Trucks (RH)

54 (18). September 7, 1953, RH, Fenway Park vs. Boston Red Sox, Pitcher: Mel Parnell (LH)

55 (19). September 9, 1953, RH, Yankee Stadium vs. Chicago White Sox, Pitcher: Billy Pierce (LH)

56 (20). September 12, 1953, RH, Yankee Stadium vs. Detroit Tigers, Pitcher: Billy Hoeft (LH)

57 (21). September 20, 1953, RH, Fenway Park vs. Boston Red Sox, Pitcher: Mickey McDermott (LH)

Number of games in which Mickey homered in 1953: 21
Yankees record in 1953 in games in which Mickey homered: 15-6 (.714)

1954: 27 Home Runs

58 (1). April 19, 1954, RH, Fenway Park vs. Boston Red Sox, Pitcher: Mel Parnell (LH)

59 (2). April 21, 1954, RH, Yankee Stadium vs. Boston Red Sox, Pitcher: Lou Kiely (LH)

60 (3). May 7, 1954, RH, Yankee Stadium vs. Philadelphia A's, Pitcher: Morrie Martin (LH)

61 (4). May 21, 1954, LH, Yankee Stadium vs. Boston Red Sox, Pitcher: Frank Sullivan (RH)

62 (5). May 22, 1954, LH, Yankee Stadium vs. Boston Red Sox, Pitcher: Tex Clevenger (RH)

63 (6). May 23, 1954, RH, Yankee Stadium vs. Boston Red Sox, Pitcher: Bill Henry (LH)

64 (7). May 25, 1954, LH, Griffith Stadium vs. Washington Senators, Pitcher: Sonny Dixon (RH)

65 (8). May 29, 1954, LH, Fenway Park vs. Boston Red Sox, Pitcher: Sid Hudson (RH)

66 (9). May 30, 1954, LH, Fenway Park vs. Boston Red Sox, Pitcher: Willard Nixon (RH)

67 (10). June 6, 1954, LH, Yankee Stadium vs. Baltimore Orioles, Pitcher: Don Larsen (RH)

68 (11). June 10, 1954, LH, Yankee Stadium vs. Detroit Tigers, Pitcher: Ralph Branca (RH)

69 (12). June 20, 1954, LH, Comiskey Park vs. Chicago White Sox, Pitcher: Mike Fornieles (RH)

70 (13). June 26, 1954, LH, Municipal Stadium vs. Cleveland Indians, Pitcher: Bob Hooper (RH)

71 (14). June 30, 1954, LH, Fenway Park vs. Boston Red Sox, Pitcher: Willard Nixon (RH)

72 (15). July 1, 1954, LH, Fenway Park vs. Boston Red Sox, Pitcher: Frank Sullivan (RH)

73 (16). July 3, 1954, LH, Yankee Stadium vs. Washington Senators, Pitcher: Bob Porterfield (RH)

74 (17). July 5, 1954, LH, Connie Mack Stadium vs. Philadelphia A's, Pitcher: Arnie Portocarrero (RH)

75 (18). July 7, 1954, LH, Yankee Stadium vs. Boston Red Sox, Pitcher: Tom Brewer (RH)

76 (19). July 19, 1954, RH, Yankee Stadium vs. Detroit Tigers, Pitcher: Ted Gray (LH)

77 (20). July 22, 1954, LH, Yankee Stadium vs. Chicago White Sox, Pitcher: Don Johnson (RH)

78 (21). July 28, 1954, RH, Comiskey Park vs. Chicago White Sox, Pitcher: Jack Harshman (LH)

79 (22). August 5, 1954, LH, Municipal Stadium vs. Cleveland Indians, Pitcher: Early Wynn (RH)

80 (23). August 5, 1954, LH, Municipal Stadium vs. Cleveland Indians, Pitcher: Ray Narleski

81 (24). August 8, 1954, RH, Briggs Stadium vs. Detroit Tigers, Pitcher: Billy Hoeft (LH)

82 (25). August 12, 1954, LH, Yankee Stadium vs. Philadelphia A's, Pitcher: Arnie Portocarrero (RH)

83 (26). August 15, 1954, LH, Yankee Stadium vs. Boston Red Sox, Pitcher: Hal "Skinny" Brown (RH)

84 (27). September 2, 1954, LH, Yankee Stadium vs. Cleveland Indians, Pitcher: Bob Lemon (RH)

Number of games in which Mickey homered in 1954: 26
Yankees record in 1954 in games in which Mickey homered: 21-5 (.846)

1955: 37 Home Runs (League Leader)
85 (1). April 13, 1955, LH, Yankee Stadium vs. Washington Senators, Pitcher: Ted Abernathy (RH)

86 (2). April 18, 1955, LH, Memorial Stadium vs. Baltimore Orioles, Pitcher: Harry Byrd (RH)

87 (3). April 28, 1955, LH, Municipal Stadium vs. Kansas City A's, Pitcher: Charlie Bishop (RH)

88 (4). May 3, 1955, LH, Municipal Stadium vs. Cleveland Indians, Pitcher: Mike Garcia (RH)

89 (5). May 6, 1955, LH, Fenway Park vs. Boston Red Sox, Pitcher: Frank Sullivan (RH)

90 (6). May 7, 1955, LH, Fenway Park vs. Boston Red Sox, Pitcher: Ike Delock (RH)

91 (7). May 11, 1955, LH, Yankee Stadium vs. Cleveland Indians, Pitcher: Early Wynn (RH)

92 (8). May 13, 1955, LH, Yankee Stadium vs. Detroit Tigers, Pitcher: Steve Gromek (RH)

93 (9). May 13, 1955, LH, Yankee Stadium vs. Detroit Tigers, Pitcher: Steve Gromek (RH)

94 (10). May 13, 1955, RH, Yankee Stadium vs. Detroit Tigers, Pitcher: Bob Miller (LH)

95 (11). May 18, 1955, LH, Yankee Stadium vs. Chicago White Sox, Pitcher: Mike Fornieles (RH)

96 (12). June 3, 1955, RH, Comiskey Park vs. Chicago White Sox, Pitcher: Jack Harshman (LH)

97 (13). June 5, 1955, RH, Comiskey Park vs. Chicago White Sox, Pitcher: Billy Pierce (LH)

98 (14). June 6, 1955, RH, Briggs Stadium vs. Detroit Tigers, Pitcher: Bob Miller (LH)

99 (15). June 17, 1955, LH, Yankee Stadium vs. Chicago White Sox, Pitcher: Dick Donovan (RH)

100 (16). June 19, 1955, LH, Yankee Stadium vs. Chicago White Sox, Pitcher: Sandy Consuegra (RH)

101 (17). June 21, 1955, RH, Yankee Stadium vs. Kansas City A's, Pitcher: Alex Kellner (LH)

102 (18). June 22, 1955, LH, Yankee Stadium vs. Kansas City A's, Pitcher: Art Ditmar (RH)

103 (19). July 10, 1955, RH, Griffith Stadium vs. Washington Senators, Pitcher: Dean Stone (LH)

104 (20). July 10, 1955, RH, Griffith Stadium vs. Washington Senators, Pitcher: Dean Stone (LH)

105 (21). July 10, 1955, LH, Griffith Stadium vs. Washington Senators, Pitcher: Ted Abernathy (RH)

106 (22). July 28, 1955, LH, Yankee Stadium vs. Chicago White Sox, Pitcher: Connie Johnson (RH)

107 (23). July 31, 1955, RH, Yankee Stadium vs. Kansas City A's, Pitcher: Alex Kellner (LH)

108 (24). August 4, 1955, LH, Yankee Stadium vs. Cleveland Indians, Pitcher: Ray Narleski (RH)

109 (25). August 7, 1955, LH, Yankee Stadium vs. Detroit Tigers, Pitcher: Frank Lary (RH)

110 (26). August 7, 1955, LH, Yankee Stadium vs. Detroit Tigers, Pitcher: Babe Birrer (RH)

111 (27). August 14, 1955, RH, Memorial Stadium vs. Baltimore Orioles, Pitcher: Ed Lopat (LH)

112 (28). August 15, 1955, LH, Memorial Stadium vs. Baltimore Orioles, Pitcher: Ray Moore (RH)

113 (29). August 15, 1955, RH, Memorial Stadium vs. Baltimore Orioles, Pitcher: Art Schallock (LH)

114 (30). August 16, 1955, LH, Fenway Park vs. Boston Red Sox, Pitcher: Frank Sullivan (RH)

115 (31). August 19, 1955, LH, Yankee Stadium vs. Baltimore Orioles, Pitcher: Jim Wilson (RH)

116 (32). August 21, 1955, RH, Yankee Stadium vs. Baltimore Orioles, Pitcher: Ed Lopat (LH)

117 (33). August 24, 1955, LH, Briggs Stadium vs. Detroit Tigers, Pitcher: Steve Gromek (RH)

118 (34). August 28, 1955, LH, Comiskey Park vs. Chicago White Sox, Pitcher: Connie Johnson (RH)

119 (35). August 31, 1955, LH, Municipal Stadium vs. Kansas City A's, Pitcher: Arnie Portocarrero (RH)

120 (36). September 2, 1955, LH, Yankee Stadium vs. Washington Senators, Pitcher: Bob Porterfield (RH)

121 (37). September 4, 1955, LH, Yankee Stadium vs. Washington Senators, Pitcher: Pedro Ramos (RH)

Number of games in which Mickey homered in 1955: 32
Yankees record in 1955 in games in which Mickey homered: 27-5 (.844)

1956: 52 Home Runs (League Leader)

122 (1). April 17, 1956, LH, Griffith Stadium vs. Washington Senators, Pitcher: Camilo Pascual (RH)

123 (2). April 17, 1956, LH, Griffith Stadium vs. Washington Senators, Pitcher: Camilo Pascual (RH)

124 (3). April 20, 1956, LH, Yankee Stadium vs. Boston Red Sox, Pitcher: Ike Delock (RH)

125 (4). April 21, 1956, LH, Yankee Stadium vs. Boston Red Sox, Pitcher: George Susce (RH)

126 (5). May 1, 1956, LH, Yankee Stadium vs. Detroit Tigers, Pitcher: Steve Gromek (RH)

127 (6). May 2, 1956, LH, Yankee Stadium vs. Detroit Tigers, Pitcher: Frank Lary (RH)

128 (7). May 3, 1956, RH, Yankee Stadium vs. Kansas City A's, Pitcher: Art Ceccarelli (LH)

129 (8). May 5, 1956, LH, Yankee Stadium vs. Kansas City A's, Pitcher: Lou Kretlow (RH)

130 (9). May 5, 1956, LH, Yankee Stadium vs. Kansas City A's, Pitcher: Moe Burtschy (RH)

131 (10). May 8, 1956, LH, Yankee Stadium vs. Cleveland Indians, Pitcher: Early Wynn (RH)

132 (11). May 10, 1956, LH, Yankee Stadium vs. Cleveland Indians, Pitcher: Bob Lemon (RH)

133 (12). May 14, 1956, LH, Municipal Stadium vs. Cleveland Indians, Pitcher: Bob Lemon (RH)

134 (13). May 16, 1956, RH, Municipal Stadium vs. Cleveland Indians, Pitcher: Bud Daley (LH)

135 (14). May 18, 1956, RH, Comiskey Park vs. Chicago White Sox, Pitcher: Billy Pierce (LH)

136 (15). May 18, 1956, LH, Comiskey Park vs. Chicago White Sox, Pitcher: Dixie Howell (RH)

137 (16). May 21, 1956, LH, Municipal Stadium vs. Kansas City A's, Pitcher: Moe Burtschy (RH)

138 (17). May 24, 1956, LH, Briggs Stadium vs. Detroit Tigers, Pitcher: Duke Mass (RH)

139 (18). May 29, 1956, LH, Yankee Stadium vs. Boston Red Sox, Pitcher: Willard Nixon (RH)

140 (19). May 30, 1956, LH, Yankee Stadium vs. Washington Senators, Pitcher: Pedro Ramos (RH)

141 (20). May 30, 1956, LH, Yankee Stadium vs. Washington Senators, Pitcher: Camilo Pascual (RH)

142 (21). June 5, 1956, LH, Yankee Stadium vs. Kansas City A's, Pitcher: Lou Kretlow (RH)

143 (22). June 14, 1956, LH, Yankee Stadium vs. Chicago White Sox, Pitcher: Jim Wilson (RH)

144 (23). June 15, 1956, LH, Municipal Stadium vs. Cleveland Indians, Pitcher: Mike Garcia (RH)

145 (24). June 16, 1956, RH, Municipal Stadium vs. Cleveland Indians, Pitcher: Herb Score (LH)

146 (25). June 18, 1956, LH, Briggs Stadium vs. Detroit Tigers, Pitcher: Paul Foytack (RH)

147 (26). June 20, 1956, RH, Briggs Stadium vs. Detroit Tigers, Pitcher: Billy Hoeft (LH)

148 (27). June 20, 1956, RH, Briggs Stadium vs. Detroit Tigers, Pitcher: Billy Hoeft (LH)

149 (28). July 1, 1956, RH, Yankee Stadium vs. Washington Senators, Pitcher: Dean Stone (LH)

150 (29). July 1, 1956, LH, Yankee Stadium vs. Washington Senators, Pitcher: Bud Byerly (RH)

151 (30). July 14, 1956, RH, Yankee Stadium vs. Cleveland Indians, Pitcher: Herb Score (LH)

152 (31). July 18, 1956, LH, Yankee Stadium vs. Detroit Tigers, Pitcher: Paul Foytack (RH)

153 (32). July 22, 1956, LH, Yankee Stadium vs. Kansas City A's, Pitcher: Art Ditmar (RH)

154 (33). July 30, 1956, LH, Municipal Stadium vs. Cleveland Indians, Pitcher: Bob Lemon (RH)

155 (34). July 30, 1956, LH, Municipal Stadium vs. Cleveland Indians, Pitcher: Bob Feller (RH)

156 (35). August 4, 1956, LH, Briggs Stadium vs. Detroit Tigers, Pitcher: Virgil Trucks (RH)

157 (36). August 4, 1956, LH, Briggs Stadium vs. Detroit Tigers, Pitcher: Virgil Trucks (RH)

158 (37). August 5, 1956, LH, Briggs Stadium vs. Detroit Tigers, Pitcher: Jim Bunning (RH)

159 (38). August 8, 1956, LH, Griffith Stadium vs. Washington Senators, Pitcher: Camilo Pascual (RH)

160 (39). August 9, 1956, LH, Griffith Stadium vs. Washington Senators, Pitcher: Hal Griggs (RH)

161 (40). August 11, 1956, LH, Yankee Stadium vs. Baltimore Orioles, Pitcher: Hal "Skinny" Brown (RH)

162 (41). August 12, 1956, RH, Yankee Stadium vs. Baltimore Orioles, Pitcher: Dan Ferrarese (LH)

163 (42). August 14, 1956, RH, Yankee Stadium vs. Boston Red Sox, Pitcher: Mel Parnell (LH)

164 (43). August 23, 1956, RH, Yankee Stadium vs. Chicago White Sox, Pitcher: Paul LaPalme (LH)

165 (44). August 25, 1956, LH, Yankee Stadium vs. Chicago White Sox, Pitcher: Dick Donovan (RH)

166 (45). August 28, 1956, LH, Yankee Stadium vs. Kansas City A's, Pitcher: Art Ditmar (RH)

167 (46). August 29, 1956, RH, Yankee Stadium vs. Kansas City A's, Pitcher: Jack McMahan (LH)

168 (47). August 31, 1956, LH, Griffith Stadium vs. Washington Senators, Pitcher: Camilo Pascual (RH)

169 (48). September 13, 1956, LH, Municipal Stadium vs. Kansas City A's, Pitcher: Tom Gorman (RH)

170 (49). September 16, 1956, LH, Municipal Stadium vs. Cleveland Indians, Pitcher: Early Wynn (RH)

171 (50). September 18, 1956, RH, Comiskey Park vs. Chicago White Sox, Pitcher: Billy Pierce (LH)

172 (51). September 21, 1956, LH, Fenway Park vs. Boston Red Sox, Pitcher: Frank Sullivan (RH)

173 (52). September 28, 1956, LH, Yankee Stadium vs. Boston Red Sox, Pitcher: Bob Porterfield (RH)

Number of games in which Mickey homered in 1956: 45
Yankees record in 1956 in games in which Mickey homered: 30-15 (.667)

1957: 34 Home Runs
174 (1). April 22, 1957, RH, Griffith Stadium vs. Washington Senators, Pitcher: Chuck Stobbs (LH)
175 (2). April 24, 1957, LH, Yankee Stadium vs. Baltimore Orioles, Pitcher: Connie Johnson (RH)
176 (3). May 5, 1957, RH, Comiskey Park vs. Chicago White Sox, Pitcher: Billy Pierce (LH)
177 (4). May 8, 1957, LH, Municipal Stadium vs. Cleveland Indians, Pitcher: Early Wynn (RH)
178 (5). May 12, 1957, LH, Memorial Stadium vs. Baltimore Orioles, Pitcher: Hal "Skinny" Brown (RH)
179 (6). May 16, 1957, RH, Yankee Stadium vs. Kansas City A's, Pitcher: Alex Kellner (LH)
180 (7). May 19, 1957, LH, Yankee Stadium vs. Cleveland Indians, Pitcher: Bob Lemon (RH)
181 (8). May 25, 1957, LH, Yankee Stadium vs. Washington Senators, Pitcher: Pedro Ramos (RH)
182 (9). May 26, 1957, LH, Yankee Stadium vs. Washington Senators, Pitcher: Camilo Pascual (RH)
183 (10). May 29, 1957, LH, Griffith Stadium vs. Washington Senators, Pitcher: Pedro Ramos (RH)
184 (11). June 2, 1957, LH, Yankee Stadium vs. Baltimore Orioles, Pitcher: Hal "Skinny" Brown (RH)
185 (12). June 5, 1957, LH, Municipal Stadium vs. Cleveland Indians, Pitcher: Early Wynn (RH)
186 (13). June 6, 1957, LH, Municipal Stadium vs. Cleveland Indians, Pitcher: Mike Garcia (RH)

187 (14). June 7, 1957, LH, Briggs Stadium vs. Detroit Tigers, Pitcher: Jim Bunning (RH)

188 (15). June 10, 1957, LH, Briggs Stadium vs. Detroit Tigers, Pitcher: Frank Lary (RH)

189 (16). June 11, 1957, LH, Comiskey Park vs. Chicago White Sox, Pitcher: Jim Wilson (RH)

190 (17). June 12, 1957, RH, Comiskey Park vs. Chicago White Sox, Pitcher: Jack Harshman (LH)

191 (18). June 12, 1957, LH, Comiskey Park vs. Chicago White Sox, Pitcher: Bob Keegan (RH)

192 (19). June 14, 1957, RH, Municipal Stadium vs. Kansas City A's, Pitcher: Gene Host (LH)

193 (20). June 22, 1957, RH, Yankee Stadium vs. Chicago White Sox, Pitcher: Jack Harshman (LH)

194 (21). June 23, 1957, LH, Yankee Stadium vs. Chicago White Sox, Pitcher: Dick Donovan (RH)

195 (22). July 1, 1957, LH, Memorial Stadium vs. Baltimore Orioles, Pitcher: George Zuverink (RH)

196 (23). July 11, 1957, LH, Municipal Stadium vs. Kansas City A's, Pitcher: Tom Morgan (RH)

197 (24). July 12, 1957, LH, Municipal Stadium vs. Kansas City A's, Pitcher: Ralph Terry (RH)

198 (25). July 21, 1957, LH, Municipal Stadium vs. Cleveland Indians, Pitcher: Ray Narleski (RH)

199 (26). July 23, 1957, LH, Yankee Stadium vs. Chicago White Sox, Pitcher: Bob Keegan (RH)

200 (27). July 26, 1957, LH, Yankee Stadium vs. Detroit Tigers, Pitcher: Jim Bunning (RH)

201 (28). July 31, 1957, RH, Yankee Stadium vs. Kansas City A's, Pitcher: Wally Burnette (LH)

202 (29). August 2, 1957, RH, Yankee Stadium vs. Cleveland Indians, Pitcher: Don Mossi (LH)

203 (30). August 7, 1957, LH, Yankee Stadium vs. Washington Senators, Pitcher: Tex Clevenger (RH)

204 (31). August 10, 1957, LH, Memorial Stadium vs. Baltimore Orioles, Pitcher: Ray Moore (RH)
205 (32). August 13, 1957, LH, Fenway Park vs. Boston Red Sox, Pitcher: Frank Sullivan (RH)
206 (33). August 26, 1957, LH, Briggs Stadium vs. Detroit Tigers, Pitcher: Frank Lary (RH)
207 (34). August 30, 1957, RH, Yankee Stadium vs. Washington Senators, Pitcher: Chuck Stobbs (LH)

Number of games in which Mickey homered in 1957: 33
Yankees record in 1957 in games in which Mickey homered: 20-13 (.613)

1958: 42 Home Runs (League Leader)
208 (1). April 17, 1958, LH, Fenway Park vs. Boston Red Sox, Pitcher: Tom Brewer (RH)
209 (2). May 9, 1958, LH, Yankee Stadium vs. Washington Senators, Pitcher: Pedro Ramos (RH)
210 (3). May 18, 1958, LH, Griffith Stadium vs. Washington Senators, Pitcher: Pedro Ramos (RH)
211 (4). May 20, 1958, LH, Comiskey Park vs. Chicago White Sox, Pitcher: Dick Donovan (RH)
212 (5). June 2, 1958, LH, Yankee Stadium vs. Chicago White Sox, Pitcher: Jim Wilson (RH)
213 (6). June 3, 1958, LH, Yankee Stadium vs. Chicago White Sox, Pitcher: Dick Donovan (RH)
214 (7). June 4, 1958, RH, Yankee Stadium vs. Chicago White Sox, Pitcher: Billy Pierce (LH)
215 (8). June 5, 1958, LH, Yankee Stadium vs. Chicago White Sox, Pitcher: Early Wynn (RH)
216 (9). June 6, 1958, RH, Yankee Stadium vs. Cleveland Indians, Pitcher: Dick Tomanek (LH)
217 (10). June 6, 1958, RH, Yankee Stadium vs. Cleveland Indians, Pitcher: Dick Tomanek (LH)

218 (11). June 8, 1958, LH, Yankee Stadium vs. Cleveland Indians, Pitcher: Jim "Mudcat" Grant (RH)

219 (12). June 13, 1958, RH, Yankee Stadium vs. Detroit Tigers: Billy Hoeft (LH)

220 (13). June 24, 1958, LH, Comiskey Park vs. Chicago White Sox, Pitcher: Early Wynn (RH)

221 (14). June 29, 1958, LH, Municipal Stadium vs. Kansas City A's, Pitcher: Ralph Terry (RH)

222 (15). July 1, 1958, LH, Memorial Stadium vs. Baltimore Orioles, Pitcher: Connie Johnson (RH)

223 (16). July 1, 1958, RH, Memorial Stadium vs. Baltimore Orioles, Pitcher: Jack Harshman (LH)

224 (17). July 3, 1958, LH, Griffith Stadium vs. Washington Senators, Pitcher: Russ Kemmerer (RH)

225 (18). July 3, 1958, LH, Griffith Stadium vs. Washington Senators, Pitcher: Russ Kemmerer (RH)

226 (19). July 4, 1958, RH, Griffith Stadium vs. Washington Senators, Pitcher: Chuck Stobbs (LH)

227 (20). July 5, 1958, LH, Yankee Stadium vs. Boston Red Sox, Pitcher: Dave Sisler (RH)

228 (21). July 6, 1958, LH, Yankee Stadium vs. Boston Red Sox, Pitcher: Ike Delock (RH)

229 (22). July 11, 1958, LH, Yankee Stadium vs. Cleveland Indians, Pitcher: Ray Narleski (RH)

230 (23). July 14, 1958, LH, Yankee Stadium vs. Chicago White Sox, Pitcher: Early Wynn (RH)

231 (24). July 15, 1958, LH, Yankee Stadium vs. Detroit Tigers, Pitcher: Frank Lary (RH)

232 (25). July 23, 1958, LH, Briggs Stadium vs. Detroit Tigers, Pitcher: Bill Fischer (RH)

233 (26). July 24, 1958, LH, Briggs Stadium vs. Detroit Tigers, Pitcher: Paul Foytack (RH)

234 (27). July 28, 1958, RH, Municipal Stadium vs. Kansas City A's, Pitcher: Dick Tomanek (LH)

235 (28). July 28, 1958, LH, Municipal Stadium vs. Kansas City A's, Pitcher: Ray Herbert (RH)

236 (29). August 4, 1958, LH, Memorial Stadium vs. Baltimore Orioles, Pitcher: Charlie Beamon (RH)

237 (30). August 5, 1958, LH, Memorial Stadium vs. Baltimore Orioles, Pitcher: Connie Johnson (RH)

238 (31). August 9, 1958, LH, Yankee Stadium vs. Boston Red Sox, Pitcher: Dave Sisler (RH)

239 (32). August 11, 1958, LH, Yankee Stadium vs. Baltimore Orioles, Pitcher: Connie Johnson (RH)

240 (33). August 12, 1958, RH, Yankee Stadium vs. Baltimore Orioles, Pitcher: Ken Lehman (LH)

241 (34). August 16, 1958, LH, Fenway Park vs. Boston Red Sox, Pitcher: Tom Brewer (RH)

242 (35). August 17, 1958, LH, Fenway Park vs. Boston Red Sox, Pitcher: Ike Delock (RH)

243 (36). August 22, 1958, LH, Yankee Stadium vs. Chicago White Sox, Pitcher: Early Wynn (RH)

244 (37). August 27, 1958, LH, Yankee Stadium vs. Kansas City A's, Pitcher: Tom Gorman (RH)

245 (38). September 2, 1958, LH, Yankee Stadium vs. Boston Red Sox, Pitcher: Dave Sisler (RH)

246 (39). September 3, 1958, LH, Yankee Stadium vs. Boston Red Sox, Pitcher: Frank Sullivan (RH)

247 (40). September 9, 1958, LH, Municipal Stadium vs. Cleveland Indians, Pitcher: Cal McLish (RH)

248 (41). September 17, 1958, LH, Briggs Stadium vs. Detroit Tigers, Pitcher: Jim Bunning (RH)

249 (42). September 24, 1958, LH, Fenway Park vs. Boston Red Sox, Pitcher: Tom Gorman (RH)

Number of games in which Mickey homered in 1958: 38 (plus one game suspended)

Yankees record in 1958 in games in which Mickey homered: 26-12-1 (.605)

1959: 31 Home Runs
250 (1). April 21, 1959, LH, Griffith Stadium vs. Washington Senators, Pitcher: Pedro Ramos (RH)
251 (2). April 23, 1959, LH, Griffith Stadium vs. Washington Senators, Pitcher: Russ Kemmerer (RH)
252 (3). April 29, 1959, LH, Comiskey Park vs. Chicago White Sox, Pitcher: Ray Moore (RH)
253 (4). May 10, 1959, RH, Yankee Stadium vs. Washington Senators, Pitcher: Chuck Stobbs (LH)
254 (5). May 12, 1959, LH, Yankee Stadium vs. Cleveland Indians, Pitcher: Cal McLish (RH)
255 (6). May 20, 1959, LH, Yankee Stadium vs. Detroit Tigers, Pitcher: Frank Lary (RH)
256 (7). May 23, 1959, LH, Memorial Stadium vs. Baltimore Orioles, Pitcher: George Zuverink (RH)
257 (8). May 24, 1959, RH, Memorial Stadium vs. Baltimore Orioles, Pitcher: Billy O'Dell (LH)
258 (9). May 30, 1959, LH, Griffith Stadium vs. Washington Senators, Pitcher: Dick Hyde (RH)
259 (10). June 3, 1959, LH, Briggs Stadium vs. Detroit Tigers, Pitcher: Ray Narleski (RH)
260 (11). June 9, 1959, LH, Yankee Stadium vs. Kansas City A's, Pitcher: Murray Dickson (RH)
261 (12). June 11, 1959, LH, Yankee Stadium vs. Kansas City A's, Pitcher: Ned Garver (RH)
262 (13). June 13, 1959, LH, Yankee Stadium vs. Detroit Tigers, Pitcher: Jim Bunning (RH)
263 (14). June 17, 1959, LH, Yankee Stadium vs. Chicago White Sox, Pitcher: Ray Moore (RH)
264 (15). June 18, 1959, LH, Yankee Stadium vs. Chicago White Sox, Pitcher: Jerry Staley (RH)
265 (16). June 22, 1959, LH, Municipal Stadium vs. Kansas City A's, Pitcher: Ray Herbert (RH)
266 (17). June 22, 1959, LH, Municipal Stadium vs. Kansas City A's, Pitcher: Bob Grim (RH)

267 (18). June 23, 1959, RH, Municipal Stadium vs. Kansas City A's, Pitcher: Rip Coleman (LH)

268 (19). July 16, 1959, LH, Yankee Stadium vs. Cleveland Indians, Pitcher: Gary Bell (RH)

269 (20). July 19, 1959, RH, Yankee Stadium vs. Chicago White Sox, Pitcher: Billy Pierce (LH)

270 (21). August 4, 1959, LH, Yankee Stadium vs. Detroit Tigers, Pitcher: Frank Lary (RH)

271 (22). August 5, 1959, RH, Yankee Stadium vs. Detroit Tigers, Pitcher: Don Mossi (LH)

272 (23). August 16, 1959, LH, Yankee Stadium vs. Boston Red Sox, Pitcher: Jerry Casale (RH)

273 (24). August 16, 1959, LH, Yankee Stadium vs. Boston Red Sox, Pitcher: Bill Monbouquette (RH)

274 (25). August 26, 1959, LH, Municipal Stadium vs. Cleveland Indians, Pitcher: Gary Bell (RH)

275 (26). August 29, 1959, LH, Griffith Stadium vs. Washington Senators, Pitcher: Hal Griggs (RH)

276 (27). September 7, 1959, LH, Fenway Park vs. Boston Red Sox, Pitcher: Jerry Casale (RH)

277 (28). September 10, 1959, LH, Yankee Stadium vs. Kansas City A's, Pitcher: Ray Herbert (RH)

278 (29). September 13, 1959, RH, Yankee Stadium vs. Cleveland Indians, Pitcher: Jack Harshman (LH)

279 (30). September 15, 1959, RH, Yankee Stadium vs. Chicago White Sox, Pitcher: Billy Pierce (LH)

280 (31). September 15, 1959, LH, Yankee Stadium vs. Chicago White Sox, Pitcher: Bob Shaw (RH)

Number of games in which Mickey homered in 1959: 29
Yankees record in 1959 in games in which Mickey homered: 19-10 (.652)

1960: 40 Home Runs (League Leader)

281 (1). April 22, 1960, LH, Yankee Stadium vs. Baltimore Orioles, Pitcher: Hoyt Wilhelm (RH)

282 (2). May 13, 1960, RH, Griffith Stadium vs. Washington Senators, Pitcher: Jim Kaat (LH)

283 (3). May 17, 1960, LH, Municipal Stadium vs. Cleveland Indians, Pitcher: Gary Bell (RH)

284 (4). May 20, 1960, LH, Comiskey Park vs. Chicago White Sox, Pitcher: Early Wynn (RH)

285 (5). May 29, 1960, RH, Yankee Stadium vs. Washington Senators, Pitcher: Jim Kaat (LH)

286 (6). May 29, 1960, RH, Yankee Stadium vs. Washington Senators, Pitcher: Hal Woodeschick (LH)

287 (7). June 1, 1960, LH, Memorial Stadium vs. Baltimore Orioles, Pitcher: Hal "Skinny" Brown (RH)

288 (8). June 5, 1960, LH, Yankee Stadium vs. Boston Red Sox, Pitcher: Tom Brewer (RH)

289 (9). June 8, 1960, LH, Yankee Stadium vs. Chicago White Sox, Pitcher: Bob Shaw (RH)

290 (10). June 8, 1960, LH, Yankee Stadium vs. Chicago White Sox, Pitcher: Ray Moore (RH)

291 (11). June 9, 1960, RH, Yankee Stadium vs. Chicago White Sox, Pitcher: Frank Baumann (LH)

292 (12). June 10, 1960, RH, Yankee Stadium vs. Cleveland Indians, Pitcher: Dick Stigman (LH)

293 (13). June 17, 1960, LH, Comiskey Park vs. Chicago White Sox, Pitcher: Turk Lown (RH)

294 (14). June 18, 1960, LH, Comiskey Park vs. Chicago White Sox, Pitcher: Bob Rush (RH)

295 (15). June 21, 1960, LH, Briggs Stadium vs. Detroit Tigers, Pitcher: Frank Lary (RH)

296 (16). June 21, 1960, LH, Briggs Stadium vs. Detroit Tigers, Pitcher: Frank Lary (RH)

297 (17). June 28, 1960, RH, Yankee Stadium vs. Kansas City A's, Pitcher: Bud Daley (LH)

298 (18). June 30, 1960, LH, Yankee Stadium vs. Kansas City A's, Pitcher: Bob Trowbridge (RH)

299 (19). July 3, 1960, RH, Yankee Stadium vs. Detroit Tigers, Pitcher: Pete Burnside (LH)

300 (20). July 4, 1960, RH, Griffith Stadium vs. Washington Senators, Pitcher: Hal Woodeschick (LH)

301 (21). July 15, 1960, RH, Briggs Stadium vs. Detroit Tigers, Pitcher: Don Mossi (LH)

302 (22). July 18, 1960, RH, Municipal Stadium vs. Cleveland Indians, Pitcher: Dick Stigman (LH)

303 (23). July 20, 1960, LH, Municipal Stadium vs. Cleveland Indians, Pitcher: Gary Bell (RH)

304 (24). July 24, 1960, LH, Yankee Stadium vs. Chicago White Sox, Pitcher: Russ Kemmerer (RH)

305 (25). July 26, 1960, RH, Yankee Stadium vs. Cleveland Indians, Pitcher: Dick Stigman (LH)

306 (26). July 28, 1960, LH, Yankee Stadium vs. Cleveland Indians, Pitcher: Jim Perry (RH)

307 (27). July 31, 1960, LH, Yankee Stadium vs. Kansas City A's, Pitcher: Johnny Kucks (RH)

308 (28). August 15, 1960, LH, Yankee Stadium vs. Baltimore Orioles, Pitcher: Jerry Walker (RH)

309 (29). August 15, 1960, LH, Yankee Stadium vs. Baltimore Orioles, Pitcher: Hoyt Wilhelm (RH)

310 (30). August 26, 1960, LH, Yankee Stadium vs. Cleveland Indians, Pitcher: Jim Perry (RH)

311 (31). August 28, 1960, LH, Yankee Stadium vs. Detroit Tigers, Pitcher: Phil Regan (RH)

312 (32). September 6, 1960, LH, Yankee Stadium vs. Boston Red Sox, Pitcher: Billy Muffett (RH)

313 (33). September 10, 1960, LH, Briggs Stadium vs. Detroit Tigers, Pitcher: Paul Foytack (RH)

314 (34). September 11, 1960, RH, Municipal Stadium vs. Cleveland Indians, Pitcher: Carl Mathias (LH)

315 (35). September 17, 1960, LH, Yankee Stadium vs. Baltimore Orioles, Pitcher: Chuck Estrada (RH)

316 (36). September 20, 1960, RH, Yankee Stadium vs. Washington Senators, Pitcher: Jack Kralick (LH)

317 (37). September 21, 1960, LH, Yankee Stadium vs. Washington Senators, Pitcher: Pedro Ramos (RH)

318 (38). September 24, 1960, RH, Fenway Park vs. Boston Red Sox, Pitcher: Ted Wills (LH)

319 (39). September 28, 1960, RH, Griffith Stadium vs. Washington Senators, Pitcher: Chuck Stobbs (LH)

320 (40). September 28, 1960, RH, Griffith Stadium vs. Washington Senators, Pitcher: Chuck Stobbs (LH)

Number of games in which Mickey homered in 1960: 36
Yankees record in 1960 in games in which Mickey homered: 28-8 (.778)

1961: 54 Home Runs
321 (1). April 17, 1961, LH, Yankee Stadium vs. Kansas City A's, Pitcher: Jerry Walker (RH)

322 (2). April 20, 1961, LH, Yankee Stadium vs. Los Angeles Angels, Pitcher: Eli Grba (RH)

323 (3). April 20, 1961, LH, Yankee Stadium vs. Los Angeles Angels, Pitcher: Eli Grba (RH)

324 (4). April 21, 1961, RH, Memorial Stadium vs. Baltimore Orioles, Pitcher: Steve Barber (LH)

325 (5). April 23, 1961, LH, Memorial Stadium vs. Baltimore Orioles, Pitcher: Chuck Estrada (RH)

326 (6). April 26, 1961, LH, Tiger Stadium vs. Detroit Tigers, Pitcher: Jim Donahue (RH)

327 (7). April 26, 1961, RH, Tiger Stadium vs. Detroit Tigers, Pitcher: Hank Aguirre (LH)

328 (8). May 2, 1961, LH, Metropolitan Stadium vs. Minnesota Twins, Pitcher: Camilo Pascual (RH)

329 (9). May 4, 1961, LH, Metropolitan Stadium vs. Minnesota Twins, Pitcher: Ted Sadowski (RH)

330 (10). May 16, 1961, RH, Yankee Stadium vs. Washington Senators,
Pitcher: Hal Woodeschick (LH)

331 (11). May 29, 1961, LH, Fenway Park vs. Boston Red Sox, Pitcher:
Ike Delock (RH)

332 (12). May 30, 1961, LH, Fenway Park vs. Boston Red Sox, Pitcher:
Gene Conley (RH)

333 (13). May 30, 1961, LH, Fenway Park vs. Boston Red Sox, Pitcher:
Mike Fornieles (RH)

334 (14). May 31, 1961, LH, Fenway Park vs. Boston Red Sox, Pitcher:
Billy Muffett (RH)

335 (15). June 5, 1961, LH, Yankee Stadium vs. Minnesota Twins,
Pitcher: Don Lee (RH)

336 (16). June 9, 1961, LH, Yankee Stadium vs. Kansas City A's, Pitcher:
Ray Herbert (RH)

337 (17). June 10, 1961, LH, Yankee Stadium vs. Kansas City A's,
Pitcher: Bill Kunkel (RH)

338 (18). June 11, 1961, LH, Yankee Stadium vs. Los Angeles Angels,
Pitcher: Eli Grba (RH)

339 (19). June 15, 1961, LH, Municipal Stadium vs. Cleveland Indians,
Pitcher: Jim "Mudcat" Grant (RH)

340 (20). June 17, 1961, LH, Tiger Stadium vs. Detroit Tigers, Pitcher:
Paul Foytack (RH)

341 (21). June 21, 1961, LH, Municipal Stadium vs. Kansas City A's,
Pitcher: Bob Shaw (RH)

342 (22). June 21, 1961, LH, Municipal Stadium vs. Kansas City A's,
Pitcher: Bob Shaw (RH)

343 (23). June 26, 1961, LH, Wrigley Field vs. Los Angeles Angels,
Pitcher: Ken McBride (RH)

344 (24). June 28, 1961, LH, Wrigley Field vs. Los Angeles Angels,
Pitcher: Ryne Duren (RH)

345 (25). June 30, 1961, LH, Yankee Stadium vs. Washington Senators,
Pitcher: Dick Donovan (RH)

346 (26). July 1, 1961, RH, Yankee Stadium vs. Washington Senators,
Pitcher: Carl Mathias (LH)

347 (27). July 1, 1961, RH, Yankee Stadium vs. Washington Senators, Pitcher: Carl Mathias (LH)

348 (28). July 2, 1961, LH, Yankee Stadium vs. Washington Senators, Pitcher: Johnny Klippstein (RH)

349 (29). July 8, 1961, LH, Yankee Stadium vs. Boston Red Sox, Pitcher: Tracy Stallard (RH)

350 (30). July 13, 1961, LH, Comiskey Park vs. Chicago White Sox, Pitcher: Early Wynn (RH)

351 (31). July 14, 1961, RH, Comiskey Park vs. Chicago White Sox, Pitcher: Juan Pizarro (LH)

352 (32). July 16, 1961, RH, Memorial Stadium vs. Baltimore Orioles, Pitcher: Steve Barber (LH)

353 (33). July 17, 1961, LH, Memorial Stadium vs. Baltimore Orioles, Pitcher: Milt Pappas (RH)

354 (34). July 18, 1961, LH, Griffith Stadium vs. Washington Senators, Pitcher: Joe McLain (RH)

355 (35). July 18, 1961, LH, Griffith Stadium vs. Washington Senators, Pitcher: Joe McLain (RH)

356 (36). July 19, 1961, LH, Griffith Stadium vs. Washington Senators, Pitcher: Dick Donovan (RH)

357 (37). July 21, 1961, LH, Fenway Park vs. Boston Red Sox, Pitcher: Bill Monbouquette (RH)

358 (38). July 25, 1961, RH, Yankee Stadium vs. Chicago White Sox, Pitcher: Frank Baumann (LH)

359 (39). July 26, 1961, LH, Yankee Stadium vs. Chicago White Sox, Pitcher: Ray Herbert (RH)

360 (40). August 2, 1961, RH, Yankee Stadium vs. Kansas City A's, Pitcher: Jim Archer (LH)

361 (41). August 6, 1961, LH, Yankee Stadium vs. Minnesota Twins, Pitcher: Pedro Ramos (RH)

362 (42). August 6, 1961, LH, Yankee Stadium vs. Minnesota Twins, Pitcher: Pedro Ramos (RH)

363 (43). August 6, 1961, LH, Yankee Stadium vs. Minnesota Twins, Pitcher: Al Schroll (RH)

364 (44). August 11, 1961, RH, Yankee Stadium vs. Washington Senators, Pitcher: Pete Burnside (LH)

365 (45). August 13, 1961, LH, Griffith Stadium vs. Washington Senators, Pitcher: Bennie Daniels (RH)

366 (46). August 20, 1961, LH, Municipal Stadium vs. Cleveland Indians, Pitcher: Jim Perry (RH)

367 (47). August 30, 1961, RH, Metropolitan Stadium vs. Minnesota Twins, Pitcher: Jim Kaat (LH)

368 (48). August 31, 1961, RH, Metropolitan Stadium vs. Minnesota Twins, Pitcher: Jack Kralick (LH)

369 (49). September 3, 1961, LH, Yankee Stadium vs. Detroit Tigers, Pitcher: Jim Bunning (RH)

370 (50). September 3, 1961, LH, Yankee Stadium vs. Detroit Tigers, Pitcher: Jerry Staley (RH)

371 (51). September 5, 1961, LH, Yankee Stadium vs. Washington Senators, Pitcher: Joe McLain (RH)

372 (52). September 8, 1961, LH, Yankee Stadium vs. Cleveland Indians, Pitcher: Gary Bell (RH)

373 (53). September 10, 1961, LH, Yankee Stadium vs. Cleveland Indians, Pitcher: Jim Perry (RH)

374 (54). September 23, 1961, LH, Fenway Park vs. Boston Red Sox, Pitcher: Don Schwall (RH)

Number of games in which Mickey homered in 1961: 47
Yankees record in 1961 in games in which Mickey homered: 39-8 (.830)

1962: 30 Home Runs

375 (1). April 10, 1962, LH, Yankee Stadium vs. Baltimore Orioles, Pitcher: Hoyt Wilhelm (RH)

376 (2). April 19, 1962, LH, Memorial Stadium vs. Baltimore Orioles, Pitcher: Chuck Estrada (RH)

377 (3). May 5, 1962, LH, Yankee Stadium vs. Washington Senators, Pitcher: Marty Kutyna (RH)

378 (4). May 6, 1962, LH, Yankee Stadium vs. Washington Senators, Pitcher: Dave Stenhouse (RH)

379 (5). May 6, 1962, RH, Yankee Stadium vs. Washington Senators, Pitcher: Pete Burnside (LH)

380 (6). May 6, 1962, LH, Yankee Stadium vs. Washington Senators, Pitcher: Jim Hannan (RH)

381 (7). May 12, 1962, LH, Municipal Stadium vs. Cleveland Indians, Pitcher: Barry Latman (RH)

382 (8). June 16, 1962, LH, Municipal Stadium vs. Cleveland Indians, Pitcher: Gary Bell (RH)

383 (9). June 23, 1962, LH, Tiger Stadium vs. Detroit Tigers, Pitcher: Paul Foytack (RH)

384 (10). June 28, 1962, RH, Yankee Stadium vs. Minnesota Twins, Pitcher: Jack Kralick (LH)

385 (11). July 2, 1962, LH, Yankee Stadium vs. Kansas City A's, Pitcher: Ed Rakow (RH)

386 (12). July 3, 1962, LH, Yankee Stadium vs. Kansas City A's, Pitcher: Jerry Walker (RH)

387 (13). July 3, 1962, LH, Yankee Stadium vs. Kansas City A's, Pitcher: Gordon Jones (RH)

388 (14). July 4, 1962, RH, Yankee Stadium vs. Kansas City A's, Pitcher: Dan Pfister (LH)

389 (15). July 4, 1962, LH, Yankee Stadium vs. Kansas City A's, Pitcher: John Wyatt (RH)

390 (16). July 6, 1962, LH, Metropolitan Stadium vs. Minnesota Twins, Pitcher: Camilo Pascual (RH)

391 (17). July 6, 1962, LH, Metropolitan Stadium vs. Minnesota Twins, Pitcher: Camilo Pascual (RH)

392 (18). July 18, 1962, LH, Fenway Park vs. Boston Red Sox, Pitcher: Galen Cisco (RH)

393 (19). July 20, 1962, RH, Yankee Stadium vs. Washington Senators, Pitcher: Steve Hamilton (LH)

394 (20). July 25, 1962, LH, Yankee Stadium vs. Boston Red Sox, Pitcher: Earl Wilson (RH)

395 (21). July 28, 1962, LH, Yankee Stadium vs. Chicago White Sox, Pitcher: Eddie Fisher (RH)

396 (22). August 17, 1962, LH, Municipal Stadium vs. Kansas City A's, Pitcher: Bill Fischer (RH)

397 (23). August 18, 1962, LH, Municipal Stadium vs. Kansas City A's, Pitcher: Diego Segui (RH)

398 (24). August 19, 1962, LH, Municipal Stadium vs. Kansas City A's, Pitcher: Jerry Walker (RH)

399 (25). August 28, 1962, LH, Yankee Stadium vs. Cleveland Indians, Pitcher: Jim "Mudcat" Grant (RH)

400 (26). September 10, 1962, RH, Tiger Stadium vs. Detroit Tigers, Pitcher: Hank Aguirre (LH)

401 (27). September 12, 1962, LH, Municipal Stadium vs. Cleveland Indians, Pitcher: Pedro Ramos (RH)

402 (28). September 18, 1962, LH, D.C. Stadium vs. Washington Senators, Pitcher: Tom Cheney (RH)

403 (29). September 18, 1962, LH, D.C. Stadium vs. Washington Senators, Pitcher: Tom Cheney (RH)

404 (30). September 30, 1962, LH, Yankee Stadium vs. Chicago White Sox, Pitcher: Ray Herbert (RH)

Number of games in which Mickey homered in 1962: 25
Yankees record in 1962 in games in which Mickey homered: 18-7 (.720)

1963: 15 Home Runs
405 (1). April 10, 1963, RH, Municipal Stadium vs. Kansas City A's, Pitcher: Ted Bowsfield (LH)

406 (2). April 11, 1963, LH, Yankee Stadium vs. Baltimore Orioles, Pitcher: Milt Pappas (RH)

407 (3). May 4, 1963, RH, Metropolitan Stadium vs. Minnesota Twins, Pitcher: Jim Kaat (LH)

408 (4). May 6, 1963, RH, Tiger Stadium vs. Detroit Tigers, Pitcher: Hank Aguirre (LH)

409 (5). May 11, 1963, LH, Memorial Stadium vs. Baltimore Orioles, Pitcher: Milt Pappas (RH)

410 (6). May 15, 1963, LH, Yankee Stadium vs. Minnesota Twins, Pitcher: Camilo Pascual (RH)

411 (7). May 21, 1963, LH, Yankee Stadium vs. Kansas City A's, Pitcher: Orlando Pena (RH)

412 (8). May 21, 1963, LH, Yankee Stadium vs. Kansas City A's, Pitcher: Diego Segui (RH)

413 (9). May 22, 1963, LH, Yankee Stadium vs. Kansas City A's, Pitcher: Bill Fischer (RH)

414 (10). May 26, 1963, RH, Yankee Stadium vs. Washington Senators, Pitcher: Don Rudolph (LH)

415 (11). June 4, 1963, RH, Memorial Stadium vs. Baltimore Orioles, Pitcher: Steve Barber (LH)

416 (12). August 4, 1963, RH, Yankee Stadium vs. Baltimore Orioles, Pitcher: George Brunet (LH)

417 (13). September 1, 1963, RH, Memorial Stadium vs. Baltimore Orioles, Pitcher: Mike McCormick (LH)

418 (14). September 11, 1963, LH, Municipal Stadium vs. Kansas City A's, Pitcher: Ed Rakow (RH)

419 (15). September 21, 1963, LH, Yankee Stadium vs. Kansas City A's, Pitcher: Moe Drabowsky (RH)

Number of games in which Mickey homered in 1963: 14
Yankees record in 1963 in games in which Mickey homered: 11-3 (.786)

1964: 35 Home Runs
420 (1). May 6, 1964, LH, D.C. Stadium vs. Washington Senators, Pitcher: Bennie Daniels (RH)

421 (2). May 6, 1964, RH, D.C. Stadium vs. Washington Senators, Pitcher: Bob Meyer (LH)

422 (3). May 8, 1964, RH, Municipal Stadium vs. Cleveland Indians, Pitcher: Tommy John (LH)

423 (4). May 9, 1964, LH, Municipal Stadium vs. Cleveland Indians, Pitcher: Pedro Ramos (RH)

424 (5). May 16, 1964, LH, Yankee Stadium vs. Kansas City A's, Pitcher: Moe Drabowsky (RH)

425 (6). May 17, 1964, RH, Yankee Stadium vs. Kansas City A's, Pitcher: John O'Donoghue (LH)

426 (7). May 23, 1964, RH, Yankee Stadium vs. Los Angeles Angels, Pitcher: Bo Belinsky (LH)

427 (8). May 24, 1964, LH, Yankee Stadium vs. Los Angeles Angels, Pitcher: Fred Newman (RH)

428 (9). June 11, 1964, LH, Fenway Park vs. Boston Red Sox, Pitcher: Bill Monbouquette (RH)

429 (10). June 11, 1964, LH, Fenway Park vs. Boston Red Sox, Pitcher: Bill Monbouquette (RH)

430 (11). June 13, 1964, RH, Yankee Stadium vs. Chicago White Sox, Pitcher: Don Mossi (LH)

431 (12). June 17, 1964, LH, Yankee Stadium vs. Boston Red Sox, Pitcher: Dick Radatz (RH)

432 (13). June 21, 1964, RH, Comiskey Park vs. Chicago White Sox, Pitcher: Juan Pizarro (LH)

433 (14). June 23, 1964, LH, Memorial Stadium vs. Baltimore Orioles, Pitcher: Chuck Estrada (RH)

434 (15). June 27, 1964, LH, Yankee Stadium vs. Detroit Tigers, Pitcher: Denny McLain (RH)

435 (16). July 1, 1964, RH, Yankee Stadium vs. Kansas City A's, Pitcher: John O'Donoghue (LH)

436 (17). July 4, 1964, LH, Yankee Stadium vs. Minnesota Twins, Pitcher: Al Worthington (RH)

437 (18). July 13, 1964, LH, Municipal Stadium vs. Cleveland Indians, Pitcher: Gary Bell (RH)

438 (19). July 24, 1964, RH, Tiger Stadium vs. Detroit Tigers, Pitcher: Hank Aguirre (LH)

439 (20). July 28, 1964, LH, Chavez Ravine vs. Los Angeles Angels, Pitcher: Dean Chance (RH)

440 (21). August 1, 1964, RH, Metropolitan Stadium vs. Minnesota Twins, Pitcher: Dick Stigman (LH)

441 (22). August 4, 1964, RH, Municipal Stadium vs. Kansas City A's, Pitcher: John O'Donoghue (LH)

442 (23). August 11, 1964, RH, Yankee Stadium vs. Chicago White Sox, Pitcher: Juan Pizarro (LH)

443 (24). August 12, 1964, LH, Yankee Stadium vs. Chicago White Sox, Pitcher: Ray Herbert (RH)

444 (25). August 12, 1964, RH, Yankee Stadium vs. Chicago White Sox, Pitcher: Frank Baumann (LH)

445 (26). August 22, 1964, LH, Fenway Park vs. Boston Red Sox, Pitcher: Jack Lamabe (RH)

446 (27). August 23, 1964, LH, Fenway Park vs. Boston Red Sox, Pitcher: Earl Wilson (RH)

447 (28). August 29, 1964, LH, Yankee Stadium vs. Boston Red Sox, Pitcher: Pete Charlton (RH)

448 (29). September 4, 1964, RH, Municipal Stadium vs. Kansas City A's, Pitcher: John O'Donoghue (LH)

449 (30). September 5, 1964, LH, Municipal Stadium vs. Kansas City A's, Pitcher: John "Blue Moon" Odom (RH)

450 (31). September 17, 1964, LH, Yankee Stadium vs. Los Angeles Angels, Pitcher: Bob Duliba (RH)

451 (32). September 19, 1964, LH, Yankee Stadium vs. Kansas City A's, Pitcher: Diego Segui (RH)

452 (33). September 22, 1964, LH, Municipal Stadium vs. Cleveland Indians, Pitcher: Dick Donovan (RH)

453 (34). September 27, 1964, LH, D.C. Stadium vs. Washington Senators, Pitcher: Bennie Daniels (RH)

454 (35). September 30, 1964, RH, Yankee Stadium vs. Detroit Tigers, Pitcher: Mickey Lolich (LH)

Number of games in which Mickey homered in 1964: 33
Yankees record in 1964 in games in which Mickey homered: 25-8 (.758)

1965: 19 Home Runs
455 (1). April 17, 1965, LH, Municipal Stadium vs. Kansas City A's, Pitcher: John Wyatt (RH)

456 (2). April 18, 1965, LH, Municipal Stadium vs. Kansas City A's, Pitcher: Moe Drabowsky (RH)

457 (3). April 21, 1965, LH, Yankee Stadium vs. Minnesota Twins, Pitcher: Camilo Pascual (RH)

458 (4). April 25, 1965, RH, Yankee Stadium vs. Los Angeles Angels, Pitcher: Rudy May (LH)
459 (5). May 10, 1965, LH, Fenway Park vs. Boston Red Sox, Pitcher: Jim Lonborg (RH)
460 (6). May 11, 1965, RH, Fenway Park vs. Boston Red Sox, Pitcher: Arnold Earley (LH)
461 (7). May 15, 1965, LH, Memorial Stadium vs. Baltimore Orioles, Pitcher: Dick Hall (RH)
462 (8). May 30, 1965, RH, Comiskey Park vs. Chicago White Sox, Pitcher: Gary Peters (LH)
463 (9). June 5, 1965, RH, Yankee Stadium vs. Chicago White Sox, Pitcher: Gary Peters (LH)
464 (10). June 18, 1965, RH, Yankee Stadium vs. Minnesota Twins, Pitcher: Mel Nelson (LH)
465 (11). June 22, 1965, RH, Yankee Stadium vs. Kansas City A's, Pitcher: John O'Donoghue (LH)
466 (12). July 15, 1965, LH, Yankee Stadium vs. Washington Senators, Pitcher: Phil Ortega (RH)
467 (13). July 25, 1965, LH, Municipal Stadium vs. Cleveland Indians, Pitcher: Lee Stange (RH)
468 (14). August 6, 1965, RH, Tiger Stadium vs. Detroit Tigers, Pitcher: Mickey Lolich (LH)
469 (15). August 7, 1965, LH, Tiger Stadium vs. Detroit Tigers, Pitcher: Fred Gladding (RH)
470 (16). August 10, 1965, RH, Yankee Stadium vs. Minnesota Twins, Pitcher: Jim Kaat (LH)
471 (17). August 18, 1965, LH, Yankee Stadium vs. Los Angeles Angels, Pitcher: Dean Chance (RH)
472 (18). September 2, 1965, RH, Chavez Ravine vs. Los Angeles Angels, Pitcher: Marcelino Lopez (LH)
473 (19). September 4, 1965, RH, Yankee Stadium vs. Boston Red Sox, Pitcher: Dennis Bennett (LH)

Number of games in which Mickey homered in 1965: 19
Yankees record in 1965 in games in which Mickey homered: 12-7 (.632)

1966: 23 Home Runs

474 (1). May 9, 1966, LH, Metropolitan Stadium vs. Minnesota Twins, Pitcher: Jim Perry (RH)

475 (2). May 14, 1966, LH, Municipal Stadium vs. Kansas City A's, Pitcher: Fred Talbot (RH)

476 (3). May 25, 1966, LH, Yankee Stadium vs. California Angels, Pitcher: Dean Chance (RH)

477 (4). May 25, 1966, LH, Yankee Stadium vs. California Angels, Pitcher: Lew Burdette (RH)

478 (5). June 1, 1966, RH, Comiskey Park vs. Chicago White Sox, Pitcher: Juan Pizarro (LH)

479 (6). June 16, 1966, RH, Yankee Stadium vs. Cleveland Indians, Pitcher: Sam McDowell (LH)

480 (7). June 23, 1966, LH, Yankee Stadium vs. Baltimore Orioles, Pitcher: Jim Palmer (RH)

481 (8). June 28, 1966, LH, Fenway Park vs. Boston Red Sox, Pitcher: Jose Santiago (RH)

482 (9). June 28, 1966, LH, Fenway Park vs. Boston Red Sox, Pitcher: Jose Santiago (RH)

483 (10). June 29, 1966, LH, Fenway Park vs. Boston Red Sox, Pitcher: Roland Sheldon (RH)

484 (11). June 29, 1966, LH, Fenway Park vs. Boston Red Sox, Pitcher: Lee Stange (RH)

485 (12). July 1, 1966, LH, D.C. Stadium vs. Washington Senators, Pitcher: Phil Ortega (RH)

486 (13). July 2, 1966, RH, D.C. Stadium vs. Washington Senators, Pitcher: Mike McCormick (LH)

487 (14). July 2, 1966, RH, D.C. Stadium vs. Washington Senators, Pitcher: Mike McCormick (LH)

488 (15). July 3, 1966, RH, D.C. Stadium vs. Washington Senators, Pitcher: Pete Richert (LH)

489 (16). July 7, 1966, LH, Yankee Stadium vs. Boston Red Sox, Pitcher: Don McMahon (RH)

490 (17). July 8, 1966, LH, Yankee Stadium vs. Washington Senators, Pitcher: Dick Bosman (RH)

491 (18). July 8, 1966, RH, Yankee Stadium vs. Washington Senators, Pitcher: Jim Hannan (RH)
492 (19). July 23, 1966, RH, Yankee Stadium vs. California Angels, Pitcher: Marcelino Lopez (LH)
493 (20). July 24, 1966, RH, Yankee Stadium vs. California Angels, Pitcher: George Brunet (LH)
494 (21). July 29, 1966, LH, Comiskey Park vs. Chicago White Sox, Pitcher: Bruce Howard (RH)
495 (22). August 14, 1966, RH, Yankee Stadium vs. Cleveland Indians, Pitcher: Jack Kralick (LH)
496 (23). August 26, 1966, RH, Yankee Stadium vs. Detroit Tigers, Pitcher: Hank Aguirre (LH)

Number of games in which Mickey homered in 1966: 18
Yankees record in 1966 in games in which Mickey homered: 11-7 (.611)

1967: 22 Home Runs
497 (1). April 29, 1967, LH, Yankee Stadium vs. California Angels, Pitcher: Jack Sanford (RH)
498 (2). April 30, 1967, LH, Yankee Stadium vs. California Angels, Pitcher: Minnie Rojas (RH)
499 (3). May 3, 1967, LH, Metropolitan Stadium vs. Minnesota Twins, Pitcher: Dave Boswell (RH)
500 (4). May 14, 1967, LH, Yankee Stadium vs. Baltimore Orioles, Pitcher: Stu Miller (RH)
501 (5). May 17, 1967, LH, Yankee Stadium vs. Cleveland Indians, Pitcher: Steve Hargan (RH)
502 (6). May 19, 1967, RH, Tiger Stadium vs. Detroit Tigers, Pitcher: Mickey Lolich (LH)
503 (7). May 20, 1967, LH, Tiger Stadium vs. Detroit Tigers, Pitcher: Denny McLain (RH)
504 (8). May 21, 1967, LH, Tiger Stadium vs. Detroit Tigers, Pitcher: Earl Wilson (RH)
505 (9). May 24, 1967, RH, Memorial Stadium vs. Baltimore Orioles, Pitcher: Steve Barber (LH)

506 (10). May 27, 1967, LH, Municipal Stadium vs. Cleveland Indians, Pitcher: Sonny Siebert (RH)

507 (11). May 28, 1967, LH, Municipal Stadium vs. Cleveland Indians, Pitcher: Gary Bell (RH)

508 (12). June 5, 1967, RH, Yankee Stadium vs. Washington Senators, Pitcher: Darold Knowles (LH)

509 (13). June 15, 1967, RH, D.C. Stadium vs. Washington Senators, Pitcher: Frank Bertaina (LH)

510 (14). June 24, 1967, LH, Yankee Stadium vs. Detroit Tigers, Pitcher: Fred Gladding (RH)

511 (15). July 4, 1967, LH, Metropolitan Stadium vs. Minnesota Twins, Pitcher: Jim "Mudcat" Grant (RH)

512 (16). July 4, 1967, LH, Metropolitan Stadium vs. Minnesota Twins, Pitcher: Jim "Mudcat" Grant (RH)

513 (17). July 16, 1967, LH, Yankee Stadium vs. Baltimore Orioles, Pitcher: Bill Dillman (RH)

514 (18). July 22, 1967, LH, Tiger Stadium vs. Detroit Tigers, Pitcher: Earl Wilson (RH)

515 (19). July 25, 1967, RH, Yankee Stadium vs. Minnesota Twins, Pitcher: Jim Kaat (LH)

516 (20). August 7, 1967, LH, Anaheim Stadium vs. California Angels, Pitcher: Minnie Rojas (RH)

517 (21). September 2, 1967, LH, Yankee Stadium vs. Washington Senators, Pitcher: Bob Priddy (RH)

518 (22). September 3, 1967, LH, Yankee Stadium vs. Washington Senators, Pitcher: Dick Bosman (RH)

Number of games in which Mickey homered in 1967: 21 (plus one game suspended)
Yankees record in 1967 in games in which Mickey homered: 9-11-1 (.450)

1968: 18 Home Runs
519 (1). April 18, 1968, LH, Anaheim Stadium vs. California Angels, Pitcher: Jim McGlothlin (RH)

520 (2). April 24, 1968, LH, Oakland Coliseum vs. Oakland A's, Pitcher: Jim Nash (RH)

521 (3). April 26, 1968, LH, Yankee Stadium vs. Detroit Tigers, Pitcher: Earl Wilson (RH)

522 (4). May 6, 1968, RH, Yankee Stadium vs. Cleveland Indians, Pitcher: Sam McDowell (LH)

523 (5). May 30, 1968, LH, Yankee Stadium vs. Washington Senators, Pitcher: Joe Coleman (RH)

524 (6). May 30, 1968, LH, Yankee Stadium vs. Washington Senators, Pitcher: Bob Humphreys (RH)

525 (7). June 7, 1968, LH, Yankee Stadium vs. California Angels, Pitcher: Jim McGlothlin (RH)

526 (8). June 11, 1968, LH, Yankee Stadium vs. Chicago White Sox, Pitcher: Joel Horlen (RH)

527 (9). June 16, 1968, RH, Anaheim Stadium vs. California Angels, Pitcher: Clyde Wright (LH)

528 (10). June 22, 1968, RH, Metropolitan Stadium vs. Minnesota Twins, Pitcher: Jim Kaat (LH)

529 (11). June 29, 1968, LH, Yankee Stadium vs. Oakland A's, Pitcher: John "Blue Moon" Odom (RH)

530 (12). August 10, 1968, RH, Yankee Stadium vs. Minnesota Twins, Pitcher: Jim Merritt (LH)

531 (13). August 10, 1968, RH, Yankee Stadium vs. Minnesota Twins, Pitcher: Jim Merritt (LH)

532 (14). August 12, 1968, RH, Anaheim Stadium vs. California Angels, Pitcher: George Brunet (LH)

533 (15). August 15, 1968, LH, Oakland Coliseum vs. Oakland A's, Pitcher: John "Blue Moon" Odom (RH)

534 (16). August 22, 1968, RH, Metropolitan Stadium vs. Minnesota Twins, Pitcher: Jim Merritt (LH)

535 (17). September 19, 1968, LH, Tiger Stadium vs. Detroit Tigers, Pitcher: Denny McLain (RH)

536 (18). September 20, 1968, LH, Yankee Stadium vs. Boston Red Sox, Pitcher: Jim Lonborg (RH)

Number of games in which Mickey homered in 1968: 16 (plus one game suspended)
Yankees record in 1968 in games in which Mickey homered: 8-8-1 (.500)

Career Totals:
Home Runs Hit Left-Handed - 373
Home Runs Hit Right-Handed - 163

Number of Games in which Mickey Homered: 487 (plus three games suspended)
Yankees record in games in which Mickey homered: 344-143-3 (.706)

Mickey Mantle's World Series Home Runs (18)
1. October 6, 1952, Ebbets Field vs. Brooklyn Dodgers
2. October 7, 1952, Ebbets Field vs. Brooklyn Dodgers
3. October 1, 1953, Yankee Stadium vs. Brooklyn Dodgers
4. October 4, 1953, Ebbets Field vs. Brooklyn Dodgers
5. September 30, 1955, Ebbets Field vs. Brooklyn Dodgers
6. October 3, 1956, Ebbets Field vs. Brooklyn Dodgers
7. October 7, 1956, Yankee Stadium vs. Brooklyn Dodgers
8. October 8, 1956, Yankee Stadium vs. Brooklyn Dodgers
9. October 5, 1957, County Stadium vs. Milwaukee Braves
10. October 2, 1958, County Stadium vs. Milwaukee Braves
11. October 2, 1958, County Stadium vs. Milwaukee Braves
12. October 6, 1960, Forbes Field vs. Pittsburgh Pirates
13. October 6, 1960, Forbes Field vs. Pittsburgh Pirates
14. October 8, 1960, Yankee Stadium vs. Pittsburgh Pirates
15. October 6, 1963, Dodger Stadium vs. Los Angeles Dodgers
16. October 10, 1964, Yankee Stadium vs. St. Louis Cardinals
17. October 14, 1964, Busch Stadium vs. St. Louis Cardinals
18. October 15, 1964, Busch Stadium vs. St. Louis Cardinals

Total: Left-handed - 10 / Right-handed - 8

Mickey Mantle's All-Star Game Home Runs (2)
1. July 22, 1955, County Stadium, Milwaukee - Pitcher Robin Roberts
2. July 10, 1956, Griffith Stadium, Washington - Pitcher Warren Spahn

Total: Left-Handed - 1 / Right-Handed - 1

Appendix E

Joe DiMaggio's Batting Statistics

Major League Regular Season

Year	G	AB	R	H	2B	3B	HR	RBI	AVG.	BB	K	OBP	SLG.
1936	138	637	132	206	44	15	29	125	.323	24	39	.352	.576
1937	151	621	151	215	35	15	46	167	.346	64	37	.412	.673
1938	145	599	129	194	32	13	32	140	.324	59	21	.386	.581
1939	120	462	108	176	32	6	30	126	.381	52	20	.448	.671
1940	132	508	93	179	28	9	31	133	.352	61	30	.425	.626
1941	139	541	122	193	43	11	30	125	.357	76	13	.440	.643
1942	154	610	123	186	29	13	21	114	.305	68	36	.376	.498
1943	*												
1944	*												
1945	*												
1946	132	503	81	146	20	8	25	95	.290	59	24	.367	.511
1947	141	534	97	168	31	10	20	97	.315	64	32	.391	.522
1948	153	594	110	190	26	1	39	155	.320	67	30	.396	.598
1949	76	272	58	94	14	6	14	67	.346	55	18	.459	.596
1950	139	525	114	158	33	10	32	122	.301	80	33	.394	.585
1951	116	415	72	109	22	4	12	71	.263	61	36	.365	.422
Totals	1736	6821	1390	2214	389	131	361	1537	.325	790	369	.398	.579

* Did not play because of military service

World Series

Year	Opponent	G	AB	R	H	2B	3B	HR	RBI	AVG.	BB	K	OBP	SLG.	SB
1936	New York (N)	6	26	3	9	3	0	0	3	.346	1	3	.370	.462	0
1937	New York (N)	5	22	2	6	0	0	1	4	.273	0	3	.273	.409	0
1938	Chicago	4	15	4	4	0	0	1	2	.267	1	1	.313	.467	0
1939	Cincinnati	4	16	3	5	0	0	1	3	.313	1	1	.353	.500	0
1941	Brooklyn	5	19	1	5	0	0	0	1	.263	2	2	.333	.263	1
1942	St. Louis	5	21	3	7	0	0	0	3	.333	0	1	.333	.333	0
1947	Brooklyn	7	26	4	6	0	0	2	5	.231	6	2	.375	.462	0
1949	Brooklyn	5	18	2	3	0	0	1	2	.111	3	5	.238	.278	0
1950	Philadelphia	4	13	2	4	1	0	1	2	.308	3	1	.471	.615	0
1951	New York (N)	6	23	3	6	2	0	1	5	.261	2	4	.320	.478	0
Totals		**51**	**199**	**27**	**54**	**6**	**0**	**8**	**30**	**.271**	**19**	**23**	**.338**	**.422**	**0**

BIBLIOGRAPHY

Allen, Maury. *Roger Maris: A Man for All Seasons.* New York: Donald J. Fine, 1986.

Antonucci, Thomas J., and Eric Caren. *Big League Baseball in the Big Apple: The New York Yankees.* Verplank, NY: Historical Briefs, 1995.

Appel, Marty. *Pinstripe Empire: The New York Yankees from Before the Babe to After the Boss.* New York: Bloomsbury USA, 2012.

Barra, Allen. *Yogi Berra: Eternal Yankee.* New York: W. W. Norton, 2009.

Berger, Phil. *Mickey Mantle.* New York: Park Lane Press, 1998.

Borelli, Stephen. *How About That! The Life of Mel Allen.* Champagne, IL: Sports Publishing, 2005.

Bouton, Jim. *Ball Four.* Ed. Leonard Shecter. New York: World Publishing, 1970.

Canale, Larry. *Mickey Mantle: The Classic Photography of Ozzie Sweet.* Richmond, VA: Tuff Stuff Books, 1998.

Castro, Tony. *Mickey Mantle: America's Prodigal Son.* Dulles, VA: Potomac Books, 2002.

Cataneo, David. *I Remember Joe DiMaggio: Personal Memories of the Yankee Clipper by the People Who Knew Him Best.* New York: Cumberland House Publishing, 2001.

Chadwick, Dean. *Those Damn Yankees: The Secret Life of America's Greatest Franchise.* New York: Verso, 1999.

Clavin, Tom. *The DiMaggios: Three Brothers, Their Passion for Baseball, Their Pursuit of the American Dream.* New York: Ecco, 2013.

Cramer, Richard Ben. *Joe DiMaggio: The Hero's Life.* New York: Simon & Schuster, 2000.

Creamer, Robert W. *Babe: The Legend Comes to Life.* Evanston, IL: Holtzman Press, 1974.

Creamer, Robert W. *Stengel: His Life and Times.* New York: Simon and Schuster, 1984.

Creamer, Robert W., and *Sports Illustrated. Mantle Remembered* (SI Presents). New York: Warner Books, 1995.

DiMaggio, Joe. *Lucky to Be a Yankee.* Revised Edition. New York: Grosset & Dunlap, 1957.

Durso, Joseph. *Casey: The Life and Legend of Charles Dillon Stengel.* Upper Saddle River, NJ: Prentice-Hall, 1967.

Engelberg, Morris, and Marv Schneider. *DiMaggio: Setting the Record Straight.* New York: Motorbooks International, 2003.

Falkner, David. *The Last Hero: The Life of Mickey Mantle.* New York: Simon & Schuster, 1995.

Flynn, George. *Lewis B. Hershey, Mr. Selective Service.* Chapel Hill and London: University of North Carolina Press, 1985.

Ford, Whitey, and Mickey Mantle. *Whitey and Mickey: A Joint Autobiography of the Yankee Years:* New York: Signet, 1978.

Golenbock, Peter. *Dynasty: The New York Yankees, 1949–1964.* Chicago: Contemporary Books, 2000.

Golenbock, Peter. *Wild, High and Tight: The Life and Death of Billy Martin*. New York: St. Martin's Press, 1994.

Halberstam, David. *Summer of '49*. New York: William Morrow, 2006.

Hart, Jeffrey. *When the Going Was Good: American Life in the Fifties*. New York: Crown Publishers, 1982.

Herskowitz, Mickey. *Mickey Mantle: An Appreciation*. New York: William Morrow, 1995.

Hines, Rick, Mark Larson, and Dave Platta. *Mickey Mantle Memorabilia*. New York: Krause, 1993.

Kahn, Roger. *October Men*. New York: Harcourt, 2003.

Kennedy, Kostya. *56: Joe DiMaggio and the Last Magic Number in Sports*. New York: Sports Illustrated, 2011.

Kerrane, Kevin. *Dollar Sign on the Muscle*. New York: Beaufort, 1984.

Lansky, Sandra, and William Stadiem. *Daughter of the King: Growing up in Gangland*. New York: Weinstein Books, 2014.

Leavy, Jane. *The Last Boy: Mickey Mantle and the End of America's Childhood*. New York: Harper, 2010.

Leinwand, Gerald. *Heroism in America*. New York: Franklin Watts, 1996.

Linn, Ed. *Hitter: The Life and Turmoils of Ted Williams*. New York: Harcourt Brace & Co., 1993.

Mantle, Merlyn, Mickey Mantle Jr., David Mantle, and Dan Mantle. *A Hero All His Life*. New York: Harper Collins, 1996.

Mantle, Mickey, and Robert W. Creamer. *The Quality of Courage: Heroes In and Out of Baseball*. Garden City, NY: Doubleday, 2005.

Mantle, Mickey, with Herb Gluck. *The Mick*. New York: Doubleday, 1985.

Mantle, Mickey, and Mickey Herskowitz. *All My Octobers*. New York: Harper Collins, 1994.

Mantle, Mickey, and Phil Pepe. *My Favorite Summer, 1956*. New York: Doubleday, 1991.

Mays, Willie, and Lou Sahadi. *Say Hey: The Autobiography of Willie Mays*. New York: Simon and Schuster, 1988.

Robinson, Ray. *Iron Horse: Lou Gehrig in His Time*. New York: W.W. Norton & Co., 1990.

Schaap, Dick. *Mickey Mantle, the Indispensable Yankee*. New York: Bartholomew House, 1961.

Schoor, Gene. *The Illustrated History of Mickey Mantle*. New York: Carroll & Graf, 1996.

Smith, Marshall, and John Rohde. *Memories of Mickey Mantle: My Very Best Friend*. Bronxville, NY: Adventure Quest, 1996.

Sweet, Ozzie, and Larry Canale. *Mickey Mantle: The Yankee Years, the Classic Photography of Ozzie Sweet*. Richmond, VA: Tuff Stuff Publications 1998.

Talese, Gay. *Fame and Obscurity*. New York: World Publishing, 1970.

Talese, Gay. *The Silent Season of a Hero: The Sports Writing of Gay Talese*. New York: Walker Books, 2010.

Thorn, John, ed. *Glory Days: New York Baseball, 1947–1957*. New York: HarperCollins, 2008.

Index

ABOUT THE AUTHOR

Tony Castro is the author of the critically acclaimed and best-selling *Mickey Mantle: America's Prodigal Son,* hailed by the *New York Times* as the best biography ever written about the Hall of Fame legend. He is also the author of the rite of passage memoir *The Prince of South Waco: American Dreams and Great Expectations* and the landmark civil rights history *Chicano Power: The Emergence of Mexican America,* which *Publishers Weekly* called "brilliant . . . a valuable contribution to the understanding of our time."

A former staff writer at *Sports Illustrated* and a syndicated political columnist, Castro has written for the *Washington Post,* the *Los Angeles Times,* and the *Dallas Morning News.* He is a graduate of Baylor and a Nieman Fellow at Harvard University. With his wife and two sons and black Labrador Jeter, he lives in Los Angeles, California.